THE JEWISH SPIRIT

THE JEWISH SPIRIT

A CELEBRATION IN STORIES & ART

EDITED BY ELLEN FRANKEL

A FAIR STREET/WELCOME BOOK

STEWART, TABORI & CHANG
NEW YORK

CONTENTS

V. COMMUNITY

VI. IN THE HEART OF WISDOM

VII. THE END OF DAYS

הללויה

הללו עבדי ייַ הללו את

שֵׁם ייַ יְהִי שֵׁם ייַ מְבֹרָךְ

מֵעַתָה וְעַד עוֹלָם מִמִּזְרַח

שֶׁמֶשׁ וְעַד מְבוֹאוֹ מְהֻלָּל

שֵׁם ייַ רָם עַל כָּל גּוֹיִם ייַ

עַל הַשָּׁמַיִם כְּבוֹדוֹ מִי

INTRODUCTION

Ⓗow magical are stories!

Just as a simple alphabet generates the complex miracle of language, so too a people's stock of stories creates an entire world. Stories transport us to the outer reaches of our imagination, mark out the beginning and end of human time, explain the world to us, and reassure us with visions of justice and order. Stories dam the rushing flow of our lives so that they seem to us inextricably linked chains of lakes, rivers, and waterfalls rather than untidy bogs. Sustained by our people's stories, each of us ventures boldly into the uncharted future, confident that we are on our way home.

A people's tales are its memory, its conscience, the imaginative channel to its place in the world. In these tales are embedded the formative experiences of the nation, the primal sensibilities that first shaped and even now continue to shape a particular people's vision of the world. Such tales teach each generation how to live and what to believe, whom to trust and whom to fear, when to laugh and why to cling fast to hope.

If such a treasury of tales reflects the unique history and customs of a specific community, what then characterizes *Jewish* tales? Not language, since we Jews have told our stories in a score of tongues over the millenia. Not place, since we have wandered the earth, borrowing clothes, foods, customs, and landscapes from every nation among whom we've dwelled. Even our plots and characters have been appropriated from other tale traditions—India's *Pachatantra*, Persia's *Kalila* and *Dimna*, the *Arabian Nights*, Aesop's fables, European folklore.

No, the trademark of the Jewish tale is its special point of view, a paradoxical blend of resignation and optimism. Many of our stories tell of heroes, masters of cunning and spiritual courage; other stories deflate their characters, recounting tales of failure, sexual trespass, intellectual conceit, spiritual arrogance, and foolishness. And it is precisely this double-edged vision that has been the secret of Jewish survival.

Jewish storytellers have developed several special techniques to tell their tales. For example, some use *prooftexts*, citing a biblical source in order to anchor a character's words or deeds in the past, a proverbial Golden Age when larger-than-life ancestors walked the earth. Such scriptural allusions lend authority to the teller's words and also link the tale to the golden chain of tradition, an unbroken strand stretching back through the generations.

Another technique is *midrash*, from the Hebrew verb meaning to search out, a process of reading between the lines of an ancient story—primarily those of the Bible and especially the Torah—to fill in the missing pieces, unravel ambiguities or contradictions, rationalize redundancy, revitalize old forms. These imaginative reconstructions are not meant to replace previous tales or to invalidate their truths; rather, they establish a continuity with the past, proving to contemporary listeners that "there is nothing new under the sun," that the "Story" continues to unfold in our own lives. Allied to this technique is the frequent disregard of chronology, especially in more traditional tales. Thus, Moses and Rabbi Akiva, living centuries apart, meet and converse; such biblical heroes as Abraham and Isaac study Torah in Eastern European yeshivahs; ancient prophets roam the earth, performing miracles and pricking modern consciences.

Although classical midrashim date back to the first centuries of the common era, the genre has proved endlessly fertile and surprisingly contemporary. Many modern short story writers, poets, playwrights, and storytellers have turned to the ancient technique of midrash to recast old tales in new forms. Jewish feminists have found the model especially resonant for their agendas, giving voices to muted figures such as the biblical matriarchs Miriam and Zipporah. The genre is naturally subversive and playful.

Jewish literature has developed other written genres besides these ancient forms. In the Middle Ages a Jewish scribe named Berechiah ben Natronai ha-Nakdan— Benedictus the Punctuator—wrote Jewish fables modeled on the myths of the Greeks and Romans, French fabliaux, and Persian moral tales. He created Jewish versions of such familiar stories as "The Country Mouse and the City Mouse" and "The Fox and the Grapes." These terse narratives, written in elegant literary Hebrew laced with biblical allusions, demonstrated both craft and ethical probity, cast in an undeniably Jewish voice.

In our own time, in the wake of the Enlightenment and the Zionist movement, Jewish writers have developed a new Jewish literature, written in Hebrew (liberated from its sacred ghetto), Yiddish, or in the vernaculars of their native country. Those stories written in Jewish languages (Hebrew and Yiddish) carry echoes of other Jewish books—especially the Bible,

prayerbook, and rabbinic texts; those written in non-Jewish languages (primarily European languages, Russian, and English) resonate to other literary traditions as well. What all of them share is their modern sensibility, the bittersweet recognition that the Jewish people no longer live isolated from the secular world, that many tantalizing fruits, including forbidden ones, are now within reach.

And what do Jewish stories speak about?

They speak of origins—how the world began and foundered, how the first families emerged, begat offspring, and negotiated the inevitable pitfalls of human nature. Other stories dramatize ethical dilemmas—how communities treat their less fortunate members, how individuals plot their courses and lose their way, how the vicissitudes of fortune test a person's mettle. Still others provide parables to guide our behavior, often using humor—as in the foolish escapades of Chelm, the broad burlesques of Sephardic folktales, or the sentimental comedy of Sholom Aleichem—to sweeten a bitter pill. Taken as a whole, the corpus of Jewish tales depicts the universal human condition, but the picture is often refracted through the prism of exile and estrangement that characterizes so much of the Jewish experience.

For the Jewish people, uprooted so often from home throughout the long centuries of a restless history, stories have served to orient and guide us back onto a familiar path. Like the other portable baggage of Jewish tradition—an elaborate code of laws, the Hebrew language, the prayerbook, the Jewish calendar, and a comprehensive ritual life—stories are easily packed, carried, and unpacked when our people reaches the next watering hole. All it takes is a teller, a listener, and a moment to catch our breath.

Like Native American peoples, we Jews have stories about everything—about the beginning of the world and the creation of life; about coming of age, marrying, and begetting children; about fools, sages, and tricksters; about spirits, death, and the afterworld.

Yet in many respects, Jewish stories are also quite different. Unlike Native American or African American story traditions that are primarily oral, Jews have long had a written as well as an oral literature. More than two thousand years ago, we began writing our stories down—first in scrolls made of cured animal skin, then in codices, and finally in books. Of course, even when the stories took fixed form, oral storytelling never ceased—but in time, a hierarchy arose that placed a higher value on the written text than on spoken tales. These written narratives begin with the Torah (literally, the Teaching), which comprises the Pentateuch and other books of the Hebrew Bible, and include stories drawn from the rabbinic anthology of law and lore known as the Talmud and the collective body of legends known as the Midrash. Although oral tales have often been regarded as the stepchildren of rabbinic authority, they have been lovingly embraced by the people, retold and singularly embellished by each community in the farflung Jewish diaspora.

In this volume you will find both kinds of ancient tale: those, though once told in tents, in the marketplace, and in the ancient rabbinical academies, that have long since been committed to writing; and those that still echo in living memory. What distinguishes these two genres of stories from each other are their differing narrative conventions, the rules by which the storyteller plays the game.

Written versions of Jewish stories tend to be more tightly constructed and generally more solemn in tone; their oral counterparts are usually looser, earthier, and frequently funny. Written tales comport themselves with a certain degree of dignity; oral tales, in contrast, flap their arms and carry on, emitting groans and smells, grimaces and winks, imprinting all of our senses with vivid memories.

You will also find in this collection a second kind of written narrative: the literary tale. These stories, products of our own time, are born of the intercourse between Jewish culture and the modern secular world. Unlike oral and written folktales, they never had a spoken life. They were born on the printed page, designed for eyes, not ears. They, too, have their own set of narrative conventions that sensitize the reader to their purpose: They develop character as well as plot, abound in sensuous details as well as actions, and employ a richer lexicon and more elaborate sentences. Literary tales allow a solitary author to speak to a solitary reader; folktales, on the other hand, are a communal affair. The storyteller gathers an audience around her and spins her yarn, playing the crowd and enjoying its responses. In contrast, the writer of literature writes—to paraphrase that grand performance artist of the written word, Gertrude Stein—"for [her]self and strangers." Or at least, for cousins once removed.

The Jewish Spirit is the first collection of Jewish stories organized according to the phases of the life cycle: stories of creation and beginnings; stories about coming of age, including initiation into awareness and experience; stories of families, including tests of loyalty and love and the negotiation of conflicts; stories of marriage, including matchmaking and courtship, the battle of the sexes, and the tragedy and comedy of connubial life; stories of community, including the hard lot of the poor and the persecuted, the bloody legacy of anti-Semitism, and the calamitous consequences of wagging tongues and watchful eyes; stories of wisdom and old age, including reconciliation to suffering and loss, happiness with one's lot, and the ironies of ambition; and last, stories of death and life beyond death, including intimations of the messiah.

These stories come from a variety of sources and reflect a wide spectrum of narrative approaches. Some stories, such as "The Creation of Human Beings" and "Lilith," derive from the ancient treasury of rabbinic midrash and are here presented in translations faithful to early written versions. In addition, a few stories such as "The Sheep of the Hidden Valley" have been written as modern midrash, melding classical form with a contemporary sensibility. Other stories, such as "The Pomegranate Girl," are verbatim transcriptions from living storytellers, recorded by Israeli folklorists and then scrupulously translated into English. A great number of the tales—Martin Buber's "The Werewolf," a story of the young Baal Shem Tov; tales about the fools of Chelm; Hebrew fables from Medieval France; Hayyim Nachman Bialik's "Mysterious Place"; Glückel of Hameln's "The Father Bird and the Fledglings"; and many traditional folktales—are actually retellings, adapted from oral versions in an effort to improve upon the originals by eliminating repetition, archaisms, obscurities, and digressions. The five Holocaust tales in the collection defy generic classification.

They are true stories on their way to becoming legends.

We also find in this volume some of the classics of the modern short story, including stories by such renowned European writers as Sholom Aleichem, I. L. Peretz, Franz Kafka, Isaac Babel, and Theodor Herzl; by Israeli Nobel Laureate S. Y. Agnon; and by American writers such as Bernard Malamud, Francine Prose, Leslie Epstein, I. B. Singer, and Grace Paley. Although these stories are grounded in the national literatures of their authors' native lands, they also emerge out of the transnational experience of the Jewish people, deeply rooted in ancient texts, myths, and memories.

Besides striking a balance between oral and written forms, this anthology of stories balances other poles of Jewish experience: gender and ethnicity. Although Jewish men have long dominated—and in premodern times, virtually monopolized—written literature, Jewish women have always been important transmitters of oral tradition, through songs, customs, superstitions, prayers, domestic arts—and stories. Women have functioned as tellers and retellers; teachers of young children and illiterate neighbors; entertainers of new brides and weary housewives. Many of these tales feature women as heroes—resourceful, clever, brave, determined. Many provoke laughter at a man's expense. The moods of these stories are as varied as women's lives.

One of the most notable features of the Jewish people is its multicultural diversity. During two and a half millenia of exile, Jews have lived on every inhabited continent, spoken dozens of languages (including many creoles of Hebrew and native vernaculars), borrowed religious ideas, customs, symbols, and superstitions from numerous cultures, and stirred up their own gene pool many times. In our own time, the Jewish world sorts itself into three major divisions: Ashkenazi, comprising Jews of Eastern, Central, and, with certain exceptions, Western European origins; Sephardi, comprising Jews of Spanish, Portuguese, and southern Mediterranean origins; and *edot hamizrakh*, usually translated as Oriental or Eastern Jews, comprising Jews from North Africa, the Middle East, the southern lands of the former Soviet Union, and India. Most American Jews are of Ashkenazi origin; most Latin American Jews, of Sephardic. And Israel is the ultimate melting pot. Of course, within each of these sprawling kingdoms lies numerous fiefdoms and rebellious provinces who claim for themselves independent identities, pointing to their different languages, melodies, foods, and practices.

Nowhere is this diversity more evident than in the stories each community tells.

Although the tales share many plots in common—not only with those of other Jewish communities but with those of many other different cultures as well—each community puts its own stamp on its stories. Characters, proverbs and idioms, humor, the particular cast of non-Jewish characters who torment and befriend that community's Jews, cultural allusions, and philosophies of life vary depending upon the teller's longitude and latitude.

Finally, the stories in *The Jewish Spirit* are accompanied by a wide range of Jewish art. These pictures neither illustrate nor explain the stories; rather, they tell their own tales, balancing age-old tensions in Jewish tradition between word and image, idol and ideal. Taken together, these stories and pictures make a whole world, whose heart, like that flaming bush in the old story, burns and is never consumed.

Whosoever Reports a Thing, Harry Lieberman, 1976. Collection of the Museum of American Folk Art, NY.

11

ONLY THE STORY REMAINS

—HASIDIC TALE, retold by Ellen Frankel

Whenever the Jews were threatened with disaster, the Baal

Shem Tov would go to a certain place in the forest, light a fire,

and say a special prayer. Always a miracle would occur, and the dis-

aster would be averted.

In later times when disaster threatened, the Maggid of

Mezritch, his disciple, would go to the same place in the forest and

say, "Master of the Universe, I do not know how to light the fire,

but I can say the prayer." And again the disaster would be averted.

Still later, his disciple, Moshe Leib of Sasov, would go to the

same place in the forest and say, "Lord of the World, I do not know

how to light the fire or say the prayer, but I know the place and that

must suffice." And it always did.

When Israel of Riszhyn needed intervention from heaven, he

would say to God, "I no longer know the place, nor how to light

the fire, nor how to say the prayer, but I can tell the story and that

must suffice."

And it did.

OPPOSITE:

Study for the Jewish School

(Joe Singer as a Boy),

R. B. Kitaj, 1980.

The Jewish Museum, NY/

Art Resource, NY.

The Wandering of Adam and Eve,
Abel Pann, Jerusalem, 1925.
From the HUC Skirball
Cultural Center and
Museum, Los Angeles, CA.

BEGINNINGS

ACCORDING TO THE SACRED JEWISH TEACHING KNOWN AS THE TORAH, the world came into being through the speaking of two simple words: "Yehi Or!" ("Let-there-be Light!") With that first holy spark, the grand story of Creation began. Remarkably, it was only on the fourth day that God created the heavenly bodies of light—the sun, the moon, and the stars. What, then, was the light created on that very first day? What radiance lit up the world even before matter and energy were created? Jewish tradition claims that the Torah itself was that first light. And it was from the Torah that God formed all the other elements that make up our world. What all these elements share in common is language: for they all trace their origins to the words of the First Storyteller who spoke the world into being.

Yet placed alongside the fabulous mythologies of the Egyptians, Babylonians, and Canaanites, the creation saga of ancient Israel pales in comparison. For in place of warring gods and cosmic cataclysm, the Torah presents only unadorned soliloquy: God speaks, and the world materializes out of chaos. There is no conflict, no ultimate triumph of the forces of good over evil. In fact, all is quite peaceful until human beings enter the world and bring with them the return of primal chaos: Adam and Eve disobey God's rules, Cain murders his brother, Noah's generation backslides, and the builders of Babel's tower overreach their authority. If not for these human transgressions, we might suppose, the universe would have run like clockwork.

Not surprisingly, human beings have been unwilling to assume all the blame for the world's flaws. Through centuries-long conversation with the Torah, Jews have developed their own rich mythology of creation, characterized by moral complexity, literary ingenuity, and a healthy dose of wit. In this first section, we encounter several stories, mostly drawn from the Midrash, the ancient Jewish tradition of interpretation that views the reticence of the biblical text as an invitation to amplify, embellish, and invent.

We begin with several tales that fill in the details of creation missing from the first chapter of Genesis. "The Beginning" dramatizes in concrete form how God established the balance in nature. Divine mercy, personified by a host of angels and the primeval monsters, Behemoth, Leviathan, and Ziz-Shaddai, intervenes and tempers the seeming harshness of divine justice. Yet the balance between mercy and justice also has a dark side, as we see in Howard Schwartz's contemporary midrash, "The Dual History of the Prince of Darkness."

Several stories in this section speculate about the fundamental nature of living beings. "Leviathan and the Fox" is an *etiological* tale, a story that explains why and how something in our world first came to be. Here we are told how Fox cunningly outwits death, an almost universal motif wherever foxes cross human paths. In "Lilith," the rabbinic sages attempt to explain why there are competing versions of human creation in the first two chapters of Genesis. Their solution is to imagine that Adam actually had two wives. His first wife, Lilith, proved unacceptable because she demanded equal rights in the garden; but her successor, Eve, derived from Adam's rib, knew her proper place. This legend, once a misogynist rationale for male supremacy, has become in our own time a parable of female empowerment. Another midrash, "The Creation of the Soul," proposes that the human soul is born into the world fully knowing its fate but is stricken with forgetfulness at the moment of its birth. Human beings then spend the rest of their lives relearning what they once knew. Life itself, then, is an endless remembering.

The last two stories are about beginnings that emerge out of more recent history. The famous legend of the Golem, from sixteenth-century Prague, presents a half-human creature fashioned out of mud, like the first man, and brought to life through mystical incantations. Through a series of miraculous interventions, he rescues the Jewish community from the evil designs of a local priest. In contrast, Theodor Herzl's "The Menorah" tells of the animation of a human spirit, as a secularist takes upon himself a religious identity. This modern spiritual awakening, like the creation of the cosmos itself, begins with the kindling of light.

THE BEGINNING

—TRADITIONAL MIDRASH, retold by Ellen Frankel

Alphabet of Creation,
Ben Shahn, 1963.
Fukushima Prefectural
Museum of Art, Japan.
© 1997 Estate of Ben
Shahn/Licensed by
VAGA, NY.

Before the heavens and the earth were made, while all still whirled in the chaos of first things, God fashioned the Torah. Eons before the earth cooled and life burst forth upon its fertile soil, the letters of the Torah blazed forth, black fire upon white fire, lighting up the entire universe with its glory.

And then God created a world. But alas! It was not a perfect world, and so God destroyed it. Nine hundred and seventy-four generations sprang forth and perished, and still God labored toward perfection. Until at last God understood that the lower world would always be incomplete and flawed. So God spread over this last created world the Divine Wings of mercy and goodness and shielded it from the harsh glare of heaven's own justice. And so, this world did not perish like the others. It sparkled radiantly in the blackness, a blue-green gem in the diadem of God's love. And God saw that it was a good world.

But Divine Goodness did not end there. For God promised to continue protecting this newborn, imperfect world. Had God not done so, the evil spirits and fierce beasts would soon have put an end to the weaker creatures,

including frail beings like ourselves. And so God decreed that each Nisan, at the time of spring, the holy seraphim would swoop down upon the evil spirits and demons and monsters of the night and prevent them from harming humankind. And to this day, the seraphim cover us all with their majestic wings, and there we shelter, unafraid.

And so, too, in Tammuz, at the time of summer, God commanded mighty Behemoth, who dwells in the Thousand Mountains and feasts on the shady jujube tree, to lift up its great horny head and roar but once, but so terrible is this roar that lions and leopards and bears cower in their lairs and lose heart, and so the gentle beasts can nurture their young in peace.

And in Tishrei, at the coming of autumn, the great bird Ziz-Shaddai flaps its monstrous wings and lets out such a fearsome shriek that the falcon and the hawk and the eagle tremble in their nests and fear to prey upon the weaker birds lest the Ziz swoop down upon them and gobble them whole. And so the little birds escape their enemies' sharp talons.

And in winter, in the month of Tevet, the sea boils and fumes, and the mighty Leviathan, whose fins flash with a brilliant flame and whose length exceeds a hundred miles, passes gas in the depths and frightens the bigger fish into their caves, so that the smaller ones can swim unafraid. Even the shark and whale shudder when Leviathan churns the ocean with his great tail and gnashes his ten thousand teeth.

And to watch over all, God appointed the Angels of Mercy surrounding the Heavenly Throne, Michael and Gabriel and Raphael and Uriel, and God banished the Angels of Destruction to the far reaches of heaven, so that above—as below—peace might prevail.

THE DUAL HISTORY OF THE PRINCE OF DARKNESS

—BY HOWARD SCHWARTZ

Long before the creation of light came the creation of darkness. This realm was ruled by the Prince of Darkness, who was served by a legion of angels who drew their sustenance from darkness. There are those who believe that the Prince of Darkness was Samael, the archangel who fell from heaven and now rules the underworld, and there are others who insist that the Prince of Darkness had no other name. Both sources agree that when the Holy One revealed his decision to create the world from light, the Prince of Darkness raised his voice to ask, *Why not from darkness?* But from here on the history is told in ways that are very different. Those who consider the Prince to be the evil angel claim that the Holy One and the angels who advised him regarded this objection with the greatest concern, since at that time all of creation consisted of nothing more than a great span of darkness. And there was no doubt that the Prince of Darkness, as ruler of all that then existed, was powerful enough to create another world whose source would stem from darkness rather than from light. These angels are said to have convinced the Holy One of this great danger to the future of the world he wanted, and those who tell this story claim that the Holy One then banished the Prince of Darkness and all of his angels to a dungeon, where they languish to this day, now known as the Watchers, their faces haggard and their lips sealed. And they also believe that these prisoners will remain silent until the end of time, when the Prince of Darkness will once more raise his voice and claim to have taken part in the creation. Then, it is assumed, the Holy One will destroy both him and all of his angels, and in the absence of darkness a veil of light will come to surround the world.

Untitled,
Orly Maiberg, 1997.
Courtesy of the artist.

But there are others who tell this story, and though they agree that the Prince did propose that the world be derived from darkness, they insist that this suggestion did not provoke either the Holy One or any of his angels. Rather, they believe that the Holy One considered this question for nine or ten centuries and then announced what he had decided to do: No, he had not changed his mind about creating the world from light, but he had decided to derive this light from darkness, so that it would be written, *With darkness over the surface of the deep, God said, Let there be light,* and in this way all would understand that light must draw its source from darkness, and that this darkness must always precede the light. And these same sources believe that far from objecting to this decision, the Prince of Darkness and all his angels accepted it from the first. For among them it was understood that eventually everything must come back to the seeds of its own creation, and that in the end the darkness that had preceded the light from which the cosmos was created would also succeed it, and that a time would come again when the Prince of Darkness would once more rule over the world.

LEVIATHAN AND THE FOX

—*BY MICHA JOSEF BERDYCZEWSKI*, translated by I. M. Lask

Nebuchadnezzar asked Ben Sira: "Why are the images in the world to be found in the sea as well, save the likenesses of the fox and the mole, which are not in the sea?" "Because," said he, "the fox is shrewder than all other creatures."

When the Angel of Death was fashioned and raised his eyes and saw the many creatures found in the world, he promptly said to Him: "Lord of the Universe, give me authority to slay them." And the Holy and Blessed One answered: "Fling a pair of each of the creatures into the sea and you shall hold sway over those who are left." This he did at once and flung a pair of each species into the sea, where he drowned them. When the fox saw this, what did he do? He promptly stood stock still and began to weep. "Why are you weeping?" the Angel of Death asked him; and he answered: "Because of my companion whom you have flung into the sea." "And where is your companion then?" asked the angel. Thereupon the fox went over to the seashore and the Angel of Death saw the fox's reflection in the sea, so he thought that he had flung some other pair instead of him and said to him: "Clear away from here." Thereupon the fox fled and saved himself.

The mole met him and he told her what had happened and what he had done. She went and did the same and also escaped.

A year later Leviathan gathered all the creatures in the sea together. The only ones missing were the fox and the mole, which had never entered the water. He sent to inquire and was told what the fox had done in his wisdom, together with the mole. And they told him that the fox was exceedingly wise. When Leviathan heard that the fox was clever, he became envious of him and sent big fishes after him and commanded them to mislead him and to bring him to his place.

They went and found him strolling by the seashore. When the fox saw the fishes playing there, he was surprised and joined them. When they saw him, they asked him: "Who are you?" "I am a fox," said he. "Why," they told him, "do you know how greatly you are held in honor, for it is to you that we have come." "How is that?" he asked them. "Leviathan," they explained, "is sick and on the verge of death, and has ordered that none may reign in his place save the fox; for he has heard that you are wise and more understanding than all creatures. So come with us, since we have been sent in your honor." "How can I enter the sea without perishing?" he asked them. "Ride upon one of us," they said, "and he will carry you above the surface so that the sea does not touch you with a single drop even on the tip of your paw until you reach the kingdom. There we shall bring you down, though you will feel nothing, and you will reign over them all and be king and rejoice all your life, and you will no longer need to go in search of food, nor will savage beasts that are larger than you come and strike you and consume you."

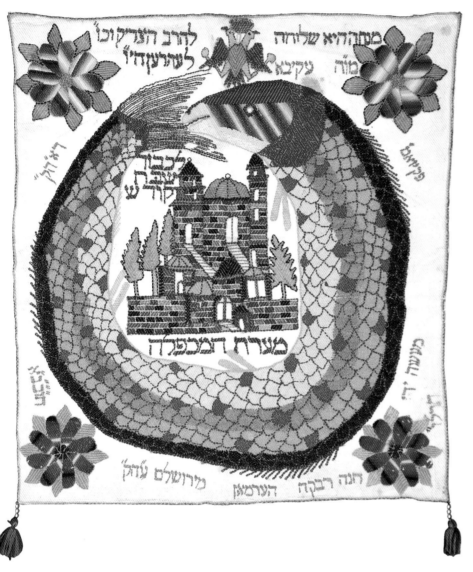

Sabbath Cloth,
19th century.
Collection Israel Museum,
Jerusalem.

would have honored me. But as it is you are going wrong." "You do not have your heart with you?" they cried. "Oh no," said he, "for it is our practice to leave our hearts in our own places when we go hither and thither. If we need it we take it, and if not, we let it remain in our own place."

"Well then," said they, "what shall we do now?" "My place and dwelling," he informed them, "are by the seashore. If you like you can take me back to the spot where you found me, and I shall take my heart and come with you and give it to Leviathan so that he honors me and you, too. But if you conduct me thus without a heart, he will be angry with you and consume you. As for me, I do not need to be afraid, because I shall tell him: 'My lord, they did not tell me to begin with, and when they did tell me I advised them to go back with me so that I could take my heart, but they did not wish to.'" Thereupon the fish said: "He speaks well." And they turned back to the spot whence they had taken him on the seashore. There he climbed off the fish's back and began dancing and rolling in the sand and laughing. "Come, take your heart quickly," they said to him, "and let us go." "Clear off, you fools!" said he. "If my heart had not been with me, I would not have entered the sea with you. Or do you have any creature that moves about and does not have its heart with it?" "You have tricked us," said they. "Oh, you fools!" he answered. "I laughed at the Angel of Death, and can most certainly laugh at you."

Shamefacedly, they returned and told the tale to Leviathan. "Indeed," said he, "he is cunning and you are silly, and of you the verse was uttered: The waywardness of the silly shall slay them'" (Prov. 1.32). And he ate them up.

Ever since, every species of all creatures, and even of Adam and his wife, is to be found in the sea with the exception of the fox and the mole. You will not find them there.

When he heard their words he believed them and rode on one of them, and they set out across the sea. When he reached the waves, he began to regret it. He felt uneasy and said: "Woe is me! What have I done? These fish have mocked me more than all the mockery I have ever made of other creatures, and now I have fallen into their hands and how can I be delivered?" So he said to them: "Since I have now come with you and am in your power, tell me the truth. Why do you desire me?" "We shall tell you the truth," they answered. "Leviathan has heard that you are exceedingly wise, so he has declared: 'I shall rip his belly open and eat his heart and then I shall be wise.'" "Now why did you not tell me the truth earlier?" said he to them. "For then I would have brought my heart with me and I would have given it to King Leviathan and he

LILITH

—TRADITIONAL MIDRASH, retold by Ellen Frankel

H ow lonely Adam was that first day as he watched the animals parade by, two by two, each with a companion. And God took pity on him and made him a partner, scooping out another handful of dust from the earth. This creature was named Lilith and she became Adam's wife.

Because this first woman was equal to Adam in every way, having been made by God out of the same earth and on the same day as her husband, she insisted on enjoying equal footing with him in the Garden: sharing the labor and its reward, working side by side to tend the growing things entrusted into their care.

Also in the ways of love between a man and a woman, Lilith wished to share equally, sometimes lying on top of her lover and sometimes below him. For were they not full partners in creation?

RIGHT: *Amulet*, Central Europe, 19th century. From the HUC Skirball Cultural Center and Museum, Los Angeles, CA.

But this was too much for Adam to bear, and he complained to God, saying, "Is this why I have been created—to share *everything* with her? When I asked for a companion, I did not mean this!"

When Lilith heard Adam's complaint, she decided to leave the Garden, where she was not welcome, and make a new home for herself far away. Pronouncing the Awesome Name, she flew away to the shores of the Sea of Reeds.

Amulet, Germany, 18th century. From the HUC Skirball Cultural Center and Museum, Los Angeles, CA. Kirschstein Collection.

Instantly Adam was sorry that he had driven her away, and he once more cried out to God, "My wife has deserted me! Again, I am all alone!"

So God sent three angels, Senoy, Sansenoy, and Semangelof, to fetch Lilith back to Eden. But she was not willing to return, for she knew that Adam did not desire her the way she was.

"If you do not return with us," threatened the angels, "you will lose one hundred of your children each day until you change your mind."

"So be it," replied Lilith. And she sent them back to Eden empty-handed. And soon the angels' dire prophecy came to pass.

From that day on, in revenge for her hurt pride and slaughtered children, Lilith has prowled through the night, looking for newborn babies to harm. With her long black hair and great flapping wings, she will sometimes swoop down on day-old baby boys or on baby girls during their first twenty days of life, and suck the breath out of them.

But at heart she is not cruel. For out of compassion for her sister creatures, she has betrayed her own power: "If you inscribe the names of the three angels, Senoy, Sansenoy, and Semangelof, in an amulet and tie this charm around your children's neck," she has whispered to the mothers of these innocent babies, "I promise not to harm even one hair on their heads."

And she has never failed to keep her word.

THE CREATION OF THE SOUL

—TRADITIONAL MIDRASH, adapted by Ellen Frankel

All human souls were created on the first day of Creation before anything else in the world. In that first hour, God placed these souls in the highest heaven where they remain until called to enter the body chosen for them.

When a baby is conceived, the Angel of Pregnancy and Birth brings the fertilized egg before God who decides its fate: whether it will be a boy or girl, rich or poor, strong or weak, beautiful or ugly, fat or thin, wise or foolish. But God leaves one decision entirely to the unborn soul: whether it will be righteous or wicked. For it is written: everything is in the hands of Heaven, except the fear of Heaven.

Then God sends the Angel of Souls to the highest heaven to bring back the soul destined for that body, and God commands: "Enter into that seed." But the soul always rebels, for compared to the celestial world, the lower world is but a poor place, full of sorrow and pain.

But God reproves the soul, saying, "It was for this very seed that you were created!" So the soul enters the unborn child and nestles quietly under the mother's breast. And above its head God kindles a light.

The next morning a second angel carries the soul to the Garden of Eden, where it sees all the Righteous enjoying eternal happiness.

"If you follow God's Law and live justly," explains the angel, "you will one day join these happy creatures here. But if not . . ."

And that night, the angel takes the soul to Gehinnom, where it sees the Angels of Hell whipping wicked souls with burning lashes.

"This is what awaits those who devote their lives to sin and injustice," the angel says. "It is up to you to choose."

Zodiac Circle, Mark Podwal, 1995. From the HUC Skirball Cultural Center and Museum, Los Angeles, CA. Courtesy of Forum Gallery, NY. Museum commission with funds provided in honor of Marian and Don De Witt by their children and families.

Between morning and night of that day, the angel reveals to the unborn soul its future life: where it will live and where it will die and where it will be buried. Then the angel returns the soul to the womb where God shuts it up with doors and bars. There it dwells for nine months, the first three months in the lower part of the womb, the next three in the middle part, and the last three in the upper part.

When it is time for the baby to leave the warm refuge of the womb, the angel bids it to come forth. But the soul protests: "Oh, no! That will be too much to bear!"

But the angel silences it, saying: "So God has decreed. Against your will you were formed, and against your will you will be born. And against your will you will one day die. Such is your fate."

Then the angel strikes the newborn baby under the nose, leaving a small cleft there. Then he extinguishes the light shining above its head, and instantly the soul forgets everything it has learned during the previous nine months. And then the baby emerges into the world, crying and afraid.

Each soul spends the rest of its time on earth recovering all that it once knew.

Spiral of Life,
David Sharir, 1986.
Courtesy of Pucker
Gallery, Boston, MA.

THE GOLEM

—*CZECH FOLKTALE*, adapted by Nathan Ausubel

Rabbi Yehuda Loew, known to the pious as the *"Maharal,"* came to Prague from Nikolsburg, Posen, in the year 5332 of the Creation (1572 C.E.) in order to become rabbi of the community there. The whole world resounded with his fame because he was deeply learned in all branches of knowledge and knew many languages. Is it any wonder then that he was revered by the wise men among the Gentiles? Even King Rudolf of Bohemia esteemed him highly. Because of these reasons the Maharal was able to wage war successfully against the enemies of Israel who tried to besmirch Jewish honor with their false blood accusations.

After much sad experience, in the course of which these frightful slanders were fully exposed in the brilliant light of truth, King Rudolf assured Rabbi Yehuda Loew that never again would he permit any blood accusations to be charged against the Jews in his kingdom. When the Maharal first came to Prague the blood accusation was a very common occurrence there and much innocent Jewish blood was spilled because of it. Immediately on his arrival, Rabbi Yehuda Loew announced that he would fight against this unholy calumny with all his power in order to silence the enemies of his people who so tirelessly plotted for its destruction.

One day, King Rudolf sent his carriage to fetch the Maharal for an audience with him. They talked together for a whole hour but what was said during their meeting nobody knows to this very day.

The Maharal returned home in a gay mood. He told his intimates: "I have already half destroyed the filthy myth of the blood accusation! With God's help I hope soon to wash away entirely this hideous stain from our innocent people."

And the Maharal's hope was soon fulfilled. To his joy, and to the joy of *all* the Jews of Bohemia, the King issued a decree ten days later announcing that no one, besides the particular individual charged in a blood accusation, had to stand trial. Prior to that *all* the Jews were collectively charged with the alleged crime. Furthermore, the decree said that the individual accused could not be condemned unless there was positive proof of his guilt in the crime. The King also ordered that, during any trial on such a charge, the Rabbi of Prague had to be present. Nor could the verdict be valid unless the King himself countersigned the judge's sentence.

One would have thought that the King's decree would put an end to the shameless slander that the Jews had a custom which required them to use Christian blood in the baking of the Passover *matzos*. But the enemies of Israel were endlessly resourceful that way. All that it required for a Christian who wished to destroy a Jew was stealthily to plant a dead child in his house and the hue and cry of the blood accusation was on again. Only in rare cases was it possible for the Jew to extricate himself from the fine meshes of the net his enemies entangled him in.

There was one man in the kingdom of Bohemia of whom the Maharal stood in great dread. This was the priest Thaddeus. He was not only an implacable enemy of the Jews but a clever sorcerer besides. He was determined to carry on a war to the death against the Maharal. The Maharal too girded himself for battle against this enemy.

One night, the Maharal called upon Heaven to answer him in a dream how best he could wage successful war against his enemy Thaddeus. And the answer came to him in the alphabetically arranged words of the Cabala: "Create a Golem out of clay who will destroy all the enemies of Israel!"

The Maharal knew that in the Hebrew words of this formula there were stored enough mystical secrets by means of whose powers he could create a Golem. He then confided his secret to Isaac ben Shimshon ha-Cohen, his son-in-law, and to his principal disciple, Jacob ben Chayyim ha-Levi. He told them that he would require their help because they were born under the constellation of Fire and Water respectively; the Maharal himself was born under the constellation of Air. To the making of the Golem all the four elements of Fire, Water, Air and Earth were necessary. He then cautioned the two against revealing his plan to anyone and instructed them that, during the next seven days, they were to purify their bodies and souls with ablutions, fasting, prayer and austerities.

It was on the second day in the month of Adar in the year 5340 of Creation (1580 C.E.) that the momentous event took place. At four in the morning the three made their way out of the city to the Moldau. There, on the clay bank of the river, they molded the figure of a man three ells in length. They fashioned for him hands and feet and a head, and drew his features in clear human relief.

Having done this, the three stationed themselves at the feet of the prostrate Golem. The Maharal then ordered Isaac ben Shimshon ha-Cohen to encircle the figure seven times from right to left. He also revealed to him the cabalistic incantations he was to pronounce while doing so.

No sooner had the Maharal's son-in-law completed his task when the Golem began to glow like fire. Then the Maharal asked Jacob ben Chayyim ha-Levi to do the same circling, but he instructed him to utter different cabalistic formulae and to encircle the figure from left to right. As soon as he was through, the fire in the Golem was quenched and a cloud of steam arose from its body. When it cleared, they saw that hair had grown on its head and that nails had appeared on its fingers and toes.

OPPOSITE:
Message I (detail),
Grisha Bruskin, 1990.
© 1997 Grisha Bruskin/
Licensed by VAGA, NY/
Courtesy Marlborough
Gallery, NY.

Next, the Maharal himself began to circle around the Golem seven times. Then with one voice, all three recited the Scriptural passage from Genesis 2:7: "And he breathed into his nostrils the breath of life; and man became a living soul."

Immediately, the Golem opened his eyes and looked at the three men wonderingly.

"Get up on your feet!" commanded the Maharal.

The Golem stood up and they dressed him in clothes they had brought with them, clothes that were fitting for a *shammes*.

Most wonderful to relate—when they had left Prague two hours before they were only three, but when six o'clock struck there were four of them returning!

On the way home the Maharal said to the Golem: "Know that we have created you so that you may protect the defenseless Jews against their enemies. Your name is Joseph and you will

serve me as *shammes* in the House of Judgment. You must obey me no matter what I tell you to do, even should I ask you to jump into fire and water!"

Although the Golem could not speak, for the power of speech is God's alone to give, he, nonetheless, understood what the Maharal said to him. He had a remarkable sense of hearing and could detect sounds from a very great distance.

To his two disciples the Maharal said that he had named the Golem Joseph because he had implanted in him the spirit of Joseph Shida, he who was half-man and half-demon, and who had saved the sages of the Talmud from many trials and dangers.

When the Maharal came home he told his wife, Perele the *Rebbitzen*, pointing to the Golem, that he had met the poor unfortunate (plainly a mute idiot) on the street, and that he felt very sorry for him, and so he brought him home with him.

"He will serve me as *shammes* in the House of Judgment," he said.

At the same time the Maharal forbade anyone to give the Golem any menial tasks to perform for he had not created him for that.

And so the Golem sat always in a corner of the House of Judgment, with expressionless face cupped in his hands, just like a clay Golem who has no thought in his head. Because he behaved like a mute idiot, people began to call him derisively *"Yosele Golem."* Others called him "Dumb Yosele."

Despite the Maharal's orders against giving Yosele Golem any tasks to perform, his wife, Perele the *Rebbitzen*, disobeyed him. One day, just before Passover, she motioned to him to fetch water from the well and to fill the two big barrels in the pantry with water for the holy day.

Yosele Golem quickly snatched two buckets and ran with them to the well. As the *Rebbitzen* was preoccupied with other matters she did not observe what he was doing.

To the well and back again he ran so many times that, without anyone noticing it, the barrels began to overflow and soon the water spread through the house. At this the servants raised a great outcry and ran to tell the Maharal.

When Rabbi Yehuda Loew came and saw what Yosele Golem had done he burst out laughing and said to the *Rebbitzen*: "My, my, what a wonderful water-carrier you got yourself for Passover!"

He then went and took away the buckets from the Golem and led him back into his corner in the House of Judgment.

From that time on the *Rebbitzen* never again asked Yosele Golem to do anything for her. But when the story got around in Prague everybody laughed. It even gave rise to a new saying: "You're as good a watchmaker as Yosele Golem is a water-carrier!"

The Maharal employed the Golem to protect the Jews of Prague against the dangers that threatened them. With his assistance he was able to perform many miracles. Most of all he used him in his war against the blood accusations which were again rife in the land and which caused so much sorrow to the Jews. In such cases, when the Maharal had to send Yosele Golem on a dangerous mission, he found it advisable to make him invisible by means of an amulet upon which was written a cabalistic word.

In the period before Passover, which coincides with the Christian Easter, a time when the blood accusation was usually brought, the Maharal made Yosele Golem put on a disguise. He had him dress up like a Christian and made him wear a rope around his middle in order that he might look like any ordinary Gentile porter.

The Maharal ordered him to guard the Ghetto of Prague like the apple of his eye, to roam all its streets at night and to be on the lookout against those who might wish to do evil to the Jews. He was to examine the contents of every passing wagon and of every bundle carried by a passerby. If he but suspected someone of making preparations for bringing a blood accusation against the Jews he was to bind the malefactor with his rope and bring him straightway to the city watch in the *Rathaus*.

It so happened that the leading Jew of Prague in communal matters was the wealthy *Reb* Mordchi Meisel. One of his debtors, a Christian who ran a slaughter-house, owed him five thousand crowns. Time and again *Reb* Mordchi demanded of the slaughterer that he return the money, but each time the latter declined to pay on some pretext or other.

Now the slaughter-house was situated outside the city, and the slaughterer was in the habit of conveying meat into the city through the Jewish ghetto. This put the idea into his head of accusing Reb Mordchi of having used Christian blood for the baking of *matzos*.

Several days before Passover, the child of a Christian neighbor of the slaughterer's died. It was buried in the Christian cemetery. Late that night, the slaughterer stole into the cemetery and dug up the child. He then killed a pig in the slaughter-house and cleaned out its insides. He cut the throat of the dead child and wrapping it in the folds of a *tallit*, he placed it inside the pig. Afterwards, he rode to town, intending to secrete the body in *Reb* Mordchi's house while he slept.

When the slaughterer was near *Reb* Mordchi's house, Yosele Golem, who was then roaming the streets, suddenly appeared and insisted on examining the contents of his wagon. When he saw the dead child in the pig's carcass, he quickly bound the slaughterer with his rope and carried him to the town watch right in the *Rathaus*. He dumped him in the courtyard and hurried away.

A great commotion was heard in the *Rathaus*. The watch was called out. They brought lights, and saw before them the slaughterer, lying tied hand and foot and looking bruised and swollen. They examined the pig and found the dead child in its carcass. Seeing that it was wrapped in a Jewish *tallit*, the chief of the watch clearly saw that it was a blood accusation plot.

After close questioning the slaughterer confessed what he was up to. When he was asked who had brought him to the city watch he answered: "It was a Christian porter who was mute. He was an enormous fellow who looked more like a devil than a man!"

No one had any idea who this strange creature could be. A great terror fell upon all enemies of Israel. Only Thaddeus the priest understood from what quarter this secret power could have come. So he had the rumor spread in town that the Maharal was a sorcerer, in order to discredit him in the eyes of all upright Christians who respected him. And he intensified his struggle against him and all the Jews with a consuming hatred.

❖

When King Rudolf saw that there was no foundation whatsoever for any of the blood accusations he became angry at the priest Thaddeus. The pleas and persuasion of the Maharal at last had their effect. The King issued a solemn decree under his own seal, forbidding anyone in his realm from ever raising the blood accusation against any Jew or group of Jews. Neither were the courts of the kingdom to honor such charges because the sin of accusing the innocent with crimes they had not committed always falls like a blight upon the entire nation.

Once again Passover came around but not one blood accusation was raised in the Kingdom of Bohemia that year. It seemed as if King Rudolf's decree had effectively silenced the enemy. Thereupon, the Maharal called his son-in-law and his disciple, both of whom had assisted in the creation of the Golem, and said to them: "I have called you to tell you that the Golem is no longer needed. The lie of the blood accusation will never be raised in this country again."

This took place on the night of *Lag Ba-Omer* in the year 5350 of the Creation (1590 C.E.).

That night, the Maharal said to Yosele Golem: "Don't sleep tonight in the House of Judgment but instead go up into the attic of the Synagogue and make your bed there!"

Ever-obedient, Yosele Golem did as the Maharal told him.

After midnight, accompanied by his son-in-law and his disciple, the Maharal ascended to the attic of the Synagogue and stationed himself before the sleeping giant. They now took their places in reverse position to that when they created him. They stood at his head and gazed into his face.

Then they began to circle around him, beginning from left to right. They did this seven times, intoning cabalistic incantations and formulae in the meantime.

All this time, the old *shammes*, *Reb* Abraham Chayyim, whom the Maharal had brought to assist him, stood at a discreet distance from the Golem, lighting him up with two waxen candles. Upon the completion of the seventh encirclement the Golem lay rigid in death. He looked again like a hunk of hardened clay.

The Maharal took the two candles from the *shammes* and had him divest the Golem of his clothes, except for the shirt. They then took some old discarded prayer shawls and wrapped them securely around him. Afterwards, they covered him with thousands upon thousands of discarded leaves from old prayer books so that he was altogether hidden from sight.

The Maharal also told the *shammes* not to breathe a word to any living soul of what he had seen that night and to burn the Golem's clothes when no one saw. Then they all descended from the attic. They washed their hands and uttered prayers of purification, as one usually does after being near a corpse.

In the morning, the Maharal had a report spread throughout Prague that his *shammes*, Yosele Golem, had quarreled with him and had left the city at night. Everybody accepted the report as true except the three who had the privilege of going up to the attic with the Maharal the previous night.

One week later, the Maharal had a proclamation posted and read in the *Altneuschul*, forbidding any Jew, on pain of excommunication, ever to go up to the Synagogue attic.

The reverence for Rabbi Yehuda Loew was so great that no one dared look for the Golem in the attic. It is believed that he is still lying there, buried deep under a heap of torn leaves from old prayer books, and only waiting for the coming of the Messiah, or for the time when new dangers appear to menace the existence of Israel, to rise again and smite the foe.

THE MENORAH

—*BY THEODOR HERZL*, translated by Henry Zohn

Once there was a man who deep in his soul felt the need to be a Jew. His material circumstances were satisfactory enough. He was making an adequate living and was fortunate enough to have a vocation in which he could create according to the impulses of his heart. You see, he was an artist. He had long ceased to trouble his head about his Jewish origin or about the faith of his fathers, when the age-old hatred reasserted itself under a fashionable slogan. Like many others, our man, too, believed that this movement would soon subside. But instead of getting better, it got worse. Although he was not personally affected by them, the attacks pained him anew each time. Gradually his soul became one bleeding wound.

This secret psychic torment had the effect of steering him to its source, namely, his Jewishness, with the result that he experienced a change that he might never have in better days because he had become so alienated: he began to love Judaism with great fervor. At first he did not fully acknowledge this mysterious affection, but finally it grew so powerful that his vague feelings crystallized into a clear idea to which he gave voice: the thought that there was only one way out of this Jewish suffering—namely, to return to Judaism.

When his best friends, whose situation was similar to his, found out about this, they shook their heads and thought that he had gone out of his mind. How could something that only meant an intensification and deepening of the malady be a remedy? He, on the other hand, thought that the moral distress of modern Jews was so acute because they had lost the spiritual counterpoise which our strong forefathers had possessed. People ridiculed him behind his back, some even laughed right in his face, but he did not let the silly remarks of people whose judgment he had never before had occasion to value throw him off his course, and he bore their malicious or good-natured jests with equanimity. And since his behavior otherwise was not irrational, people in time left him to his whim, although some used a stronger term, *idée fixe*, to describe it.

In his patient way our man over and over again displayed the courage of his convictions. There were a number of changes which he himself found hard to accept, although he was stubborn enough not to let on. As a man and

Lamp,
Rome, 1st–3rd century.
The Jewish Museum, NY/
Art Resource, NY.

an artist of modern sensibilities he was deeply rooted in many non-Jewish customs, and he had absorbed ineradicable elements from the cultures of the nations among which his intellectual pursuits had taken him. How was this to be reconciled with his return to Judaism? This gave rise to many doubts in his own mind about the soundness of his guiding idea, his *idée maitresse*, as a French thinker has called it. Perhaps the generation that had grown up under the influence of other cultures was no longer capable of that return which he had discovered as the solution. But the next generation, provided it were given the right guidance early enough, would be able to do so. He therefore tried to make sure that his own children, at least, would be shown the right way; he was going to give them a Jewish education from the very beginning.

In previous years he had let the festival which for centuries had illuminated the marvel of the Maccabees with the glow of candles pass by unobserved. Now, however, he used it as an occasion to provide his children with a beautiful memory for the future. An attachment to the ancient nation was to be instilled early in these young souls. A menorah was acquired, and when he held this nine-branched candelabrum in his hands for the first time, a strange mood came over him. In his remote youth, in his father's house, such little lights had burned and there was something intimate and homelike about the holiday. This tradition did not seem chill or dead. The custom of kindling one light with another had been passed on through the ages.

The ancient form of the menorah also gave him food for thought. When had the primitive structure of this candelabrum first been devised? Obviously, its form had originally been derived from that of a tree: the sturdy stem in the center; four branches to the right and four to the left, each below the other, each pair on the same level, yet all reaching the same height. A later symbolism added a ninth, shorter branch which jutted out in front and was called the *shammash* or servant. With what mystery had this simple artistic form, taken from nature, been endowed by successive generations? And our friend, who was, after all, an artist, wondered whether it would not be possible to infuse new life into the rigid form of the menorah, to water its roots like those of a tree. The very sound of the name, which he now pronounced in front of his children every evening, gave him pleasure. Its sound was especially lovely when it came from the mouth of a child.

The first candle was lit and the origin of the holiday was retold: the miracle of the little lamp which had burned so much longer than expected, as well as the story of the return from the Babylonian exile, of the Second Temple, of the Maccabees. Our friend told his children all he knew. It was not much but for them it was enough. When the second candle was lit, they repeated what he had told them, and although they had learned it all from him, it seemed to him quite new and beautiful. In the days that followed he could hardly wait for the evenings, which became ever brighter. Candle after candle was lit in the menorah, and together with his children the father mused upon the little lights. At length his reveries became more than he could or would tell them, for his dreams would have been beyond their understanding.

When he had resolved to return to the ancient fold and openly acknowledge his return, he had only intended to do what he considered honorable and sensible. But he had never dreamed that on his way back

Hanukkah Lamp,
c. 1900.
Erich Lessing/
Art Resource, NY.

32

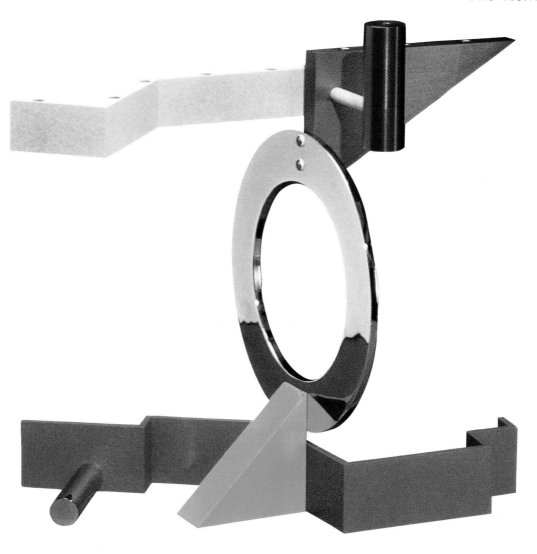

Hanukkah Lamp,
Peter Shire, 1986.
From the HUC Skirball
Cultural Center and
Museum, Los Angeles, CA.
Museum commission
with funds provided by
Marvin and Judy Zeidler.

home he would also find gratification for his longing for beauty. Yet what befell him was nothing less. The menorah with its growing brilliance was indeed a thing of beauty, and inspired lofty thoughts. So he set to work and with an expert hand sketched a design for a menorah which he wanted to present to his children the following year. He made a free adaptation of the motif of the eight arms of equal height which projected from the central stem to the right and to the left, each pair on the same level. He did not consider himself bound by the rigid traditional form, but created again directly from nature, unconcerned with other interpretations which, of course, continued to be no less valid on that account. What he was aiming for was vibrant beauty. But even as he brought new motion into the rigid forms, he still observed their tradition, the refined old style of their arrangement. It was a tree with slender branches; its ends opened up like calyxes, and it was these calyxes that were to hold the candles.

With such thoughtful occupation the week passed. There came the eighth day, on which the entire row of lights is kindled, including the faithful ninth candle, the *sham-mash*, which otherwise serves only to light the others. A great radiance shone forth from the menorah. The eyes of the children sparkled. For our friend, the occasion became a parable for the enkindling of a whole nation. First one candle; it is still dark and the solitary light looks gloomy. Then it finds a companion, then another, and yet another. The darkness must retreat. The young and the poor are the first to see the light; then the others join in, all those who love justice, truth, liberty, progress, humanity and beauty. When all the candles are ablaze everyone must stop in amazement and rejoice at what has been wrought. And no office is more blessed than that of a servant of light.

A$_{\text{CCORDING}}$ TO J$_{\text{EWISH}}$ T$_{\text{RADITION}}$, coming of age obligates children to assume for themselves full legal and ritual responsibility for their actions. A girl is considered religiously mature at twelve; a boy, at thirteen. Until modern times, this transitional moment was marked rather simply by Jewish communities: A boy was called publicly to the Torah to recite the prescribed blessings; then the family celebrated their son's new status with a festive communal meal. Until recently, girls had no equivalent public ritual. Typically, female childhood simply ended at puberty or shortly thereafter when the young girls were married. In our own times, bar and bat mitzvah ceremonies have developed into elaborate communal spectacles, demanding of the initiate extensive preparation and public performance; of the family, considerable outlays of capital, time, and effort; and of the community, participation and gift-giving. Then as now, what really matters when children reach the age of commandments (*mitzvot*) is that they accept responsibility for their own choices.

COMING OF AGE

In many other traditional cultures, male initiation rites typically involve tests of physical prowess—killing a totem animal, bartering trophies for a bride, engaging in combat, surviving in the wild. But for Jews, living landless and disempowered during centuries of diaspora, such trials of manhood have not been an option. Instead of proving themselves through feats of strength, Jewish boys—and on rare occasions, girls—have earned their admission as adult members of the tribe by triumphing over adversity through displays of wit, virtue, and spiritual courage.

The stories in this section feature many different models of coming of age. In "Cracker, or Because of the Calf and Something More," "The Box with Bones," and "The Adventures of Hershel Summerwind," the simple wisdom of a good heart prevails over avarice, malice, and a young man's own natural foolishness. In "The Prince Who Thought He Was a Rooster" by Rabbi Nachman of Bratzlav, a prince's madness gives way to reason when an adult meets him where he is, respecting the young prince's own unique way of being in the world. In each of these stories, children teach their parents that growing up is often not a straight path and seldom one of the parents' own choosing.

What happens when the obstacles facing a young person have been set there not by human forces but by supernatural ones, perhaps by the Evil One himself? Is a good heart sufficient to see one through such a trial? In "The Werewolf," young Israel ben Eliezer, known as the Ba'al Shem Tov, the "Master of the Good Name," confronts Satan and conquers him through the power of compassion. But in Isaac Babel's "The Story of My Dovecote," the young protagonist just barely escapes the satanic pogrom in his village. What saves him is not his good heart or his wits, but only blind fortune that takes his grandfather in his stead. With this sacrificial death comes the end of his childhood. A milder kind of disillusionment marks childhood's end for Teresa Filipine in Kadia Molodowsky's "The Lost Shabes," as the young girl gains a new country at the expense of an old one.

As we reflect on these tales, we may recall our own coming of age. Whether we negotiate this rite of passage with a light heart or with our heart in our mouth, whether we come to a place of power or disenchantment, we each must follow the path charted uniquely for us, and we each must travel it alone.

THE WEREWOLF

—*BY MARTIN BUBER*, translated by Maurice Friedman

When death overtook the old Rabbi Eliezer, the father of the child Israel, he surrendered to it, without a struggle, the soul which had grown weary during many earthly years of wandering and affliction and longed for the fire-spring of renewal. But his dim eyes still sought again and again the fair head of the boy; and when the hour of deliverance appeared, he took him once again in his arms and held with fervent force this light of his last days, that had risen so late for him and his aging wife. He gave him a penetrating look as if he wished to summon up the still-slumbering spirit behind the brow and he spoke.

"My child, the Adversary will confront you in the beginning, at the turning, and at the fulfilment; in the shadow of a dream and in living flesh. He is the abyss over which you must fly. There will be times when you will descend into his last concealment like a flash of lightning, and he will disperse before your power like a thin cloud; and there will be times when he will surround you with vapors of thick darkness, and you will have to stand your ground alone. But those and these times will disappear, and you will be victor in your soul. For know that your soul is an ore that no one can crush and only God can melt. Therefore, fear not the Adversary."

The child read with astonished eyes the words from the withered mouth. The words sank in and remained.

When Rabbi Eliezer had passed away, the pious people of the community took on themselves the care of the boy out of the love that they had had for his father. And when it was time, they sent him to school. But he did not like the noisy and confined place; he escaped again and again into the forest where he delighted in the trees and the animals and moved familiarly in the green woodland without the least fear of night and weather. When they brought him back with sharp reprimands, he kept still for as much as several days under the monotonous sing-song of the teacher; but then he slipped off as softly as a cat and threw himself into the forest. After awhile the men who took care of him decided that they had looked after him enough; besides this, their trouble over the wild creature was completely wasted. So they let him go, and he remained unchecked in the wilds and grew up under the speechless modes of the creatures.

When he was twelve, he hired himself out as helper to the teacher to lead the boys from their houses to school and home again. Then the people in the dull little town saw a remarkable transformation take place. Day by day Israel led a singing procession of children through the streets to school, and later led them home again by a wide detour through meadow and forest. The boys no longer hung their wan, heavy heads as before. They shouted merrily and carried flowers and green branches in their hands. In their hearts burned devotion. So great was the

Trees,
Samuel Halpert, 1917.
The Jewish Museum, NY/
Art Resource, NY.

soaring flame that it broke through the thick smoke of misery and confusion that presses down on the earth and flamed into heaven. And behold, there shone forth above a resplendent reflection.

But the Adversary swelled up with disquietude and hatred and ascended unto heaven. Here he complained about that which was beginning to take place below and which threatened to cheat him of his work. He demanded that he be allowed to descend and measure his strength against the premature messenger, and his request was granted.

So he descended and mingled with the creatures of the earth. He moved among them, listened to them, tested and weighed, but for a long time he encountered no one who might serve the purpose of his venture. At last, in the forest in which Israel had spent the days of his childhood, the Adversary found a charcoal burner, a shy, unsociable fellow who avoided other men. This man was at times compelled to change at night into a werewolf that swept down from afar and rushed around the homesteads, sometimes falling upon an animal and striking terror into a late wanderer, yet never harming any human being. His simple heart writhed under the bitter compulsion; trembling and resisting, he lay hidden in a thicket when the mania overtook him and he could not subdue it. It was thus that the Adversary found him sleeping one night, already in the convulsions of the approaching transformation, and deemed him suitable for his instrument. He thrust his hand into the man's breast, took out his heart and hid it in the earth. Then he sank into the creature his own, a heart out of the heart of darkness.

As Israel led the singing children at sunrise in a wide arc around the little town, the werewolf burst out of the still night-bound forest and rushed in among the troop with foaming mouth and livid misshapenness. The children ran in all directions, some fell senseless to the earth, others clung wailing to their leader. The animal disappeared meanwhile and no calamity took place. Israel collected and comforted the little ones; still the incident brought severe confusion and alarm to the city, especially since several of the children fell into a high fever from fright, burning in anxious dreams and moaning in the darkened rooms. No mother permitted her child on the streets any longer, and no one knew what to do.

Then the word of his dying father came back to the young Israel and now for the first time took on meaning. So he trudged from house to house and swore to the despairing parents that they might again entrust the small ones to him, for he was certain that he could protect them from the monster. None was able to withstand him.

He gathered the children around him and spoke to them as to the grown-ups, indeed more powerfully still, and their souls opened wide to him. He led them again at an early hour to the meadow, bid them wait for him there, and went alone to the forest. As he drew near, the animal burst forth; it stood in front of the trees and grew before his eyes into the heavens, so that it

Children's Portrait (detail),
Jan Rauchwerger, 1993.
Collection of the
Gottesman Family,
Tel Aviv.
Courtesy of the artist.

covered the forest with its body and the field with its claws, and the bloody drivel from its mouth flowed around the rising sun. Israel did not give way, for the word of his father was with him. It seemed to him as if he were going farther and farther and were entering into the body of the werewolf. There was no halt or hindrance to his step until he came to the dark, glowing heart, from whose mournful mirror all beings of the world were reflected, discolored by a burning hatred. He grasped the heart and closed his fingers tight around it. Then he felt it throb, saw drops run down and sensed the infinite suffering that was within it from the beginning. He laid it gently on the earth, which at once swallowed it, found himself alone at the edge of the forest, breathed freely once again, and returned to the children.

On the way they saw the charcoal burner lying dead at the edge of the forest. Those who came across him were astonished by the great peacefulness of his countenance and no longer understood the fear of him that they had experienced, for in death he appeared like a great, clumsy child.

From that day on the boys forgot their singing and began to resemble their fathers and their fathers' fathers. Growing up, they passed over the land with their heads bowed between their shoulders as their fathers had done.

CRACKER, OR BECAUSE OF THE CALF AND SOMETHING MORE

—YEMENITE FOLK TALE, retold by S. D. Goitein

Once upon a time there were a man and his wife who had only one child and were exceedingly poor. The man died, leaving nothing but a calf. After his father died the son asked his mother what his name was, and she told him, "You don't have any name." Then he said, "Give me some money with which to buy one." She said, "We have no money, but if you care to take the calf, you are welcome to it." The son took the calf and went along till he met seven robbers. They asked him what he wanted, and when he had told them, they took away the calf, and said, "You are called Cracker." Full of delight he hastened back to his mother, and cried out, "Mother, now I have got a name." "Well, what is it?" asked the mother. "Oh, dear!" he said, "I have forgotten it." So he forthwith hurried back to the robbers and asked them about his name. They gave him a pitcher, and said, "When you get back to your mother smash the pitcher, and the pitcher will go 'crack' and you will remember your name." He did as he was told, but his mother was very angry, and said, "Alas! You have done away with our only possession and you have simply been made a fool of." He answered, "Now, Mother, you'll see, they will catch it because of the calf and something more."

As soon as his mother had given him some broken bracelets, he planted them in the soil of their garden and began to water the spot. The seven robbers came by and asked him what he was doing. He said, "This soil has the property, when wheat is sown in it, of bringing forth silver." "How is that?" they asked. Then he pulled a few pieces of the broken bracelets out of the ground and showed them to the robbers. As soon as they saw it, they bought the piece of ground at a high price. They sowed wheat, but the earth gave nothing but wheat. Then they denounced

A Street in the Village,
Issachar Ryback, 1917.
The Ryback Museum,
Bat-Yam, Israel.

Cracker to the judge. But he brought witnesses that the robbers had seen for themselves how silver grew from the ground; they just didn't have the same luck that he had. The judge dismissed them, and Cracker consoled them by saying that he had an even better proposition for them. He took a donkey and stuck a nugget of gold into his backside; then when he prodded its behind with a stick, the donkey dropped the gold. As soon as the seven robbers saw that Cracker's donkey dropped gold, they bought it for a great sum of money. But Cracker said, "Take care, for this donkey eats only almonds and raisins and passes gold but once a week. For this he must be taken into the best room in the upper story where fine rugs have to be spread and many porcelain cups put, and many lamps have to be lit there and mirrors put all about the room." The robbers did exactly as Cracker had explained and they waited all night long expectantly at the door of the room. Now as soon as the donkey saw the many lamps gleaming in the mirrors and his own reflection coming at him from all sides, he went mad and raged around the room until all the lamps, mirrors, and porcelain cups were broken and the rugs were torn to shreds. But when they heard the noise the robbers were highly delighted; they thought, What a lot of gold the donkey has produced, only listen how it chinks and clatters! But when, in the morning, they went into the room and saw what the donkey had done, they ran straightway to the judge to denounce Cracker. But he brought witnesses that the donkey had produced gold in front of the robbers' eyes. If the robbers had not succeeded, they just hadn't had the same luck as he had had. The judge realized that Cracker was right and dismissed the robbers.

When they saw that they could not get hold of Cracker by lawful means, they seized him and stuffed him into a sack, intending to drown him in a pond. On the way they came to an inn, and, going in to refresh them-

Merchant of Bastille,
Marc Chagall, 1912.
Giraudon/Art Resource, NY.
© 1997 Artists Rights
Society, NY/ADAGP, Paris.

selves, they left Cracker lying outside. Cracker shouted for help. By chance, a herdsman whom he knew passed by with his flock, and asked him, "What is the matter?" Then Cracker cried, "Woe is me! They want to marry me to the daughter of the Sultan and have put me into this accursed sack to take me to her." The herdsman said, "Do you want to exchange with me?" "With pleasure," said Cracker. The herdsman undid the sack and let Cracker out, then crept into it himself. Cracker tied it up, took the flock, and made off. But the robbers picked up the sack with the herdsman in it and threw it into the pond.

Next day the robbers again passed by this pond and great was their astonishment at sud-

denly seeing Cracker, with a huge flock, standing before them. "How did you get here?" they called out. "Is it the Day of Resurrection already?" "Far from it," replied Cracker, "but don't you know that at the bottom of the pond the most beautiful treasures can be got?" He led them down to the edge of the pond, where the reflection of the beasts of his herd could be seen, and shouted out, "Just look down there! I got the whole of this herd of sheep and oxen from down there, so now I have all that I want, thank you!" Then the robbers' mouths watered, and they said to Cracker, "Perhaps you will be good enough to throw us into the pond so that we may get a fine herd like that, too?" Cracker was ready and willing and he wanted to set to work at

once, but they suggested, "Had we better perhaps wait till evening for this?" "On no account," replied Cracker, "the water herds hide during the night, and then you will get nothing." "Well, if there's no other way . . ." said the robbers, and let themselves be thrown into the water one by one. After this had been accomplished Cracker went to the robbers' house, took everything that was in it, and carried it all to his mother, saying, "Look, Mother, this was because of the calf and something more."

From now on they were rich, and lived happily to the end of their days. On their roof is sheep dung, but on ours are almonds and raisins.

THE BOX WITH BONES

—POLISH FOLKTALE, told by David Fishlein,
translated by Gene Baharav

There once lived a very rich couple. They had an only son who was not too bright. When he grew up, the mother asked her husband, a merchant, to look out for the boy and find him a trade. "Good," the husband agreed and sent his son to a fair in one of the towns near the capital. Arriving at the fair, the son saw someone selling pipes; children gathered round the pipe-seller, grabbing them out of his hand, so eager were they to buy them. The son said in his heart, "I shall buy a box full of pipes, and on my return home I shall make a fortune." So he bought a box of pipes and returned home. When he opened the box, what did he find? All the pipes were broken.

Said his father, the merchant, to his wife, "I could have told you that would happen."

Now let us leave the rich merchant, his wife, and his son, and go to another place where a Jew was living on a farm leased from a gentile landlord. This Jew lost a large sum of money in business, and he still had a big debt to settle with his landlord. What did the landlord do? He decided to keep the Jew in a storeroom and to starve him to death if he still refused to pay the debt. The Jew died in captivity, whereupon the landlord collected his bones in a box and ordered one of his servants to sell it at the fair.

Wooden Case,
Yemen, 1930s.
Collection Israel Museum,
Jerusalem.

In the meantime the rich merchant's wife once again asked her husband to fix up her son in business. Again the father took no notice of her pleading. But what does one not do for peace in a family? The father agreed, and once again the son was sent to the fair. He walked to and fro and saw a peasant crying out his wares in a loud voice, "A box of Jewish bones for sale! A box of Jewish bones for sale!"

Of course, these were the bones of the poor Jewish farmer who had passed away in captivity. The boy did not think twice and bought the bones. With the help of the burial society he brought the bones to a Jewish cemetery and buried them there. Then he returned home, saying to his father, "I have done a good deed. I bought Jewish bones and buried them in the Jewish cemetery."

That night in a dream, a man appeared before the rich merchant and bade him, "If you want your son to succeed, do as I tell you. Rinse your hands when you wake up in the morning and then leave the house. Suggest to the first Jew you meet on your way that he become your son's partner and go with him to the fair. You will see what a successful partnership this will be."

In the morning the father arose with a light heart and said to himself, "Dreams are bubbles."

Yet the same man appeared to him once again the next night in his sleep and on the third night too. The following morning the merchant did as the man in the dream advised him. He rinsed his hands and then left his house. And lo! he saw a Jew with a staff in his hand and a bag on his shoulders. He approached him: "Where to?"

"To the fair."

"Why must you go on foot?" asked the merchant. "Be my son's partner, and you will get a cart drawn by horses. It will be better for both of you."

The wayfarer agreed. And so it was. The horses were harnessed to the cart, and the two partners went on their way with other merchants. They went on until they found themselves in a dense forest. Then the merchant's son and his partner left the others and drove along till they came to a sturdy tree. There they stopped, and the partner got out of the cart, saying to the merchant's son, "Stay here till I come." Then he set off in the direction of a small house. He approached it, and looking through a chink in the walls, he saw thieves busy inside. In one of the corners there were hands, legs, and heads, as well as silver and precious stones, piled up.

He entered the house and said, "I am one of your trade. Let us become partners. The merchants, who are on their way here, have with them rich treasures of gold. If you send me your men one by one, we shall get rid of all the merchants."

One by one the robbers came to him, and one by one the partner beheaded them. Then he returned to the merchant's son, saying, "Now let us be off!"

They rode to the robbers' den, filled a jar with gold and precious stones, and set off on their way.

In the meantime the Sabbath approached, and they arrived at an inn owned by a Jew. There they asked the innkeeper to put them up for the night.

"I have no food," the innkeeper informed them.

"Take three rubles, and prepare everything for the Sabbath," the partners proposed.

So they stayed with the Jew. On Friday night, when they sat down for supper, they saw that their host was serving food to a hand, stretched out through a half-closed door. And so it happened at every meal. It is not customary to ask questions on Sabbath, so they kept quiet, but on Saturday evening they asked the innkeeper, "Tell us, please, whose hand was that stretching out for food at mealtimes?"

The host answered, "Even if you fill my house with silver and gold, I shall never reveal this secret."

But they did not stop inquiring and nagging until he answered, "That is my daughter. Three times she was wedded, and on each wedding night her husband died."

Said the partner, "Never mind; I have a husband for your daughter."

"What are you thinking of? He will surely die," exclaimed the host in fear.

"Do not worry. Nothing will happen to him," replied the partner, and he kept on repeating his offer until the innkeeper agreed to his daughter's marriage with the merchant's son.

They fixed a date for the wedding and when it drew near, the innkeeper said to his wife, "Buy candles because soon there will be another death in this house." The wife bought candles, and both of them began to lament the death to be.

After the wedding ceremony the partner said to the merchant's son, "Now is the time for us to part and to divide all our possessions." So they began dividing their treasures: "A ring for you and a ring for me, silver for you and silver for me, gold for you and gold for me." So they continued until everything had been divided between them.

Then said the partner, "Now we shall divide your bride, half for me and half for you."

"How can we?" shouted the merchant's son. "How can one divide a woman into two? Either I pay you for your share or you take her for yourself!"

But the partner did not agree. "We shall cut her into two," he insisted. Then he tied her to a tree, took out a shiny knife and got ready to sever the girl. But before he had time to do so, a big frightened snake popped out of the girl's mouth, and the partner cut it into pieces.

In the morning the bride's parents were overcome with joy when they saw their daughter safe and sound. On the same day the partner approached the merchant's son and said to him, "Go home and live a life of happiness and contentment. And tell your father that your partner is none other than the Jew who appeared three times in his dreams. And he is the very Jew whose bones you bought and buried in the Jewish cemetery. Thus I have repaid you for your good deed."

The partner finished speaking and disappeared.

THE ADVENTURES OF HERSHEL SUMMERWIND

—BY *ITZIK MANGER*, translated by Irving Howe

These stories were told to me by Hershel Summerwind in Pantule's Inn, where the Jewish porters, water-carriers, and ordinary laborers would gather to drink tea in the late afternoon. All of Hershel's stories were outlandish, yet all were true, for they had really happened to him.

If you still see the stars in heaven, do you know whom to thank for that? No one but Hershel Summerwind!

It took place once upon a time when he, Hershel, was still a snip of a schoolboy, not more than eleven. Hershel was the greatest prankster in the world: he earned an endless number of slaps from the rabbi and was always the first to taste each new cat-o'-nine-tails. But the rabbi's slaps were nothing at all compared to his stepmother's pinches. Hershel was born an orphan—his mother had died in childbirth—and his stepmother, whom his father brought from another town, wasn't exactly wild about him. Some folks even said she had her reasons.

All day long Hershel made life miserable for her. If she sent him on an errand he'd make tracks and return only for supper. When his father came home from the market place, worn and weary, his stepmother would pour out a heartful of complaints: Hershel did this and Hershel did that.

But his father, who was sweet-tempered by nature, never beat him. True, he was upset by Hershel's pranks, but after the stepmother had finished chanting Hershel's praises the father would smile sadly. "You'll see, Zlate, our Hershel will make good. But how good that will be, God alone knows!"

When she saw that her husband dismissed the problem as a joke, the stepmother took things into her own hands. She was good at pinching, so she pinched. And each time she pinched him, Hershel saw Cracow and Lemberg spring up before his eyes. His answer to her pinches was still more tricks and pranks.

That's the sort of fellow he was—the biggest prankster in the world.

In the house a rooster roamed about, behaving as if he owned the place, doing whatever he wanted and dirtying up wherever he liked. No one asked him any questions, no one bothered him. Hershel, the stepmother would treat like a dog, but the rooster she cuddled as if it were a pigeon.

The stepmother, who believed in ghosts, spirits, and transmigration of souls, became convinced that the rooster was none other than a reincarnation of her first husband Mendel. She recognized him by his profile and the way his head trembled: her Mendel to the marrow!

When no one was home she actually called him "Mendel," and, wiping her eyes on her apron, she would say, "You're paying, Mendel, you're paying! You had to become a rooster, woe is me! Who told you to chase the girls, Mendel? I warned you, and now you've come back as a rooster."

A minute later: "It's lucky you fell into my hands and I recognized you. Some place else you'd have been slaughtered long ago."

In turn Mendel seemed clearly to feel that the stepmother was his friend. Whether he also recognized her as his wife, Hershel Summerwind doesn't know to this day, and whatever Hershel doesn't know he isn't the man to talk about.

No matter how many roosters were slaughtered, Mendel remained alive, guarded and cherished by the stepmother. That Hershel Summerwind hated Mendel goes without saying, and whenever he could he made life miserable for him. Tearing out feathers one by one, that too goes without saying. If the rooster fell into a doze Hershel would wake him up. If he met the rooster in the yard Hershel chased him until he fluttered onto the fence, hoarsely crowing and pleading for help.

When the stepmother heard Mendel's anguished cries she would rush out, more dead than alive, to save him from Hershel's vengeance. And each time she heard the rooster crowing, it seemed to her still another sign that she had come upon a reincarnation of her first husband, blessed be his memory. For that was just the way *he* used to crow when called upon to recite a chapter from the Torah on the Sabbath!

Once it happened that the devilish Hershel was chasing the rooster through the yard. Seeing the rooster flee, his wings stiff

with terror, Hershel felt a tremendous pleasure, and as he scampered after Mendel he chanted a rhyme of his own composition:

"Mendel, may your growth be stunted, I hope you'll be forever hunted!"

In the face of such danger the rooster jumped onto the fence, crowing and begging the stepmother for help, but even then Hershel did not leave him alone. Besides, this time the stepmother wasn't home, having gone out to buy something and having stopped on the way to chat with Gittel the soothsayer about ghosts, spirits, and the transmigration of souls. When she came home she found Hershel aflame with excitement, happily chasing the rooster, who seemed scarcely able to catch his breath. That Hershel got his goes without saying. The stepmother twisted his ears with a vengeance; he barely escaped with his life. Running away, he stuck out his tongue at her and burst into loud song:

"Mendel, may your growth be stunted, I hope you'll be forever hunted!"

The stepmother pressed the rescued rooster to her bosom and murmured, "You're paying, Mendel, you're paying!" And to the fleeing Hershel she cried out, "Wait till you come home for supper! Wait!"

Hershel didn't, of course, come home for supper. Hungrily he wandered through the streets, and in his imagination he saw Mendel the rooster pecking grains of food while the stepmother encouraged him, "Eat, Mendel, eat! May you grow fat and healthy!"

By now Hershel regretted the whole thing: what was the good of it? Hunger gnawed at him, but he was afraid to go home. Only at night, when everyone was asleep, did Hershel return, quietly, on tiptoe; he crept up to the garret and went to bed on an empty stomach.

He had a strange dream. He is a young rooster himself, a trickster. The stepmother, a fat respectable hen, takes him to school for the first time, and the teacher—heaven forbid!—is Mendel the rooster. Mendel, as usual, holds his head to one side. He asks Hershel, "Which is the *aleph?*" Immediately afterward he pecks at Hershel's head. "Which is the *gimmel?*" And again he pecks at Hershel's head.

Frightened, Hershel woke up and looked around him. Yes, he was still in the attic, it was only a dream. He caught his breath and cocked his ear. Who was pecking now?

Slowly he crawled over to the attic window and stuck out his head. At first Hershel was stunned. The sky was full of stars, but on the black chimney stood Mendel the rooster, pecking at the stars with his sharp beak, thinking apparently—the foolish rooster!—that the stars were grains of food.

Hershel immediately sensed the danger. If he allowed Mendel to keep pecking at the stars, the rooster would spoil the whole starry night—and not only this one, but all starry nights, for as is well known, one night bequeaths the stars to the next.

Hershel climbed out of the attic window and on his belly slowly edged his way up the chimney, so that Mendel should not hear him. And Mendel was so absorbed with his gluttony that he heard nothing at all.

Suddenly Hershel grabbed Mendel by the wings—and the rooster became so frightened that he threw up all the stars he had already swallowed!

Twirling the frightened rooster around his head, Hershel sang a new rhyme that suddenly came into his head:

"Mendel munches stars like mutton,
He has no rival as a glutton."

The stars in heaven winked slyly, and Hershel understood their meaning: "Hershel, we'll never forget you for this favor."

At first the rooster was stunned. The meal of stars he had been devouring with such zest came to an end so quickly he hardly knew what was happening to him. Only when Hershel began to twirl him through the air and dance around the chimney like a wild Indian did Mendel set up a fearful crowing.

All the roosters of the town answered him, as is the custom of roosters, and there was such a bedlam that the people of the town awoke, thinking it was already dawn, and began the ceremony of washing their fingers before eating.

Hershel's stepmother, when she heard the desperate cries of her reincarnated Mendel, rushed to his rescue. In her nightgown, with a rake in hand, she climbed up to the attic and barely squeezed herself through the little window. What Hershel caught you can imagine for yourself; the stepmother wasn't miserly.

To this day Hershel Summerwind can show you the black and blue marks of those blows. But it was worth it, he added. "After all, I saved the stars."

From that night on Mendel began to ail. In a few weeks he shook his head for the last time in a corner of the yard, and into what kind of creature he has since been reincarnated no one knows. But Hershel survived his stepmother's blows. Proof? He is still alive to tell us true stories of things that happened to him.

THE PRINCE WHO THOUGHT HE WAS A ROOSTER

—BY RABBI NACHMAN OF BRATZLAV, retold by Rabbi Jack Reimer

Once there was a prince who fell into the delusion of thinking he was a rooster. He took off all his clothes, sat under the table, and refused to eat any food but corn seeds. The king sent for many doctors and many specialists, but none of them could cure him.

Finally a wise man appeared before the king, and said: "I think that I can cure the prince." The king gave him permission to try.

The wise man took off his clothes, crawled under the table and began to munch on corn seeds. The prince looked at him suspiciously, and said: "Who are you, and what are you doing here?"

The wise man answered: "Who are you, and what are you doing here?"

"I am a rooster," answered the prince belligerently.

"Oh really? So am I," answered the wise man quietly.

The two of them sat together under the table until they became accustomed to each other. When the wise man felt that the prince was used to his presence, he signaled for some clothing. He put on the clothing, and then he said to the prince: "Don't think that roosters can't wear clothing if they want to. A rooster can wear clothes and be a perfectly good rooster just the same."

The prince thought about this for a while, and then he too agreed to put on clothes.

After a time, the wise man signaled to have food put under the table. The prince became alarmed and he said: "What are you doing?" The wise man reassured him. "Don't be upset. A rooster can eat the food that human beings eat if he wants to, and still be a good rooster." The prince considered this statement for a time, and then he too signaled for food.

Then the wise man said to the prince: "Do you think that a rooster has to sit under the table all the time? A rooster can get up and walk around if he wants to and still be a good rooster." The prince considered these words for a time, and then he followed the wise man up from the table, and began to walk.

After he began dressing like a person, eating like a person, and walking like a person, he gradually recovered his senses and began to live like a person.

In the same way, said Rabbi Nachman, the *tzaddik* must go down to the level of the people if he is to raise them.

OPPOSITE: *The Rooster*, Marc Chagall, 1928. Scala/Art Resource, NY. © 1997 Artists Rights Society, NY/ADAGP, Paris.

THE STORY OF MY DOVECOTE

—BY ISAAC BABEL

When I was a kid I longed for a dovecote. Never in all my life have I wanted a thing more. But not till I was nine did father promise the wherewithal to buy the wood to make one and three pairs of pigeons to stock it with. It was then 1904, and I was studying for the entrance exam to the preparatory class of the secondary school at Nikolayev in the Province of Kherson, where my people were at that time living. This province of course no longer exists, and our town has been incorporated in the Odessa Region.

I was only nine, and I was scared stiff of the exams. In both subjects, Russian language and arithmetic, I couldn't afford to get less than top marks. At our secondary school the *numerus clausus* was stiff: a mere five percent. So that out of forty boys only two that were Jews could get into the preparatory class. The teachers used to put cunning questions to Jewish boys; no one else was asked such devilish questions. So when father promised to buy the pigeons he demanded top marks with distinction in both subjects.

Tefillin Bag,
Russia, 1900.
The Jewish Museum, NY/
Art Resource, NY.

He absolutely tortured me to death. I fell into a state of permanent daydream, into an endless, despairing, childish reverie. I went to the exam deep in this dream, and nevertheless did better than everybody else.

I had a knack for book-learning. Even though they asked cunning questions, the teachers could not rob me of my intelligence and my avid memory. I was good at learning, and got top marks in both subjects. But then everything went wrong. Khariton Efrussi, the corn-dealer who exported wheat to Marseille, slipped someone a 500-rouble bribe. My mark was changed from A to A-, and Efrussi Junior went to the secondary school instead of me. Father took it very badly. From the time I was six he had been cramming me with every scrap of learning he could, and that A- drove him to despair. He wanted to beat Efrussi up, or at least bribe two longshoremen to beat Efrussi up, but mother talked him out of the idea, and I started studying for the second exam the following year, the one for the lowest class. Behind my back my people got the teacher to take me in one year through the preparatory and first-year courses simultaneously, and conscious of the family's despair, I got three whole books by heart. These were Smirnovsky's *Russian Grammar*, Yevtushevsky's *Problems*, and Putsykovich's *Manual of Early Russian History*. Children no longer cram from these books, but I learned them by heart line upon line, and the following year in the Russian exam Karavayev gave me an unrivaled A+.

This Karavayev was a red-faced, irritable fellow, a graduate of Moscow University. He was hardly more than thirty. Crimson glowed in his manly cheeks as it does in the cheeks of peasant children. A wart sat perched on one cheek, and from it there sprouted a tuft of ash-colored cat's whiskers. At the exam, besides Karavayev, there was the Assistant Curator Pyatnitsky, who was reckoned a big noise in the school and throughout the province. When the Assistant Curator asked me about Peter the Great a feeling of complete oblivion came over me, an awareness that the end was near: an abyss seemed to yawn before me, an arid abyss lined with exultation and despair.

About Peter the Great I knew things by heart from Putsykovich's book and Pushkin's verses. Sobbing, I recited these verses, while the faces before me suddenly turned upside down, were shuffled as a pack of cards is shuffled. This card-shuffling went on, and meanwhile, shivering, jerking my back straight, galloping headlong, I was shouting Pushkin's stanzas at the top of my voice. On and on I yelled them, and no one broke into my crazy mouthings. Through a crimson blindness, through the sense of absolute freedom that had filled me, I was aware of nothing but Pyatnitsky's old face with its silver-touched beard bent toward me. He didn't interrupt me, and merely said to Karavayev, who was rejoicing for my sake and Pushkin's:

"What a people," the old man whispered, "those little Jews of yours. There's a devil in them!"

And when at last I could shout no more, he said:

"Very well, run along, my little friend."

I went out from the classroom into the corridor, and there, leaning against a wall that needed a coat of whitewash, I began to awake from my trance. About me Russian boys were playing, the school bell hung not far away above the stairs, the caretaker was snoozing on a chair with a broken seat. I looked at the caretaker, and gradually woke up. Boys were creeping toward me from all sides. They wanted to give me a jab, or perhaps just have a game, but Pyatnitsky suddenly loomed up in the corridor. As he passed me he halted for a moment, the frock coat flowing down his back in a slow heavy wave. I discerned embarrassment in that large, fleshy, upper-class back, and got closer to the old man.

"Children," he said to the boys, "don't touch this lad." And he laid a fat hand tenderly on my shoulder.

"My little friend," he went on, turning me towards him, "tell your father that you are admitted to the first class."

On his chest a great star flashed, and decorations jingled in his lapel. His great black uniformed body started to move away on its stiff legs. Hemmed in by the shadowy walls, moving between them as a barge moves through a deep canal, it disappeared in the doorway of the headmaster's study. The little servingman took in a tray of tea, clinking solemnly, and I ran home to the shop.

In the shop a peasant customer, tortured by doubt, sat scratching himself. When he saw me my father stopped trying to help the peasant make up his mind, and without a moment's hesitation believed everything I had to say. Calling to the assistant to start shutting up shop, he dashed out into Cathedral Street to buy me a school cap with a badge on it.

My poor mother had her work cut out getting me away from the crazy fellow. She was pale at the moment, she was experiencing destiny. She kept smoothing me, and pushing me away as though she hated me. She said there was always a notice in the paper about those who had been admitted to the school, and that God would punish us, and that folk would laugh at us if we bought a school cap too soon. My mother was pale; she was experiencing destiny through my eyes. She looked at me with bitter compassion as one might look at a little cripple boy, because she alone knew what a family ours was for misfortunes.

All the men in our family were trusting by nature, and quick to ill-considered actions. We were unlucky in everything we undertook. My grandfather had been a rabbi somewhere in the Belaya Tserkov region. He had been thrown out for blasphemy, and for another forty years he lived noisily and sparsely, teaching foreign languages. In his eightieth year he started going off his head. My Uncle Leo, my father's brother, had studied at the Talmudic Academy in Volozhin. In 1892 he ran away to avoid doing military service, eloping with the daughter of someone serving in the commissariat in the Kiev military district. Uncle Leo took this woman to California, to Los Angeles, and there he abandoned her, and died in a house of ill fame among Negroes and Malays. After his death the American police sent us a heritage from Los Angeles, a large trunk bound with brown iron hoops. In this trunk there were dumbbells, locks of women's hair, uncle's *tallit*, horsewhips with gilt handles, scented tea in boxes trimmed with imitation pearls. Of all the family there remained only crazy Uncle Simon-Wolf, who lived in Odessa, my father, and I. But my father had faith in people, and he used to put them off with the transports of first love. People could not forgive him for this, and used to play him false. So my father believed that his life was guided by an evil fate, an

inexplicable being that pursued him, a being in every respect unlike him. And so I alone of all our family was left to my mother. Like all Jews I was short, weakly, and had headaches from studying. My mother saw all this. She had never been dazzled by her husband's pauper pride, by his incomprehensible belief that our family would one day be richer and more powerful than all others on earth. She desired no success for us, was scared of buying a school jacket too soon, and all she would consent to was that I should have my photo taken.

On September 20, 1905, a list of those admitted to the first class was hung up at the school. In the list my name figured too. All our kith and kin kept going to look at this paper, and even Shoyl, my grand-uncle, went along. I loved that boastful old man, for he sold fish at the market. His fat hands were moist, covered with fish-scales, and smelt of worlds chill and beautiful. Shoyl also differed from ordinary folk in the lying stories he used to tell about the Polish Rising of 1861. Years ago Shoyl had been a tavernkeeper at Skvira. He had seen Nicholas I's soldiers shooting Count Godlevski and other Polish insurgents. But perhaps he hadn't. *Now* I know that Shoyl was just an old ignoramus and a simple-minded liar, but his cock-and-bull stories I have never forgotten: they were good stories. Well now, even silly old Shoyl went along to the school to read the list with my name on it, and that evening he danced and pranced at our pauper ball.

My father got up at the ball to celebrate my success, and asked all his pals—grain-dealers, real-estate brokers, and the traveling salesmen who sold agricultural machinery in our parts. These salesmen would sell a machine to anyone. Peasants and landowners went in fear of them: you couldn't break loose without buying something or other. Of all Jews, salesmen are the widest-awake and the jolliest. At our party they sang Hasidic songs consisting

of three words only but which took an awful long time to sing, songs performed with endless comical intonations. The beauty of these intonations may only be recognized by those who have had the good fortune to spend Passover with the Hasidim or who have visited their noisy Volhynian synagogues. Besides the salesmen, old Lieberman who had taught me the Torah and ancient Hebrew honored us with his presence. In our circle he was known as Monsieur Lieberman. He drank more Bessarabian wine than he should have. The ends of the traditional silk tassels poked out from beneath his waistcoat, and in ancient Hebrew he proposed my health. In this toast the old man congratulated my parents and said that I had vanquished all my foes in single combat: I had vanquished the Russian boys with their fat cheeks, and I had vanquished the sons of our own vulgar parvenus. So too in ancient times David King of Judah

had overcome Goliath, and just as I had triumphed over Goliath, so too would our people by the strength of their intellect conquer the foes who had encircled us and were thirsting for our blood. Monsieur Lieberman started to weep as he said this, drank more wine as he wept, and shouted *"Vivat!"* The guests formed a circle and danced an old-fashioned quadrille with him in the middle, just as at a wedding in a little Jewish town. Everyone was happy at our ball. Even mother took a sip of vodka, though she neither liked the stuff nor understood how anyone else could—because of this she considered all Russians cracked, and just couldn't imagine how women managed with Russian husbands.

But our happy days came later. For mother they came when of a morning, before I set off for school, she would start making me sandwiches; when we went shopping to buy my school things—pencil box, money box, satchel, new books in cardboard bindings, and exercise books in shiny covers. No one in the world has a keener feeling for new things than children have. Children shudder at the smell of newness as a dog does when it scents a hare, experiencing the madness which later, when we grow up, is called inspiration. And mother acquired this pure and childish sense of the ownership of new things. It took us a whole month to get used to the pencil box, to the morning twilight as I drank my tea on the corner of the large, brightly-lit table and packed my books in my satchel. It took us a month to grow accustomed to our happiness, and it was only after the first half-term that I remembered about the pigeons.

I had everything ready for them: one rouble fifty and a dovecote made from a box by Grandfather Shoyl, as we called him. The dovecote was painted brown. It had nests for twelve pairs of pigeons, carved strips on the roof, and a special grating that I had devised to facilitate the capture of strange birds. All was in readiness. On Sunday, October 20, I set out for the bird market, but unexpected obstacles arose in my path.

The events I am relating, that is to say my admission to the first class at the secondary school, occurred in the autumn of 1905. The Emperor Nicholas was then bestowing a constitution on the Russian people. Orators in shabby overcoats were clambering onto tall curbstones and haranguing the people. At night shots had been heard in the streets, and so mother didn't want me to go to the bird market. From early morning on October 20 the boys next door were flying a kite right by the police station, and our water carrier, abandoning all his buckets, was

walking about the streets with a red face and brilliantined hair. Then we saw baker Kalistov's sons drag a leather vaulting-horse out into the street and start doing gym in the middle of the roadway. No one tried to stop them: Semernikov the policeman even kept inciting them to jump higher. Semernikov was girt with a silk belt his wife had made him, and his boots had been polished that day as they had never been polished before. Out of his customary uniform, the policeman frightened my mother more than anything else.

Because of him she didn't want me to go out, but I sneaked out by the back way and ran to the bird market, which in our town was behind the station.

At the bird market Ivan Nikodimych, the pigeon-fancier, sat in his customary place. Apart from pigeons, he had rabbits for sale too, and a peacock. The peacock, spreading its tail, sat on a perch moving a passionless head from side to side. To its paw was tied a twisted cord, and the other end of the cord was caught beneath one leg of Ivan Nikodimych's wicker chair. The moment I got there I bought from the old man a pair of cherry-colored pigeons with luscious tousled tails, and a pair of crowned pigeons, and put them away in a bag on my chest under my shirt. After these purchases I had only forty copecks left, and for this price the old man was not prepared to let me have a male and female pigeon of the Kryukov breed. What I liked about Kryukov pigeons was their short, knobbly, good-natured beaks. Forty copecks was the proper price, but the fancier insisted on haggling, averting from me a yellow face scorched by the unsociable passions of bird-snarers. At the end of our bargaining, seeing that there were

Ritual Undergarment with Fringe (Tallit Qatan), England, 1901. From the HUC Skirball Cultural Center and Museum, Los Angeles, CA. Gift of Susan Moyse Richter in honor of the Moyse Family.

no other customers, Ivan Nikodimych beckoned me closer. All went as I wished, and all went badly.

Toward twelve o'clock, or perhaps a bit later, a man in felt boots passed across the square. He was stepping lightly on swollen feet, and in his worn-out face lively eyes glittered.

"Ivan Nikodimych," he said as he walked past the bird-fancier, "pack up your gear. In town the Jerusalem aristocrats are being granted a constitution. On Fish Street Grandfather Babel has been constitutioned to death."

He said this and walked lightly on between the cages like a barefoot ploughman walking along the edge of a field.

"They shouldn't," murmured Ivan Nikodimych in his wake. "They shouldn't!" he cried more sternly. He started collecting his rabbits and his peacock, and shoved the Kryukov pigeons at me for forty copecks. I hid them in my bosom and watched the people running away from the bird market. The peacock on Ivan Nikodimych's shoulder was last of all to depart. It sat there like the sun in a raw autumnal sky; it sat as July sits on a pink riverbank, a white-hot July in the long cool grass. No one was left in the market, and not far off shots were rattling. Then I ran to the station, cut across a square that had gone topsy-turvy, and flew down an empty lane of trampled yellow earth. At the end of the lane, in a little wheeled armchair, sat the legless Makarenko, who rode about town in his wheel-chair selling cigarettes from a tray. The boys in our street used to buy smokes from him, children loved him, I dashed toward him down the lane.

"Makarenko," I gasped, panting from my run, and I stroked the legless one's shoulder, "have you seen Shoyl?"

The cripple did not reply. A light seemed to be shining through his coarse face built up of red fat, clenched fists, chunks of iron. He was fidgeting on his chair in his excitement, while his wife Kate, presenting a wadded

behind, was sorting out some things scattered on the ground.

"How far have you counted?" asked the legless man, and moved his whole bulk away from the woman, as though aware in advance that her answer would be unbearable.

"Fourteen pair of leggings," said Kate, still bending over, "six undersheets. Now I'm a-counting the bonnets."

"Bonnets!" cried Makarenko, with a choking sound like a sob, "it's clear, Catherine, that God has picked on me, that I must answer for all. People are carting off whole rolls of cloth, people have everything they should, and we're stuck with bonnets."

And indeed a woman with a beautiful burning face ran past us down the lane. She was clutching an armful of fezzes in one arm and a piece of cloth in the other, and in a voice of joyful despair she was yelling for her children, who had strayed. A silk dress and a blue blouse fluttered after her as she flew, and she paid no attention to Makarenko who was rolling his chair in pursuit of her. The legless man couldn't catch up. His wheels clattered as he turned the handles for all he was worth.

"Little lady," he cried in a deafening voice, "where did you get that striped stuff?"

But the woman with the fluttering dress was gone. Round the corner to meet her leaped a rickety cart in which a peasant lad stood upright.

"Where've they all run to?" asked the lad, raising a red rein above the nags jerking in their collars.

"Everybody's on Cathedral Street," said Makarenko pleadingly, "everybody's there, sonny. Anything you happen to pick up, bring it along to me. I'll give you a good price."

The lad bent down over the front of the cart and whipped up his piebald nags. Tossing their filthy croups like calves, the horses shot off at a gallop. The yellow lane was once more yellow and empty. Then the legless man turned his quenched eyes upon me.

"God's picked on me, I reckon," he said lifelessly. "I'm a son of man, I reckon."

And he stretched a hand spotted with leprosy toward me.

"What's that you've got in your sack?" he demanded, and took the bag that had been warming my heart.

With his fat hand the cripple fumbled among the tumbler pigeons and dragged to light a cherry-colored she-bird. Jerking back its feet, the bird lay still on his palm.

"Pigeons," said Makarenko, and squeaking his wheels he rode right up to me. "Damned pigeons," he repeated, and struck me on the cheek.

He dealt me a flying blow with the hand that was clutching the bird. Kate's wadded back seemed to turn upside down, and I fell to the ground in my new overcoat.

"Their spawn must be wiped out," said Kate, straightening up over the bonnets. "I can't a-bear their spawn, nor their stinking menfolk."

She said more things about our spawn, but I heard nothing of it. I lay on the ground, and the guts of the crushed bird trickled down from my temple. They flowed down my cheek, winding this way and that, splashing, blinding me. The tender pigeon-guts slid down over my forehead, and I closed my solitary unstopped-up eye so as not to see the world that spread out before me. This world was tiny, and it was awful. A stone lay just before my eyes, a little stone so chipped as to resemble the face of an old woman with a large jaw. A piece of string lay not far away, and a bunch of feathers that still breathed. My world was tiny, and it was awful. I closed my eyes so as not to see it, and pressed myself tight into the ground that lay beneath me in soothing dumbness. This trampled earth in no way resembled real life, waiting for exams in real life. Somewhere far away Woe rode across it on a great steed, but the noise of the hoofbeats grew weaker and died away, and silence, the bitter silence that sometimes over-whelms children in their sorrow, suddenly deleted the boundary between my body and the earth that was moving nowhither. The earth smelled of raw depths, of the tomb, of flowers. I smelled its smell and started crying, unafraid. I was walking along an unknown street set on either side with white boxes, walking in a getup of bloodstained feathers, alone between the pavements swept clean as on Sunday, weeping bitterly, fully and happily as I never wept again in all my life. Wires that had grown white hummed above my head, a watchdog trotted on in front, in the lane on one side a young peasant in a waistcoat was smashing a window frame in the house of Khariton Efrussi. He was smashing it with a wooden mallet, striking out with his whole body. Sighing, he smiled all around with the amiable grin of drunkenness, sweat, and spiritual power. The whole street was filled with a splitting, a snapping, the song of flying wood. The peasant's whole existence consisted in bending over, sweating, shouting queer words in some unknown, non-Russian language. He shouted the words and sang, shot out his blue eyes; till in the street there appeared a procession bearing the Cross and moving from the Municipal Building. Old men bore aloft the portrait of the neatly-combed Tsar, banners with graveyard saints swayed above their heads, inflamed old women flew on in front. Seeing the procession, the peasant pressed his mallet to his chest and dashed off in pursuit of the banners, while I, waiting till the tail-end of the procession had passed, made my furtive way home. The house was empty. Its white doors were open, the grass by the dovecote had been trampled down. Only Kuzma was still in the yard. Kuzma the yardman was sitting in the shed laying out the dead Shoyl.

"The wind bears you about like an evil wood-chip," said the old man when he saw me. "You've been away ages. And now look what they've done to granddad."

Kuzma wheezed, turned away from me, and started pulling a fish out of a rent in grandfather's trousers. Two pike perch had been stuck into grandfather: one into the rent in his trousers, the other into his mouth. And while grandfather was dead, one of the fish was still alive, and struggling.

"They've done grandfather in, but nobody else," said Kuzma, tossing the fish to the cat. "He cursed them all good and proper, a wonderful damning and blasting it was. You might fetch a couple of pennies to put on his eyes."

But then, at ten years of age, I didn't know what need the dead had of pennies.

"Kuzma," I whispered, "save us."

And I went over to the yardman, hugged his crooked old back with its one shoulder higher than the other, and over this back I saw grandfather. Shoyl lay in the sawdust, his chest squashed in, his beard twisted upwards, battered shoes on his bare feet. His feet, thrown wide apart, were dirty, lilac-colored, dead. Kuzma was fussing over him. He tied the dead man's jaws and kept glancing over the body to see what else he could do. He fussed as though over a newly-purchased garment, and only cooled down when he had given the dead man's beard a good combing.

"He cursed the lot of 'em right and left," he said, smiling, and cast a loving look over the corpse. "If Tartars had crossed his path he'd have sent them packing, but Russians came, and their women with them, Rooski women. Russians just can't bring themselves to forgive, I know what Rooskis are."

The yardman spread some more sawdust beneath the body, threw off his carpenter's apron, and took me by the hand.

"Let's go to father," he mumbled, squeezing my hand tighter and tighter. "Your father has been searching for you since morning, sure as fate you was dead."

And so with Kuzma I went to the house of the tax-inspector, where my parents, escaping the pogrom, had sought refuge.

PRECEDING SPREAD:
After the Pogrom,
Maurycy Minkowski, 1910.
The Jewish Museum, NY/
Art Resource, NY.

THE LOST SHABES

—BY *KADIA MOLODOWSKY*, translated by Irena Klepfisz

rs. Haynes drops in on her neighbor Sore Shapiro at least twice a day. She does it out of the goodness of her heart. She is teaching Sore Shapiro, who is all of two years in the country (dragged herself through Siberia, Japan, and finally reached New York)—she is teaching her how to be a homemaker in America while keeping in mind the role of *vaytaminz*. She sticks her head in the door (she is wearing the red bow which she never removes from her hair) and without any preliminaries begins talking about *vaytaminz*. She speaks with gusto, with heart, as if she were keeping Sore Shapiro alive.

The little red bow in Mrs. Haynes' hair looks alive as if it had swallowed all the vitamins at one time and had become fiery hot.

Mrs. Haynes comes in with her six-year-old daughter Teresa Filipine. While her mother is busy with the theory of vitamins, Teresa Filipine hangs around the kitchen testing the faucets to see if water pours out when they are turned. Every so often Mrs. Haynes calls the child to her.

—Teresa Filipine!—And seeing the child is wet, adds—You good-for-nothing.

—Why call such a small child by such a long name, Mrs. Haynes?

—What's to be done? My mother's name was Toybe Faygl. And it's forbidden to give only half a name. If you do, they say the ghost is disappointed.

Sore Shapiro calls the child by her Yiddish name Toybe Faygele, gives her a prune to eat and teaches her a rhyme:

—Toybe Faygl a girl like a bagel.

The little one repeats the rhyme, nibbles on the prune and laughs.

Teresa Filipine's grandfather calls her Toybe Faygele. He visits them every Friday night and brings her a lollipop, and Teresa Filipine understands that her grandfather and the neighbor Mrs. Shapiro have some connection to Friday night and to her Yiddish name Toybe Faygele.

Der Uilenburgersteeg, Gerard Johan Staller, 1924. Collection Jewish Historical Museum, Amsterdam.

The Rabbi and his Grandchild,
Mark Gertler, 1913.
Southampton City Art
Gallery/Bridgeman Art
Library, London.

Sometimes the little one drops in on Mrs. Shapiro by herself without her mother. She knocks on her door, and before anyone asks who's there, she gives her Yiddish name: Toybe Faygele. Sore Shapiro gives her a piece of bread with butter and talks to her in Yiddish, just like her grandfather:

—Eat, Toybe Faygele! Eat! A trifle, all they feed her constantly are *vaytaminz.*

Teresa Filipine sits on a stool and eats simply and with great pleasure. The piece of bread with butter which she eats at Mrs. Shapiro's has also something to do with her Yiddish name, with her grandfather and with Friday nights when her grandfather brings her a lollipop. Teresa Filipine eats obediently and seriously with childlike self-importance.

When her mother looks around and sees that the child has disappeared, she calls out through the open window down into the street:

—Teresa Filipine! *Kam hir!* Where are you, you good-for nothing?

Teresa Filipine hears "good-for-nothing" and knows that her mother is angry. With a sly smile, she places the piece of bread with butter on the table, stops being Toybe Faygele and immediately begins speaking English:

—*Am hir!*—and her small steps click rapidly through the stone corridor.

Mrs. Haynes asks Sore Shapiro with a friendly reproach:

—*Pliz*, don't give Teresa Filipine bread and butter. What does she get from it? A little bit of *startsh?* The child needs protein.

But Teresa Filipine doesn't know what she needs. When her mother leaves her neighbor's house, the little one slips inside, in an instant reverts to being Toybe Faygele again and finishes eating the piece of bread and butter which she had left on the table. She eats with obedient earnestness down to the very last crumb, as if she were finishing praying.

Friday night Teresa Filipine's mother lights four candles. She puts on velvet slacks, sticks a red handkerchief in the pocket of her white blouse; in the light of the candles the red bow in her hair becomes a flaming yellow. Teresa Filipine stands, looks at her mother's fingers as she lights the candles. Soon her grandfather will come, will give her a lollipop, will call her Toybe Faygele—and that's *shabes*.

One Friday evening after her mother put on her velvet slacks and lit the candles, she told Teresa Filipine that her grandfather was not coming. He is sick and is in the hospital. Teresa Filipine became lonely: without her grandfather, without her grandfather's lollipop, and without her Yiddish name Toybe Faygele, she was left with half a *shabes*. She remembered their neighbor Mrs. Shapiro. She left and knocked on her door looking for the second half of *shabes*.

—Toybe Faygele—she announced even before anyone asked who was knocking.

There were no candles on Mrs. Shapiro's table. She herself was dressed in a housecoat and not in velvet pants: it was like any other day.

—Oh, Toybe Faygele! Come in, Toybe Faygele!

Teresa Filipine stood in the middle of the room and looked around. She walked slowly into the kitchen, took a look at the table, turned around, and feeling dejected, walked towards the door.

What are you looking for, Toybe Faygele?—the neighbor asked her and followed her.

—*Nottink*—Teresa Filipine answered in English.

—So why did you come?

The child didn't answer, moved slowly closer to the exit.

From the other apartment Mrs. Haynes' voice echoed in the summer air:

—Teresa Filipine! *Ver ar u?*—and angrily threw the words good-for-nothing.

It was all like any other weekday.

This time Teresa Filipine did not run to her mother. Her small steps clicked slowly on the stone floor of the corridor. She went down to the floor below, sat down on a stone step and cried.

FAMILY IS THE KEYSTONE OF JEWISH CULTURE. The Psalms compare children to "olive saplings around [one's] table," symbolic of the continuity provided by successive generations. Honoring one's parents is one of the Ten Commandments, equivalent to prohibitions against murder, adultery, theft, and idolatry. In fact, so important is the principle of filial honor that the Bible ordains the death penalty for children who curse or rebel against their parents. Indeed, the Bible, especially the book of Genesis, is filled with stories about real families with real problems—sibling rivalry, favoritism, sexual violation, jealousy, struggles over inheritance, barrenness, disappointed expectations, and the extraordinary strength of family ties.

FAMILY

'For a people in diaspora, a strong family is the secret of survival. Unlike so many uprooted peoples from ancient times to our own, Jews have successfully maintained family coherence in exile. Over the centuries, Jewish tradition has developed many ingenious techniques for ensuring continuity within the family. In Ashkenazi communities, parents keep ancestral memories alive by naming their children after deceased relatives; in Sephardic families, they name them after themselves or other living relatives. Perhaps the most brilliant strategy for family survival has been the institution of the Passover seder, a model for teaching history, customs, and values to the next generation. At the heart of this ritual meal is the haggadah, the Jewish storybook par excellence.

In modern times, all traditional families in western cultures find themselves threatened by a multitude of pressures and seductions—competition with their children's peers for time and loyalty, the breakdown of ritual and family celebrations, the invasion of their homes by secular values and commercial enticements, the widespread disrespect of elders, and increasing social mobility with its inevitable breakup of the exended family. The stories in this section convey many important truths about how families survive. They also contain object lessons about how they fail—and how they can be redeemed.

One of the strongest forces in the world is the love of parents for children. "The Mother" provides a poignant demonstration of this truth, as a mother sacrifices her own life to give her daughter the courage to live on. "The Kiss," a hasidic tale of the Holocaust, likewise shows us how a father's love for his son can redeem life even under the most dire circumstances.

Sometimes, however, love between parents and children comes with a price. In "The Ape and the Leopard," a father who plays favorites comes to love his less favored son only when his beloved one is snatched from him. In "How Much Do You Love Me?"—a story sharing motifs with both "King Lear" and "Cinderella"—a daughter teaches her father and in-laws that actions speak louder than words when it comes to filial love. And in "The Father Bird and the Fledglings," recorded in the rich memoirs of Glückel of Hameln, a father teaches the same lesson to his three children.

Sometimes we don't appreciate the inestimable value of family unless we lack it—or risk losing it. In "True Joy," a father and mother discover only through bitter experience that the gift of parenthood is worth more than all the gold and silver in the world. We are also shown that all families, even happy ones, must struggle with conflict and differences that sometimes threaten to tear them apart. In Sholom Aleichem's "The Inheritors," the author's familiar Yiddish humor belies the heartache that so frequently accompanies family squabbles over an inheritance. Similarly, Bernard Malamud's darkly comic "The Jewbird" reveals the bitter discord at the heart of one frustrated Jewish family. And in the excerpt from Francine Prose's wicked modern fable "Electricity," a father's embrace of religion in late middle age comes too late to transmit a spiritual legacy to his children. And yet the story ends on a note of hope. For if a man entering his final phase of life can renew himself by finding faith, why not his daughter and his infant grandson? Perhaps, the story seems to suggest, the chain of tradition is not static, but rather dynamic, like a current of electricity flowing through time. Sometimes we are discrete particles, other times fluid waves of connection between those who came before and those who are yet to come. Or we are like olive trees, evergreen, living a thousand years, that propagate by putting out shoots, surviving even as our main trunk becomes hollow and dry.

THE APE AND THE LEOPARD

—BY BERECHIAH BEN NATRONAI HA-NAKDAN, retold by Ellen Frankel

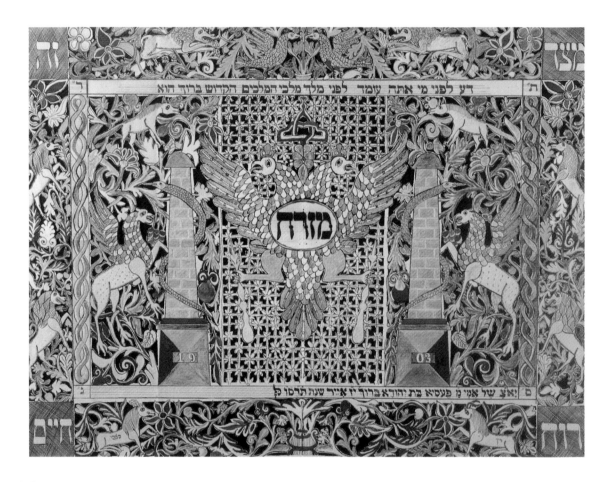

Mizrach,
Wolf Kurzman, 1903.
The Jewish Museum, NY/
Art Resource, NY.

Love your children equally, for if you love one more and put your hope in him, a sudden turn of fortune's wheel may tear him away.

There was once an ape who lived with two younger apes upon a rock. He loved the little one and hated the big one. One day a hungry leopard came forth to destroy them.

"While he eats one of us, the other two can escape," thought the ape. "I will surrender to him the one I hate."

So he put the little one under him and the larger one on his back, thinking to shake him off as he ran. But the one on his back held on tightly and would not let go. All this time the leopard continued to gain on them, until he was almost upon them. So he was forced to abandon the one he loved and flee with the other. And the leopard devoured the little one, and the other two escaped.

Then the older ape's heart turned to the one he had hated, and his hatred gave way to love. And he took pity on him, as a parent takes pity on the child who cares for him.

HOW MUCH DO YOU LOVE ME?

—EASTERN EUROPEAN FOLKTALE, retold by Beatrice Weinreich, translated by Leonard Wolf

Sabbath Candles,
Dora Holzhandler,
20th century.
Rona Gallery, London/
Bridgeman Art Library,
London.

Once upon a time there was a rabbi and his wife who had three daughters. The rabbi, wanting to know how much his daughters loved him, said to the oldest, "Rokhele dear, how much do you love me?" To which she replied, "As much as gold." He went to his second daughter. "Khavele dear, how much do you love me?" "As much as silver," she replied. Then he said, "Sorele dear, how much do you love me?" And she said, "Father, I love you as much as food that has been properly salted."

When he heard, "as much as food that has been properly salted," he drove her out of his home.

Sorele went weeping. Night overtook her and she had no place to go, but still she walked on. Then she met an old man, who was really Elijah the Prophet.

"Where are you going, my child?" he asked.

So she told him her story. "I see," he said. "Here, take this little stick. Keep on this road until you come to a house where you hear someone making the blessing over wine. Then be sure to say 'Omeyn,' amen. But no matter who asks you into the house, don't go unless it is the rabbi himself. Then, you may go in. When you are inside, go up to the attic and hide the stick there. Then whenever you need anything, take the stick out and say, 'Stick, open!' And whatever you want will appear before you."

When he had done speaking, he disappeared. She went on until she saw the house and heard someone making the *kiddush* over the wine. Three times she responded *"Omeyn."*

Hearing an *omeyn* from outside, the people in the house were startled. The rabbi's wife went out and invited the girl in, but she refused. It was not until the rabbi came out and repeated the invitation that she entered.

Inside she crouched sadly beside the oven. The rabbi's wife brought her food, but it did not cheer her. The next morning the rabbi, his wife, and his son dressed up and left the house to attend a wedding. The girl wanted to go too, so she went up to the attic and, taking out her stick, said, "Stick, open!" The stick opened, revealing a basin of water and a bar of golden soap. When the girl had washed, she said again, "Stick, open!" and it opened to present her with a costly set of clothing. The girl dressed in an exquisite gown and put on a pair of golden shoes. Looking absolutely beautiful, she went to the wedding.

There she dazzled the rabbi's son, who did not recognize her as the beggar maiden living in his own house. But though he asked her several times to say who she was, she always turned the conversation to something else.

Finally he said to his mother, "That beautiful girl won't tell me her name, but I have a plan to find out who she is."

He fetched some pitch and used it to smear the doorsill of the house. When it came time for the wedding guests to leave, the beautiful maiden started hastily toward home. But when she crossed the threshhold, one of her shoes stuck in the pitch, and she had to go on wearing a single shoe. The rabbi's son picked up the other one and put it in his pocket.

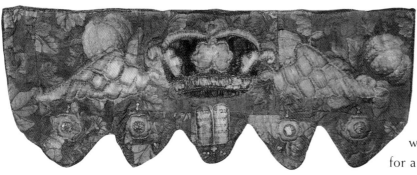

Torah Valence (Kapporet), Germany, 1735. From the HUC Skirball Cultural Center and Museum, Los Angeles, CA. Kirschstein Collection.

Meanwhile Sorele went up into the attic, changed into her old clothes, and came back down again.

The rabbi, his wife, and their son returned from the wedding. The son said, "See, I have the beautiful maiden's shoe. I'm off into the wide world to find her." He searched high and low for a maiden who could wear the golden shoe, but he couldn't find one. At last he returned home in despair.

"Let me try the shoe," Sorele said. "Perhaps it will fit me."

"Come on," he said. "As if a shoe like this could fit a beggar girl like you!"

She snatched it from him and slipped it onto her foot, where it settled as snugly as if it had been sewn for her.

Seeing this, the rabbi and his wife and son were very unhappy. How could he marry a beggar?

A few nights later they were sadder still, because each of them had been warned in a dream not to hinder their son's wedding to the poor girl. The troubled parents went for a walk to consider what to do.

Left alone in the house with the rabbi's son, Sorele said, "If you'll come to the attic with me, I'll show you who I really am."

He followed her up the stairs, and the girl said, "Stick, open!" Suddenly all sorts of wonderful clothes appeared. "Some for you," she said, "and some for me."

Each of them put on the finery and went out for a stroll.

Later, the rabbi and his wife, out on their walk, met their splendidly dressed son walking with a beautiful girl as richly garbed as he. This frightened them because of the dream that had warned them not to hinder their son's marriage to Sorele. And here he was walking about with some beautiful and wealthy girl whom they had never seen.

The two young people returned to the house and changed to their ordinary clothes. When the rabbi and his wife came home, the son said to his parents, "Stop worrying. I'm going to marry Sorele. Everything will be all right."

"Well . . . ," said his parents, in some confusion. "If you are determined, then marry her you will." And they sat down to address invitations to all the rabbis in the country.

As the wedding preparations went forward, the girl went to the kitchen and said to the cooks, "Whatever dishes you make, be sure to cook some without salt."

Came the wedding day. Rabbis from cities throughout the land arrived. To the amazement of the groom's parents, the bride, in her fine clothes, looked like a princess.

After the ceremony people sat about enjoying their food. One of the rabbis, however, did not find the menu to his liking. Seeing his unhappiness, the bride went up to him and said, "Dear guest, what's the matter? Everyone but you is eating."

"Ah," he said, "no doubt the food is very good, but the dishes have no salt."

"Father, dear Father," she said, "do you remember that I said I loved you as much as food that has been properly salted? Yet you drove me away from home."

Her father, hearing these words, dropped into a dead faint. When he came to, he told everyone that the bride was his daughter.

And there was carousing and merriment until dawn.

Elijah the Prophet gave the couple a diamond chandelier for a wedding present. And the moment they touched it, they ascended into heaven.

Torah Binder (Wimpel),
Germany, 1763.
From the HUC Skirball
Cultural Center and
Museum, Los Angeles, CA.
Kirschstein Collection.

The Sefirah of Hod (Splendor),
Diane Palley, 1995.
Courtesy of the artist.

THE FATHER BIRD AND THE FLEDGLINGS

—*BY GLÜCKEL OF HAMELN*, translated by Marvin Lowenthal

A bird once set out to cross a windy sea with its three fledglings. The sea was so wide and the wind so strong, the father bird was forced to carry his young, one by one, in his strong claws. When he was half-way across with the first fledgling the wind turned to a gale, and he said, "My child, look how I am struggling and risking my life in your behalf. When you are grown up, will you do as much for me and provide for my old age?" The fledgling replied, "Only bring me to safety, and when you are old I shall do everything you ask of me." Whereat the father bird dropped his child into the sea, and it drowned, and he said, "So shall it be done to such a liar as you." Then the father bird returned to shore, set forth with his second fledgling, asked the same question, and receiving the same answer, drowned the second child with the cry, "You, too, are a liar!" Finally he set out with the third fledgling, and when he asked the same question, the third and last fledgling replied, "My dear father, it is true you are struggling mightily and risking your life in my behalf, and I shall be wrong not to repay you when you are old, but I cannot bind myself. This, though, I can promise: when I am grown up and have children of my own, I shall do as much for them as you have done for me." Whereupon the father bird said, "Well spoken, my child, and wisely; your life I will spare and I will carry you to shore in safety."

THE MOTHER

—*LEBANESE FOLKTALE*, retold by Barbara Rush

This story took place in the north of Lebanon in the village of Hamadin. And the happening, as told, goes like this:

In the village lived a widow and her beautiful daughter, an only child. One day the girl became ill and was ordered to rest. And so she lay on her bed near the window and looked out at the only tree in the yard. Thus, days, weeks, months passed, and the autumn came. But the girl's condition didn't improve. On the contrary, she grew worse. And so, one day, as she looked at the tree, she said weakly, "You see, Mother, see those leaves. When the last leaf falls, I will die." The mother's heart grieved, and she watched anxiously as the leaves fell.

One cold night the wind howled, and the mother's heart was full of despair, as she saw the wind taking the last leaves. With every leaf her heart sank even deeper. At last there was only one leaf left. What could she do?

So the poor woman ran outside, unaware of the cold, the gusts of wind, and the storm. She approached the wall in front of the tree, and there she painted, on that wall, a picture of the last leaf. So good, so accurate was the drawing that it looked like the real leaf itself.

OPPOSITE: *Invocation*, Max Weber, 1919–20. Courtesy of Forum Gallery, NY.

When the girl awoke, she looked out the window, and there she saw one lonely leaf. Days and weeks passed. From time to time she looked out, and always she saw that last leaf, still hanging on to the branch of the tree. A new spirit entered the girl. Slowly, slowly she recovered, and at last she got well.

But the mother, by going out on that windy night, had caught cold. She developed tuberculosis, and soon died.

When the girl was able to leave her bed, she went outside to see the miracle that had occurred: Why had that leaf not fallen?

And what did she see? The painting, done by her mother, which had cost her her life for her child's sake.

Then the girl realized her mother's great love, and grieved greatly for her mother who, in her own death, had given life to her.

The Inheritors

—*BY SHOLOM ALEICHEM*, translated by Julius and Frances Butwin

The Maiers and the Schnaiers . . .

Actually there was only one Maier and one Schnaier. They were twins and they looked so much alike that there were times when it was impossible to tell which of the two was Maier and which was Schnaier. . . .

In short, the Maiers and Schnaiers had a father, and a very fine father, too. He was a virtuous and an honest man named Reb Shimshen, and he had a magnificent beard, long and rich and luxurious. In fact, it could be said without exaggeration that Reb Shimshen had more beard than face. And for that reason he was known in Kasrilevka as Reb Shimshen Beard.

And this Reb Shimshen was—I don't even know what he was. But you can be sure that all his life he struggled and sweated for a meager living, waged constant warfare against poverty. Sometimes he overcame poverty; sometimes poverty overcame him, as is usual with Kasrilevkites, who are not afraid of want, but thumb their noses at it. . . .

And Reb Shimshen lived out his life and finally he died. And when he died he was given a handsome burial. Almost the whole town followed his remains to the cemetery.

"Who is it that died?"

"Haven't you heard? Reb Shimshen."

"Which Reb Shimshen?"

"Reb Shimshen Beard."

"A great pity. So Reb Shimshen Beard is gone from us too."

That is what they said in Kasrilevka and mourned not so much for Reb Shimshen himself as for the fact that with his death there was one person less in Kasrilevka. Strange people, these Kasrilevkites! In spite of the fact that they are so poor that they almost never have enough for themselves, they would be pleased if no one among them ever died. Their only comfort is that people die everywhere, even in Paris, and that no one can buy his way out. Even Rothschild himself, who is greater than royalty, has to get up and go when the Angel of Death beckons.

Now let us turn back again to the Maiers and Schnaiers.

As long as Reb Shimshen was alive the Maiers and Schnaiers lived as one, brothers in body and soul. But when their father died they became enemies at once, ready to tear each other's beards out. Perhaps you wonder why? Well, why do sons ever fight after a father's death? Naturally, over the inheritance. It is true that Reb Shimshen did not leave behind any farms or woodlands, houses or rental property, and certainly no cash. Nor did he leave any jewelry, silver or furniture to his children—not because he was mean or avaricious, but simply because he had nothing to leave. And yet don't think that Reb Shimshen left his children absolutely nothing. He left them a treasure that could be turned

OPPOSITE: *Double Portrait (Self-Portrait with Moses Soyer)*, Raphael Soyer, 1962. Courtesy of The Estate of Raphael Soyer and Forum Gallery, NY.

to money at any time, a treasure that could be pawned, rented or sold outright. This treasure we speak of was the seat he had had in the old Kasrilevka Synagogue, a seat along the east wall right next to Reb Yozifel, the Rabbi, who was next to the Holy Ark. It is true that Kasrilevka wits have a saying that it is better to have an acre outside than a seat inside, but that is only a saying, and when the Lord is kind and a person does have his own seat, and along the east wall at that, it's not so very bad—and certainly better than nothing. . . .

In short, Reb Shimshen left behind a seat in the old Kasrilevka Synagogue. But he forgot one small detail. He didn't indicate who was to inherit the seat—Maier or Schnaier.

Obviously Reb Shimshen—may he forgive me—did not expect to die. He had forgotten that the Angel of Death lurks always behind our backs and watches every step we take, else he would surely have made a will or otherwise indicated in the presence of witnesses to which of his two sons he wanted to leave his fortune.

Well, what do you suppose? The very first Saturday after they arose from mourning, the quarrel began. Maier argued that according to law the seat belonged to him, since he was the older (by a good half-hour). And Schnaier had two arguments in his favor: first, they were not sure which of the two was older because according to their mother's story they had been exchanged as infants and he was really Maier and Maier was really Schnaier. In the second place, Maier had a rich father-in-law who also owned a seat along the east wall of the synagogue, and since the father-in-law had no sons the seat would eventually be Maier's. And when that happened Maier would have two seats by the east wall and Schnaier would have none whatever. And if that was the case, where was justice? Where was humanity?

When he heard of these goings-on, Maier's father-in-law, a man of means, but one

who had made his money only recently, entered the battle. "You've got a lot of nerve!" he exclaimed. "I am not forty yet and I have every intention of living a long time, and here you are, dividing up my inheritance already. And besides, how do you know that I won't have a son yet? I may have more than one, see!" he stormed. "This is impudence for you!"

So their neighbors tried to make peace between them, suggested that they determine how much the seat was worth and then have one brother buy his share from the other. That sounds reasonable enough, doesn't it? The only trouble was that neither brother wanted to sell his share. They didn't care a thing about the money. What was money—compared to stubbornness and pride?

"How can one's own brother be so pig-headed as to keep a person away from his rightful seat?" "Why should you have our father's place, and not I?" It became a matter not so much of having things his own way as it was of preventing the other from having his. As the saying is: If I don't, you don't either. And the rivalry between the Maiers and the Schnaiers increased in fury. Stubbornness gave way to cunning as each tried to outwit the other!

The first Sabbath Maier came early and sat down in his father's seat; and Schnaier remained standing throughout the services. The second Sabbath Schnaier came first and occupied his father's place, while Maier remained standing. The third Sabbath Maier got there still earlier, spread himself out in the seat, pulled his *tallit* over his head, and there he was. . . .

The next time it was Schnaier who hurried to get there first, sat down in the coveted seat, pulled his *tallit* over his face—and just try to budge him! The following week Maier was the first to get there. . . . This went on week after week till one fine Sabbath both of them arrived at the same time—it was still dark outside—took their posts at the door of the synagogue (it was still shut) and glared at each other like roosters ready to tear each other's eyes out. It was like this that long ago the first two brothers stood face to face in an empty field, under God's blue sky, full of anger, ready to annihilate one another, devour each other, spill innocent blood...

But let us not forget that the Maiers and Schnaiers were young men of good family, respectable and well behaved—not rowdies who were in the habit of assaulting each other in public. They waited for Ezriel, the *shammes*, to come and open the door of the synagogue. Then they would show the whole world who would get to their father's seat first—Maier or Schnaier. . . .

The minutes passed like years till Ezriel arrived with the keys. And when Ezriel, with his tangled beard, arrived he was not able to reach the door because the brothers stood against it—one with the left foot, the other with the right foot, and would not budge an inch.

"Well, what's going to happen?" said Ezriel casually, taking a pinch of snuff. "If the two of you insist on standing there like mean scarecrows I won't be able to open the door and the synagogue will have to remain closed all day. Go ahead and tell me: does that make sense?"

Apparently these words had some effect, because the Maiers and Schnaiers both moved back, one to the right, the other to the left, and made way for Ezriel and his key. And when the key turned in the lock and the door swung open, the Maiers and Schnaiers tumbled in headlong.

"Be careful, you're killing me!" yelled Ezriel the *shammes*, and before he could finish the words the poor man lay trampled under their feet, screaming in horror: "Watch out! You're trampling all over me—the father of a family!"

But the Maiers and Schnaiers cared nothing for Ezriel and his family. Their only thought was for the seat, their father's seat, and jumping over benches and praying stands they made for the east wall. There they planted themselves firmly against the wall with their shoulders and the floor with their feet and tried to shove each other aside. In the scuffle they caught each other's beards, grimaced horribly, gritted their teeth and growled: "May the plague take you before you get this seat!"

In the meantime Ezriel got up from the floor, felt to see if any of his bones were broken, and approached the brothers. He found them both on the floor clutching each other's beards. At first he tried to reason with them.

"Shame on you! Two brothers—children of the same father and mother—tearing each other's beards out! And in a Holy Place at that! Be ashamed of yourselves!"

But Ezriel gathered that at the moment his lecture was in vain. Actually, his words added fuel to the flame so that the two children of one father became so enraged that one of them clutched in his fist a tuft of black hair (from Maier's beard) and the other a tuft of red (Schnaier's beard); blue marks showed on both faces and from the nose of one streamed blood.

As long as it was merely a matter of pulling beards, slapping and pummeling each other, the *shammes* could content himself with reading a lecture. But when he saw blood streaming, Ezriel could stand it no longer, for blood, even though only from a punched nose, was an ugly thing fit for rowdies and not God-fearing men.

He wasted no time, but ran to the tap, grabbed a dipper of water, and poured it over the two brothers. Cold water has always—since the world was created—been the best means of reviving a person. A man may be in the greatest rage, but as soon as he gets a cold bath he is strangely refreshed and cool; he comes to his senses. This happened to the Maiers and the Schnaiers. At the unexpected shower of cold water to which Ezriel had

treated them, they woke up, looked each other in the eyes, and grew ashamed—like Adam and Eve when they had tasted of the forbidden fruit of the Tree of Knowledge and saw their nakedness. . . .

And that very Saturday night the Maiers and Schnaiers went together with their friends and neighbors to the home of Reb Yozifel, the Rabbi, to have the dispute settled.

If Kasrilevka had not been such a tiny place, stuck away in a forgotten corner, far from the great world, and if newspapers and periodicals had been printed there, the world

78

would have made portraits of him and spread them to the four corners of the earth. Interviewers would have plagued him, given him no rest. They would have asked him all his views—what his favorite dishes were, how many hours a day he slept, what he thought about this and that, about cigarette smoking and bicycle riding . . . But since Kasrilevka is a tiny place stuck away in a forgotten corner, far from the world, and papers and periodicals are not printed there, the world knows nothing of the existence of Reb Yozifel. The papers never mention his name. The great, the wise and the famous do not come to him, photographers and painters do not make pictures of him. Interviewers leave him alone. And Reb Yozifel lives his life quietly, modestly, without noise or fanfare. No one knows anything about him except the town of Kasrilevka, which marvels at him, glories in his wisdom, and pays him great honor (of riches there is little in Kasrilevka, but honor they will give one as much as he deserves). They say that he is a man who modestly conceals his wisdom and it is only when you come to him for judgment that you find out how deep he is, how profound, how sharp. Another Solomon!

With the Sabbath over and the benedictions completed, the Maiers and Schnaiers came to Reb Yozifel to have their dispute settled, and there they found the house already full of people. The whole town was anxious to hear how he would settle it, how he would divide one seat between two brothers.

First he gave both sides a chance to unburden themselves. Reb Yozifel works according to this theory: that before the verdict is handed down the litigants should have the right to say anything they want to—because after the verdict all the talking in the world won't help. After that he let Ezriel, the *shammes*, talk. After all, he was the chief witness. And then other townspeople had their turn—everyone who had the public welfare at

would surely have come to know the works of our Rabbi, Reb Yozifel. The papers would have been full of tales about him and his wisdom. The great, the wise and the famous of the world would have traveled far to see him in person and to hear from his own lips the words of wisdom. Photographers and painters

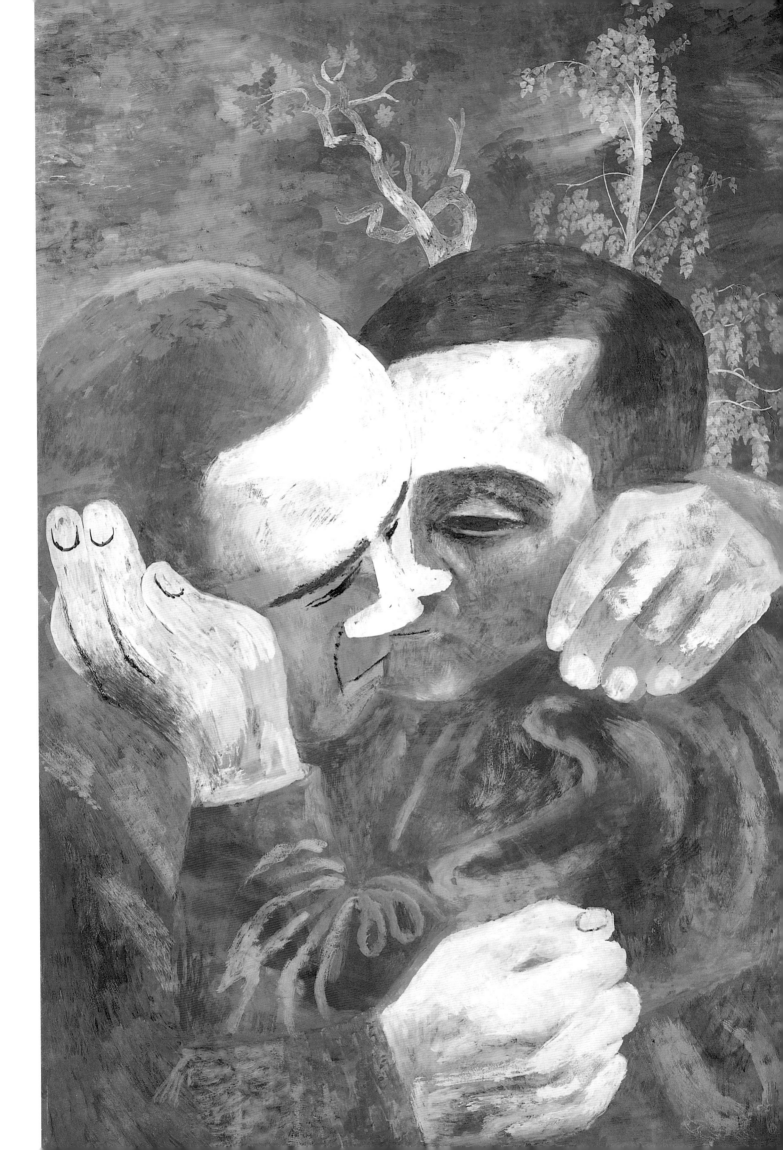

heart. And they talked as long as they wanted. Reb Yozifel is the kind of person who lets everyone talk. He is something of a philosopher. He feels this way about it: that no matter how long a person talks, he will have to stop some time.

And that is just what happened. They talked and talked and talked, and finally stopped talking. And when the last person was through, Reb Yozifel turned to the Maiers and Schnaiers and spoke to them quietly, calmly, as his custom was.

"Hear ye, my friends—this is my opinion. According to what I have heard from you and from all the other citizens it is apparent that both of you are right. You both had one father, and a very noble father, too—may he enjoy the blessings of Paradise. The only trouble is that he left you only one seat in the synagogue. Naturally, this seat is very dear to both of you. After all—it is something to own one's seat along the east wall of the old, old Kasrilevka Synagogue. You can't dismiss that with a wave of the hand. What then? Just as it is impossible for one person to use two seats, so it is impossible for two people to use a single one. On the contrary, it is much easier for one person to use two seats than for two to use one."

And so with example and precept he went on to explain the difficulty of the situation.

"But there is one way," he continued, "in which each of you can sit along the eastern wall in adjoining seats. I have come upon this solution after much reflection. And this is what I have to say. My seat in the synagogue is right next to the one your father left. One of you can have my seat and then both of you brothers can sit next to each other in peace and amity, and you will have no need to quarrel any more. And if you will ask what will I do without a seat? then I will answer you with another question: Where is it written that a rabbi or any other man, for that matter, must have his own seat and especially at the east

wall, and at the old Kasrilevka Synagogue at that? Let us stop to consider. What is a synagogue? A house of prayer. And why do we go to the synagogue? To pray. To whom? To the Almighty. And where is He found? Everywhere. All the world is filled with His glory. If that is the case, then what difference does it make whether it is east or north or south, whether it is near the Ark or by the door? The important thing is to come to the synagogue and to pray.

"Let me give you an example. Once there was a king. . . ."

And there followed another of Reb Yozifel's parables of the two servants who began to tear each other's beards in the presence of the king. And they were sent away with this admonition: "If you want to tear each other's beards, go outside and do it as much as your heart desires, but do not defile my palace. . . ."

Thus Reb Yozifel chided them gently, and then he said, "Go home now, my children, in peace and let your father be an advocate in heaven for you, for us, and for all Israel."

Thus the Rabbi handed down his verdict and all the people went home.

The following Sabbath, the Maiers and Schnaiers came to the synagogue and stationed themselves near the door. No matter how much they were entreated by the *shammes* on one side and the Rabbi on the other, they refused to occupy the seats by the east wall.

If there is anyone who would like to have his own seat by the east wall in the old, old Kasrilevka Synagogue, the seat next to Reb Yozifel, the Rabbi, at a reasonable price, let him go to Kasrilevka and see the children of Reb Shimshen Beard, either Maier or Schnaier, it does not matter which. They will sell it to you at any price you say, because neither of them uses that seat any more. It stands there—unoccupied.

What a waste!

OPPOSITE: *Brothers*, Ben Shahn, 1946. Hirshhorn Museum and Sculpture Garden. Smithsonian Institution. Gift of Joseph H. Hirshhorn, 1966. © 1997 Estate of Ben Shahn/Licensed by VAGA, NY.

TRUE JOY

—*BY KAMELIA SHAHAR*, translated by Stephen Levy

Eliyahu the Prophet and his disciple Elisha, with whom he was wandering through the roads of the Land of Israel, one day saw someone who was tilling the soil and in a very black mood, muttering and cursing at the cows. It was noon. His wife came with a meal all ready, his mother came with a jug of wine. The man stopped work, sat down, ate and drank, but neither the tasty food nor the good wine nor the kindness of his wife and mother succeeded in changing his mood.

Eliyahu the Prophet, who had been watching the man, approached him and said, "Tell me, why are you in such bad spirits? I see you're neither hungry nor thirsty. You have a wife and mother who love you and look after you. What is it you're lacking? Why are you sad?"

"And why should I be satisfied with my luck? Because I've got to walk behind my cows from morning till night to earn bread from the sweat of my brow? There are people who live in palaces, enjoying the good things of this world, while I've got to suffer and work hard for each little piece of bread! Damn the day when Adam and Eve ate the forbidden fruit! If they hadn't eaten it, we'd still be living in the Garden of Eden, without having to work in order to survive. If I'd been in Adam's place, Eve could've said whatever she wanted, I wouldn't have listened to her!"

"Me too," the wife said. "If I'd been in Eve's place, I wouldn't have listened to the snake."

"You're speaking like ignorant people," the mother said. "You shouldn't criticize the actions of others without first putting yourselves in their place."

Eliyahu the Prophet, who had been listening to the conversation in silence, said to the old woman, "One can see that you've had a lot of experience in life. And as for what concerns you," he said to the husband and wife, "in a short while you'll have the opportunity to prove if you're capable of resisting temptation." And he left.

The tiller returned to work, but he had hardly begun when he saw, buried in the earth, a little metal box! He bent down to seize it—and right there saw a second and third box. Immediately he called his wife and mother and showed them the boxes. On the first one was written: "Whoever opens me will be wealthy."

"You see?" the mother said. "Didn't I tell you that this stranger who passed through here was a messenger of God? Open it, you're going to find a treasure for sure."

He opened it and marveled at it: the little box was full of jewels. "We're rich!" he said. "Now let's see what's in the second box." Taking it in his hand, he saw that on the box was written: "If gold makes you happy, open me."

"What a question!" the man said. "The richer a person is, of course the happier he is!"

OPPOSITE:

Adam and Eve Seder Towel,

Alsace, 1829.

The Jewish Museum, NY/

Art Resource, NY.

"My son," the mother said, "that's not true. Health is a treasure more precious than all the gold in the world."

The tiller didn't respond. He opened the second little box, which was filled with ducats, and out of happiness began to sing and dance with his wife. A little afterwards, remembering the third little box, he took it in his hand to open it, but saw written on it: "Whoever opens me loses all that he has."

"I'm not so stupid as to risk all the gold and jewels we've found because of curiosity. The best thing," he said, "would be to bury the box and forget about it."

"You're stupid for not wanting to open it!" his wife exclaimed. "No doubt there's some other treasure inside of it; open it and look. If it's empty, we'll throw it away. How can we lose what we already have? It's ours! Who can take it away from us?"

At first the husband didn't want to listen to her, but she insisted so much, she begged, cried and threatened so much, that finally he was convinced and opened the little box. As soon as he did this, a fierce wind began blowing and a torrent of rain came down which carried away all the treasures they had found.

Mother and Child in Holland Park, Dora Holzhandler, 20th century. Rona Gallery, London/ Bridgeman Art Library, London.

Then Adam and Eve appeared in front of them, and at the same time a voice said, "Don't judge others till you put yourselves in their place. What happened to you happened to Adam and Eve. You couldn't resist temptation either."

The tiller's mother, seeing her son and daughter-in-law sad and humbled, told them, "My children, enough with believing only in riches. The truly happy person is the one who's content with what God gave him."

Time passed. Eliyahu the Prophet, accompanied by Elisha, came back to the same place. And this is what their eyes saw: the tiller was tilling; his mother and his wife were bringing him food, and with them was a child, who the man took in his arms, kissed and hugged.

Eliyahu said to him, "I see that you're working hard, but it seems to me that you're happy. Am I right?"

"Yes, holy man," the tiller answered. "I recognize you. God be blessed, you opened my eyes. We're happy now, we lack for nothing; most of all, God made us content by giving us a child who is more precious than all the treasures in the world."

Satisfied to have put this covetous husband and wife on the right road, Eliyahu the Prophet spread his hand, blessed them, and went away.

THE JEWBIRD

—BY BERNARD MALAMUD

The window was open so the skinny bird flew in. Flappity-flap with its frazzled black wings. That's how it goes. It's open, you're in. Closed, you're out and that's your fate. The bird wearily flapped through the open kitchen window of Harry Cohen's top-floor apartment on First Avenue near the lower East River. On a rod on the wall hung an escaped canary cage, its door wide open, but this black-type longbeaked bird—its ruffled head and small dull eyes, crossed a little, making it look like a dissipated crow—landed if not smack on Cohen's thick lamb chop, at least on the table, close by. The frozen foods salesman was sitting at supper with his wife and young son on a hot August evening a year ago. Cohen, a heavy man with hairy chest and beefy shorts; Edie, in skinny yellow shorts and red halter; and their ten-year-old Morris (after her father)—Maurie, they called him, a nice kid though not overly bright—were all in the city after two weeks out, because Cohen's mother was dying. They had been enjoying Kingston, New York, but drove back when Mama got sick in her flat in the Bronx.

"Right on the table," said Cohen, putting down his beer glass and swatting at the bird. "Son of a bitch."

"Harry, take care with your language," Edie said, looking at Maurie, who watched every move.

The bird cawed hoarsely and with a flap of its bedraggled wings—feathers tufted this way and that—rose heavily to the top of the open kitchen door, where it perched staring down.

"*Gevalt*, a pogrom!"

"It's a talking bird," said Edie in astonishment.

"In Jewish," said Maurie.

"Wise guy," muttered Cohen. He gnawed on his chop, then put down the bone. "So if you can talk, say what's your business. What do you want here?"

"If you can't spare a lamb chop," said the bird, "I'll settle for a piece of herring with a crust of bread. You can't live on your nerve forever."

"This ain't a restaurant," Cohen replied. "All I'm asking is what brings you to this address?"

"The window was open," the bird sighed; adding after a moment, "I'm running. I'm flying but I'm also running."

"From whom?" asked Edie with interest.

"Anti-Semeets."

"Anti-Semites?" they all said.

"That's from who."

"What kind of anti-Semites bother a bird?" Edie asked.

"Any kind," said the bird, "also including eagles, vultures, and hawks. And once in a while some crows will take your eyes out."

"But aren't you a crow?"

"Me? I'm a Jewbird."

Cohen laughed heartily. "What do you mean by that?"

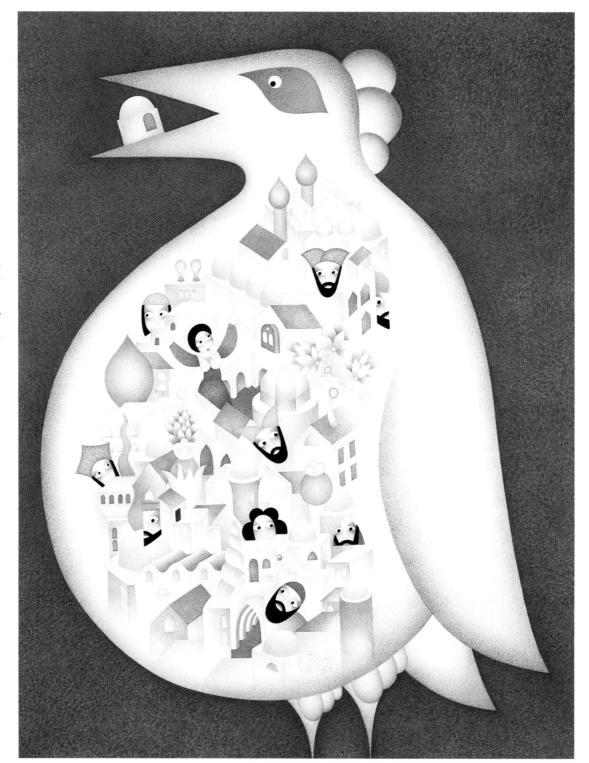

City Bird,
David Sharir, 1977.
Courtesy of Pucker
Gallery, Boston, MA.

The bird began *dovening*. He prayed without book or *tallit*, but with passion. Edie bowed her head though not Cohen. And Maurie rocked back and forth with the prayer, looking up with one wide-open eye.

When the prayer was done Cohen remarked, "No hat, no phylacteries?"

"I'm an old radical."

"You're sure you're not some kind of a ghost or dybbuk?"

"Not a dybbuk," answered the bird, "though one of my relatives had such an experience once. It's all over now, thanks God. They freed her from a former lover, a crazy jealous man. She's now the mother of two wonderful children."

"Birds?" Cohen asked slyly.

"Why not?"

"What kind of birds?"

"Like me. Jewbirds."

Cohen tipped back in his chair and guffawed. "That's a big laugh. I've heard of a Jewfish but not a Jewbird."

"We're once removed." The bird rested on

one skinny leg, then on the other. "Please, could you spare maybe a piece of herring with a small crust of bread?"

Edie got up from the table.

"What are you doing?" Cohen asked her.

"I'll clear the dishes."

Cohen turned to the bird. "So what's your name, if you don't mind saying?"

"Call me Schwartz."

"He might be an old Jew changed into a bird by somebody," said Edie, removing a plate.

"Are you?" asked Harry, lighting a cigar.

"Who knows?" answered Schwartz. "Does God tell us everything?"

Maurie got up on his chair. "What kind of herring?" he asked the bird in excitement.

"Get down, Maurie, or you'll fall," ordered Cohen.

"If you haven't got matjes, I'll take schmaltz," said Schwartz.

"All we have is marinated, with slices of onion—in a jar," said Edie.

"If you'll open for me the jar I'll eat marinated. Do you have also, if you don't mind, a piece of rye bread—the spitz?"

Edie thought she had.

"Feed him out on the balcony," Cohen said. He spoke to the bird. "After that take off."

Schwartz closed both bird eyes. "I'm tired and it's a long way."

"Which direction are you headed, north or south?"

Schwartz, barely lifting his wings, shrugged.

"You don't know where you're going?"

"Where there's charity I'll go."

"Let him stay, papa," said Maurie. "He's only a bird."

"So stay the night," Cohen said, "but no longer."

In the morning Cohen ordered the bird out of the house but Maurie cried, so Schwartz stayed for a while. Maurie was still on vacation from school and his friends were

away. He was lonely and Edie enjoyed the fun he had, playing with the bird.

"He's no trouble at all," she told Cohen, "and besides his appetite is very small."

"What'll you do when he makes dirty?"

"He flies across the street in a tree when he makes dirty, and if nobody passes below, who notices?"

"So all right," said Cohen, "but I'm dead set against it. I warn you he ain't gonna stay here long."

"What have you got against the poor bird?"

"Poor bird, my ass. He's a foxy bastard. He thinks he's a Jew."

"What difference does it make what he thinks?"

"A Jewbird, what a *chuzpah*. One false move and he's out on his drumsticks."

At Cohen's insistence Schwartz lived out on the balcony in a new wooden birdhouse Edie had bought him.

"With many thanks," said Schwartz, "though I would rather have a human roof over my head. You know how it is at my age. I like the warm, the windows, the smell of cooking. I would also be glad to see once in a while the *Jewish Morning Journal* and have now and then a schnapps because it helps my breathing, thanks God. But whatever you give me, you won't hear complaints."

However, when Cohen brought home a bird feeder full of dried corn, Schwartz said, "Impossible."

Cohen was annoyed. "What's the matter, crosseyes, is your life getting too good for you? Are you forgetting what it means to be migratory? I'll bet a helluva lot of crows you happen to be acquainted with, Jews or otherwise, would give their eyeteeth to eat this corn."

Schwartz did not answer. What can you say to a *grubber yung*?

"Not for my digestion," he later explained to Edie. "Cramps. Herring is better even if it makes you thirsty. At least rainwater don't cost anything." He laughed sadly in breathy caws.

And herring, thanks to Edie, who knew where to shop, was what Schwartz got, with an occasional piece of potato pancake, and even a bit of soupmeat when Cohen wasn't looking.

When school began in September, before Cohen would once again suggest giving the bird the boot, Edie prevailed on him to wait a little while until Maurie adjusted.

"To deprive him right now might hurt his school work, and you know what trouble we had last year."

"So okay, but sooner or later the bird goes. That I promise you."

Schwartz, though nobody had asked him, took on full responsibility for Maurie's performance in school. In return for favors granted, when he was let in for an hour or two at night, he spent most of his time overseeing the boy's lessons. He sat on top of the dresser near Maurie's desk as he laboriously wrote out his homework. Maurie was a restless type and Schwartz gently kept him to his studies. He also listened to him practice his screechy violin, taking a few minutes off now and then to rest his ears in the bathroom. And they afterwards played dominoes. The boy was an indifferent checker player and it was impossible to teach him chess. When he was sick, Schwartz read him comic books though he personally disliked them. But Maurie's work improved in school and even his violin teacher admitted his playing was better. Edie gave Schwartz credit for these improvements though the bird poohpoohed them.

Yet he was proud there was nothing lower than C minuses on Maurie's report card, and on Edie's insistence celebrated with a little schnapps.

"If he keeps up like this," Cohen said, "I'll get him in an Ivy League college for sure."

"Oh I hope so," sighed Edie.

But Schwartz shook his head. "He's a good boy—you don't have to worry. He won't be a *shicker* or a wifebeater, God forbid, but a scholar he'll never be, if you know what I mean,

although maybe a good mechanic. It's no disgrace in these times."

"If I were you," Cohen said, angered, "I'd keep my big snoot out of other people's private business."

"Harry, please," said Edie.

"My goddamn patience is wearing out. That crosseyes butts into everything."

Though he wasn't exactly a welcome guest in the house, Schwartz gained a few ounces although he did not improve in appearance. He looked bedraggled as ever, his feathers unkempt, as though he had just flown out of a snowstorm. He spent, he admitted, little time taking care of himself. Too much to think about. "Also outside plumbing," he told Edie. Still there was more glow to his eyes so that though Cohen went on calling him crosseyes he said it less emphatically.

Liking his situation, Schwartz tried tactfully to stay out of Cohen's way, but one night when Edie was at the movies and Maurie was taking a hot shower, the frozen foods salesman began a quarrel with the bird.

"For Christ sake, why don't you wash yourself sometimes? Why must you always stink like a dead fish?"

"Mr. Cohen, if you'll pardon me, if somebody eats garlic he will smell from garlic. I eat herring three times a day. Feed me flowers and I will smell like flowers."

"Who's obligated to feed you anything at all? You're lucky to get herring."

"Excuse me, I'm not complaining," said the bird. "You're complaining."

"What's more," said Cohen, "even from out on the balcony I can hear you snoring away like a pig. It keeps me awake at night."

"Snoring," said Schwartz, "isn't a crime, thanks God."

"All in all you are a goddamn pest and freeloader. Next thing you'll want to sleep in bed next to my wife."

"Mr. Cohen," said Schwartz, "on this rest assured. A bird is a bird."

"So you say, but how do I know you're a bird and not some kind of a goddamn devil?"

"If I was a devil you would know already. And I don't mean because of your son's good marks."

"Shut up, you bastard bird," shouted Cohen.

"*Grubber yung*," cawed Schwartz, rising to the tips of his talons, his long wings outstretched.

Cohen was about to lunge for the bird's scrawny neck but Maurie came out of the bathroom, and for the rest of the evening until Schwartz's bedtime on the balcony, there was pretended peace.

But the quarrel had deeply disturbed Schwartz and he slept badly. His snoring woke him, and awake, he was fearful of what would become of him. Wanting to stay out of Cohen's way, he kept to the birdhouse as much as possible. Cramped by it, he paced back and forth on the balcony ledge, or sat on the birdhouse roof, staring into space. In the evenings, while overseeing Maurie's lessons, he often fell asleep. Awakening, he nervously hopped around exploring the four corners of the room. He spent much time in Maurie's closet, and carefully examined his bureau drawers when they were left open. And once when he found a large paper bag on the floor, Schwartz poked his way into it to investigate what possibilities were. The boy was amused to see the bird in the paper bag.

"He wants to build a nest," he said to his mother.

Edie, sensing Schwartz's unhappiness, spoke to him quietly.

"Maybe if you did some of the things my husband wants you, you would get along better with him."

"Give me a for instance," Schwartz said.

"Like take a bath, for instance."

"I'm too old for baths," said the bird. "My feathers fall out without baths."

"He says you have a bad smell."

"Everybody smells. Some people smell because of their thoughts or because who they are. My bad smell comes from the food I eat. What does his come from?"

"I better not ask him or it might make him mad," said Edie.

In late November Schwartz froze on the balcony in the fog and cold, and especially on rainy days he woke with stiff joints and could barely move his wings. Already he felt twinges of rheumatism. He would have liked to spend more time in the warm house, particularly when Maurie was in school and Cohen at work. But though Edie was good-hearted and might have sneaked him in in the morning, just to thaw out, he was afraid to ask her. In the meantime Cohen, who had been reading articles about the migration of birds, came out on the balcony one night after work when Edie was in the kitchen preparing pot roast, and peeking into the birdhouse, warned Schwartz to be on his way soon if he knew what was good for him. "Time to hit the flyways."

"Mr. Cohen, why do you hate me so much?" asked the bird. "What did I do to you?"

"Because you're an A-number-one trouble maker, that's why. What's more, whoever heard of a Jewbird? Now scat or it's open war."

But Schwartz stubbornly refused to depart as Cohen embarked on a campaign of harassing him, meanwhile hiding it from Edie and Maurie. Maurie hated violence and Cohen didn't want to leave a bad impression. He thought maybe if he played dirty tricks on the bird he would fly off without being physically kicked out. The vacation was over, let him make his easy living off the fat of somebody else's land. Cohen worried about the effect of the bird's departure on Maurie's schooling but decided to take the chance, first, because the boy now seemed to have the knack of studying—give the black bird-bastard credit—and second, because Schwartz was driving him bats by being there always, even in his dreams.

The frozen foods salesman began his campaign against the bird by mixing watery cat food with the herring slices in Schwartz's dish. He also blew up and popped numerous paper bags outside the birdhouse as the bird slept, and when he had got Schwartz good and nervous, though not enough to leave, he brought a full-grown cat into the house, supposedly a gift for little Maurie, who had always wanted a pussy. The cat never stopped springing up at Schwartz whenever he saw him, one day managing to claw out several of his tailfeathers. And even at lesson time, when the cat was usually excluded from Maurie's room, though somehow or other he quickly found his way in at the end of the lesson, Schwartz was desperately fearful of his life and flew from pinnacle to pinnacle— light fixture to clothestree to doortop—in order to elude the beast's wet jaws.

Once when the bird complained to Edie how hazardous his existence was, she said, "Be patient, Mr. Schwartz. When the cat gets to know you better he won't try to catch you any more."

"When he stops trying we will both be in Paradise," Schwartz answered. "Do me a favor and get rid of him. He makes my whole life worry. I'm losing feathers like a tree loses leaves."

"I'm awfully sorry but Maurie likes the pussy and sleeps with it."

What could Schwartz do? He worried but came to no decision, being afraid to leave. So he ate the herring garnished with cat food, tried hard not to hear the paper bags bursting like firecrackers outside the birdhouse at night, and lived terror-stricken closer to the ceiling than the floor, as the cat, his tail flicking, endlessly watched him.

Weeks went by. Then on the day after Cohen's mother had died in her flat in the Bronx, when Maurie came home with a zero on an arithmetic test, Cohen, enraged, waited until Edie had taken the boy to his violin lesson, then openly attacked the bird. He chased him with a broom on the balcony and Schwartz frantically flew back and forth, finally escaping into his birdhouse. Cohen triumphantly reached in, and grabbing both skinny legs, dragged the bird out, cawing loudly, his wings wildly beating. He whirled the bird around and around his head. But Schwartz, as he moved in circles, managed to swoop down and catch Cohen's nose in his beak, and hung on for dear life. Cohen cried out in great pain, punched the bird with his fist, and tugging at its legs with all his might, pulled his nose free. Again he swung the yawking Schwartz around until the bird grew dizzy, then with a furious heave, flung him into the night. Schwartz sank like stone into the street. Cohen then tossed the birdhouse and feeder after him, listening at the ledge until they crashed on the sidewalk below. For a full hour, broom in hand, his heart palpitating and nose throbbing with pain, Cohen waited for Schwartz to return but the broken-hearted bird didn't.

That's the end of that dirty bastard, the salesman thought and went in. Edie and Maurie had come home.

"Look," said Cohen, pointing to his bloody nose swollen three times its normal size, "what that sonofabitchy bird did. It's a permanent scar."

"Where is he now?" Edie asked, frightened.

"I threw him out and he flew away. Good riddance."

Nobody said no, though Edie touched a handkerchief to her eyes and Maurie rapidly tried the nine times table and found he knew approximately half.

In the spring when the winter's snow had melted, the boy, moved by a memory, wandered in the neighborhood, looking for Schwartz. He found a dead black bird in a small lot near the river, his two wings broken, neck twisted, and both bird-eyes plucked clean.

"Who did it to you, Mr. Schwartz?" Maurie wept.

"Anti-Semeets," Edie said later.

THE KISS

—HASIDIC TALE, retold by Yaffa Eliach

I would like to tell you a story about a kiss. "Sometimes a kiss can break a man more than a vicious slap or a ringing blow," said the Rabbi of Bluzhov, Rabbi Israel Spira.

"In Lemberg, I had a foreign passport from a South American country. It was a passport for myself, my rebbetzin, of blessed memory, and for a young child. But when I received the passport, it was too late. There was no longer a rebbetzin, and my beloved grandson, as well as my daughter and son-in-law, were all gone too. Upon receiving the passport, I realized that I had an opportunity to save two Jewish souls, a middle-aged woman and a young child. When this became known, about forty children were brought to me by their parents, little boys crying and begging to be saved. They promised to be good and not to be a burden to me. How could I choose? How could I prefer one child over another?! I told the Judenrat that I was returning to my apartment and that they should bring me a child.

"Two days later, a father came with a small son, age six. 'I am Perlberger from Auschwitz,' he introduced himself. Then he went on: 'Rebbe, I am giving you my child. God should help you, so that you should be able to save my son!' He bent down, kissed the child on his head and said, 'Shraga, from this moment on, this Jew standing here next to you is your father.'

"That kiss I can't forget. Wherever I go that kiss follows me all my life. Before he shut the door behind him, the father took one more lingering look at his son. Then I heard the echo of his painful steps as he descended the stairs. A few days later, when we were deported to Bergen Belsen, a Gestapo man took a look at my passport, at the young child, and at me. He bent down to the small boy and with a big friendly grin said, 'Tell me the truth, who is this old man next to you?' Shraga glanced at me with big, childish loving eyes, took my hand in his, turned to the Gestapo man, and said 'My father.'

OPPOSITE:
Self-Portrait,
Michael Gross, 1983.
The Jewish Museum, NY/
Art Resource, NY.

"God helped us. The boy and I managed to survive Bergen Belsen together. Despite many difficulties, I studied with him every single day in camp. With God's help we were liberated by the American Army on a death train on Rosh Hodesh Iyar (April 13, 1945).

"After liberation, together with other children who survived the war, Shraga was brought to the Land of Israel. He studied at a Talmud Torah and later at the yeshiva of Hasidei Gur. He grew up into a fine, gentle lad who did very well in his studies and was liked by all.

"Shraga's father, Mr. Perlberger, also survived the war and was privileged to see his son once more, during one precious meeting. Mr. Perlberger had been in hiding for more than two years, in the pits and damp cellars on the property of Christian friends. When he was liberated he was a very sick, crippled man. Nevertheless, he soon began his search for his young son. He made his

way from Poland to Belgium, for he was told that his son and I were in Belgium. Upon reaching Belgium, he learned that I had left for America in November of 1946 and that his beloved son was in the Holy Land. Despite the British blockade around Palestine, the sick father reached the shores of the land of Israel with other illegal immigrants. When he finally reached Eretz Yisrael, he was a very sick man and near death. He saw his son one single time and then passed away. He had managed to survive all that time just to see his beloved child once more and be at peace knowing that his son was indeed alive and well. People told me that he passed away with a tranquil smile on his lips.

"Through the years I kept in touch with the boy and followed his progress in his studies. When I married the present rebbetzin, her two sons, Zvi and Yitzhak, became as dear to me as my own sons. Shraga was my third son, and our close contact continued. Years later, Shraga married a very nice girl. Their house in London became known as a home of Torah and culture.

"A few years ago Shraga came to visit me with his wife and three daughters. When we parted, he said to me, 'Rebbe-Father, I wish we had a son, to carry on my father's name!' I told him, 'Shraga, you will have a son and I will come, with God's help, to be the godfather at the boy's circumcision.' A year later I received a phone call from London. I rushed to the phone. 'Don't be afraid, nothing had happened,' I heard Shraga's reassuring voice. 'My wife just gave birth to a son.' There was a moment of silence on the other end of the line. I sensed that Shraga wanted to say something but did not dare to impose upon me.

"'I know, Shraga,' I said. 'You probably would like to refresh my memory about my promise, to be godfather to your son. Next Sunday, with God's help, I will come to the circumcision of your son. But I want you to understand that I am not coming as the Rabbi of Bluzhov. I will not take *kvitlach* nor in any other way will I act as rebbe. I am simply coming as a father to rejoice, to celebrate the birth of a child to his own son.'

"On Sunday we left for London. The overwhelming welcome at the airport is difficult to describe. The welcome at Shraga's home outdid the one at the airport. It was a beautiful reception in a house with well-behaved children, a house filled with sacred books and the comforts of life. I thanked the Lord for making me His messenger to save the father of this family. We did not sleep a wink that entire night. We were telling and recalling stories and events from our common past.

"Very early in the morning Rabbi Ashkenazi came, and in the name of the community and Hasidim begged me to remain in London for a few more days. I told him that my coming to

London was to realize what I had lost during the war and to appreciate what I had found. Our sages say that he who raises an orphan in his house is considered by the Scriptures as one who has actually given birth to him. Why does the Gemara say it? I told Rabbi Ashkenazi: it is natural for a father to raise his own biological son, but the spiritual satisfaction in raising an orphan is especially great.

"That morning, when we walked to the circumcision wearing our *shtraimlach* and dressed in our Sabbath finery, I was flanked by my three sons. I experienced the height of spiritual pleasure. That moment had no equal. I asked Rabbi Ashkenazi not to beg of me anymore to remain in London, for I wanted to retain the

Book of Mohel,
Amsterdam, 1745.
Later illustrated by
Gabriel Voel.
On loan from HUC
Francis Henry Library,
Los Angeles, from the HUC
Skirball Cultural Center and
Museum, Los Angeles, CA.

impact of the spiritual elevation of fatherhood without diluting it with anything else.

"We left for the airport and boarded the plane. That evening I prayed *Maariv*, the evening prayer, here at my *beit midrash* on 58th Street in Brooklyn.

"The great elevation of soul that I felt during my London visit was indeed part of the realization of what I have lost and the great treasures I have found. But all that time the echo of the kiss that little Shraga received on his head resounded in my ears. I saw before my eyes a father bending and kissing his beloved son, pointing to me and saying, 'From now on this man is your father.' This last kiss of a father to his son follows me all my life. But that day in London it was even more vivid than a generation ago in Lemberg.

"I hope that the merit of that kiss, which protected me in the past, gave me the great treasure of children and grandchildren who are brought up in the Jewish tradition, will protect all of us in the future."

Based on a converasation of the Grand Rabbi of Bluzhov, Rabbi Israel Spira, with his daughter-in-law, Dina Spira, May 12, 1976. I heard it at the rabbi s house.

FROM ELECTRICITY A STORY

—BY FRANCINE PROSE

Anita sails the baby over her head. "Earth to Spaceship Bertie," she says. "Earth to Spaceship Bertie. Can you read me?"

The baby's laugh sounds forced, like Johnny Carson's when he's blown a joke. Last week she caught Bertie practicing smiles in the mirror over his crib, phony social smiles for the old ladies who goo-goo him in the street, noticeably different from his real smile. It occurs to her that the baby is embarrassed for her. Lately she's often embarrassed for herself. This feeling takes her back fifteen years to her early teens, when she and her parents and her younger sister Lynne used to go places—Jones Beach, Prospect Park—and she'd see groups of kids her own age. At the time she had felt that being with her family made her horribly conspicuous; now she realizes that it probably made her invisible.

The house is quiet. Since she's been back it's the first time Anita can remember being in her parents' home without the television going. She thinks of the years her father spent trailing her and Lynne from room to room, switching lights off behind them, asking who they thought was paying the electric bills. Yet he never turned the TV off; he'd fall asleep to the *Late Show*. Now the TV is dark, the house is lit up like a birthday cake, and her father is down in the finished basement, silenced by the acoustical ceiling as he claps his hands, leaps into the air, and sings hymns in praise of God and the Baal Shem Tov.

❖

In the morning when Anita's father goes off to the *beit midrash*, the house of study, Anita and her mother and the baby watch Donahue. Today the panel is made up of parents whose children have run away and joined cults. The week Anita came home, there was a show about grown children moving back in with their parents. It reminds Anita of how in high school, and later when she used to take acid, the radio always seemed to play oddly appropriate songs. Hearing the Miracles sing "What's So Good About Goodbye?" when she was breaking up with a boyfriend had made her feel connected with lovers breaking up everywhere. But now she hates to think that her life is one of those stories which makes Donahue go all dewy-eyed with concern.

The twice-divorced mother of a Moonie is blaming everything on broken homes. "Don't you *ever* become a Moonie," Anita whispers, pressing her lips against the back of the baby's neck. Another mother is describing how her daughter calls herself Prem Ananda, wears only orange clothes, has married a boy the guru's chosen for her, and, with her doctorate in philosophy, works decorating cakes in the ashram bakery.

"Cakes?" says Anita's mother. "That's nothing. Only my Sam waits till he's fifty-seven to join a cult. After thirty-three years of marriage, he'll only make love through a hole in the sheet."

"A hole in the sheet?" Repeating this, Anita imagines Donahue repeating it, then realizes: incredibly, she and her mother have never talked about sex. Not ever. Imagining her mother or Donahue, Anita sees only close-ups, because if the camera pulled back, it would see up her mother's housedress to where the pale veined thighs dimple over the tops of her Support-hose.

Anita goes over and hugs her mother so hard that Bertie, squeezed between them, squawks like one of his bath toys. The baby starts to cry, her mother starts to cry, and Anita, not knowing what else to do, presses Bertie against her mother and pats and rubs them as if trying to burp both of them at once.

Anita takes nothing for granted. When she lifts her foot to take a step, she no longer trusts the ground to be there when she puts it down. She used to say that you could never really tell about people; now she knows it's true. She never once doubted that Jamie loved her, that he wanted the baby. When he came to visit her and Bertie in the hospital and began crying, she was so sure it was from happiness that she literally didn't hear him say he'd fallen in love with somebody else.

She'd made him repeat it till he was almost shouting and she remembered who this Lizzie was: another lawyer in his office. At a garden party that summer, Lizzie had asked to touch Anita's belly.

Just as Jamie was offering to move out of the house they had rented for its view, for their vision of children standing at the Victorian bay window watching boats sail up the Hudson, a nurse wheeled the baby in, in a futuristic clear plastic cart.

"Spaceship Bertie," said Jamie.

Anita's sister Lynne says that men do this all the time: Jamie's acting out his ambivalence about fatherhood, his jealousy of the mother-infant bond. This sounds to Anita like something from *Family Circle* or *Ladies Home Journal*. Lynne has read those magazines all her life, but now that she's going for her Master's in

Family Reunion, Jennings Tofel, 1929. Hirshhorn Museum and Sculpture Garden. Smithsonian Institution. Gift of Joseph H. Hirshhorn, 1966.

Women's Studies, she refers to it as "keeping up." Lynne can't believe that Anita never had the tiniest suspicion. A year ago, Anita would have said the same thing, but now she knows it's possible. Whenever she thinks about last summer, she feels like a Kennedy assassination buff examining the Zapruder film. But no matter how many times she rewinds it, frame by frame, she can't see the smoking gun, the face at the warehouse window. All she sees is that suddenly, everyone in the car starts moving very strangely.

Anita's mother believes her. Overnight, *her* husband turned into a born-again Hasid. Perhaps that's why she hardly sounded surprised when on the day she and Anita's father were supposed to drive up to Nyack to see the baby, Anita called to say that she and Bertie were coming to Brooklyn. Over the phone, her mother had warned her to expect changes. Daddy wasn't himself. No, he wasn't sick. Working too hard as usual, but otherwise fine. Her tone had suggested something shameful. Had he too fallen in love with somebody else?

Pulling into her parents' driveway, Anita thought: he looks the same. He opened the door for her and waited, while she unstrapped Bertie from his car seat, then sidestepped her embrace. He'd never been a comfortable hugger, but now she missed his pat-pat-pat. She held Bertie out to him; he shook his head.

"Bertie, this is your grandpa," she said. "Grandpa, this is Bertie."

"Has he been circumcised?" asked her father.

"Of course," said Anita. "Are you kidding? My doctor did it in the hospital."

"Then we'll have to have it done again," said her father. "By a *mohel*."

"Again!" yelled Anita. "Are you out of your mind?" Attracted by the noise, her mother came flying out of the house. "Sam!" She

Sabbath Wine Bottle,
Syria, 19th century.
From the HUC Skirball
Cultural Center and
Museum, Los Angeles, CA.
Kirschstein Collection.

grabbed the baby from Anita. "Can't you see she's upset?"

The commotion had comforted Anita. Everything was familiar—their voices, the pressure of her mother's plump shoulder pushing her into the house, the way she said, "Coffee?" before they'd even sat down.

"I'll get it," said Anita. "You hold the baby." But her mother headed her off at the kitchen door.

"It's arranged a little different now," she explained. "Those dishes over there by the fridge are for meat. These here by the stove are for milk."

That night they couldn't eat till her father had blessed the half grapefruits, the maraschino cherries, the boiled flank steak, potatoes and carrots, the horseradish, the unopened jar of applesauce, the kosher orange gelatin with sliced bananas. During the meal, Bertie began to fuss, and Anita guided his head up under her shirt.

"Is it all right if the baby drinks milk while I eat meat?" she asked. Her mother laughed. "Edna," said her father, "don't encourage her."

Bertie cried when Anita tried to set him down, so she was left alone with her father while her mother did the dishes.

"What *is* this?" she asked him. "You never went to *shul* in your life. Aunt Phyllis and Uncle Ron didn't speak to us for a year because on the Saturday of Cousin Simon's bar mitzvah, you *forgot*—you said—and took us all to Rip Van Winkle's Storybook Village."

"I did forget." Her father laughed. "Anyhow, we didn't miss anything. Simon was bar-mitzvahed in the Reform temple. The church."

"The church!" repeated Anita. "Dad, what's the story?"

"The story, Anita?" Her father took a deep breath. Then he said:

"Once upon a time, a jeweler was taking

the subway home to East Flatbush from his shop on 46th Street. At Nostrand, he finally got a seat and opened his *Post* when he heard loud voices at the far end of the car. Looking up, he saw three Puerto Rican kids in sneakers, jeans, and hot-pink silk jackets which said 'Men Working' on the fronts, backs and sleeves. When he realized that the jackets had been stitched together from the flags that Con Ed put up near excavations, he found this so interesting that it took him a while to notice: the kids had knives and were working their way through the car, taking money and jewelry from the passengers and dropping them in a bowling bag. Then he thought: only in New York do thieves wear clothes that glow in the dark. The boys didn't seem to be hurting anyone, but it still didn't make the jeweler comfortable. He thought: is this how it happens? One night you pick the wrong subway car, and bingo! you're an item in the morning paper.

"Halfway down the car, they'd reached an old lady—who started to scream. Then suddenly, the lights began to flash on and off in a definite pattern. Three long blinks, three short blinks, three long blinks—by the fourth SOS the muggers had their noses pressed against the door, and when it opened at the station, they ran. 'Thank God, it's a miracle!' cried the old lady.

"Meanwhile the jeweler had his head between his knees. He was trying to breathe, thinking he must have been more scared than he'd known. Then he looked up and saw a young hasidic man watching him from across the aisle.

"'It wasn't a miracle,' said the Hasid. 'I did it. Follow me out at the next stop.'

"Normally, this jeweler wasn't the type to follow a Hasid out onto the Eastern Parkway station. But all he could think of was: had his wallet been stolen, he'd have had to spend all the next day at the Motor Vehicle Bureau, replacing his license and registration. He felt that he owed somebody something, and if this

Hasid was taking credit, keeping him company was the least he could do.

"On the platform, the Hasid pointed to a bare light bulb and said, 'Look.' The light blinked on and off. Then he waved at a buzzing fluorescent light. It blinked too. 'I lied before,' said the Hasid. 'It wasn't my doing. Everything is the rebbe's . . . .'"

Anita's father stopped when her mother came in, drying her hands. "Bertie!" Anita's mother cried, picking the baby up and waltzing him into the kitchen. "Don't listen to this nonsense! A whole life ruined for one blinky light bulb!"

"It wasn't the light," said Anita's father.

Anita wanted to ask if his story really happened or if he'd made it up as a metaphor for what happened. She thought: *something* must have happened. In the old days, her father didn't make up stories. But she forgot her questions when she heard her mother in the kitchen singing "Music, Music, Music" to Bertie, singing "Put another nickel in, in the nickelodeon," sounding just like Teresa Brewer.

Now, five months later, watching the parents of cult members on Donahue, Anita decides that her father's story left out all the important parts. Such as: why he really joined. There's no overlooking the obvious reasons: old age, sickness, death. If they'd been Protestant and he'd converted to Catholicism, no one would have wondered why.

She remembers a weekend this past summer when Jamie was away on business (with Lizzie, she thinks now) and her parents came up to keep her company. Her father drove her to the supermarket to shop for their visit and for Jamie's return. At the checkout stand, the kid who packed their order insisted—over her father's protests—on wheeling the cart out and loading the bags into their (the old man's, the pregnant woman's) car. Like her father, Anita was angry at the kid. Couldn't he see that her father could have done it? Not for nothing did he swim fifteen laps at the JCC pool every Sunday morning. But the crazy thing was: for the whole way home, Anita was mad at her father too.

Her father is still in shape. And despite all the rushing to *shul* every morning and from there to work, he seems pretty relaxed. What's hurting her family, Anita decides, is the unpredictability, the shaky sense that everyone is finally unreliable. What's bothering her mother is that the man she's shared her bed with for thirty-three years has suddenly and without warning rolled to the opposite side. She must wonder if the sheet with the hole in it has been there all along.

Anita wants to tell her mother that there's no guarantee; you can't know anything about anyone. She wants to ask: what's so strange about a man wanting to sing and dance his way into heaven? But if they've never even talked about sex, how can they talk about this? . . .

Anita's wasted the morning trying to think up interesting things to tell Jamie. She's saved the last eight years up in little moments to amuse him. It's all right, though, it's not as if she's staged them for his benefit. If she didn't tell someone, she'd probably just forget.

The problem is, today she can't think of one. She blames this on living in her parents' house, where nothing interesting ever happens. She feels that living there marks her as a boring person with no interesting friends she could have stayed with. But that's not true. She and Bertie would have been welcome in the editing room of Irene's Soho loft, on the couch in Jeanie's Park Slope floor-through. But being home is easier, she doesn't have to be a good guest. If Bertie cries at night, her mother comes in and offers to sing him Teresa Brewer.

One thing she could tell Jamie is what she's noticed at the Pathmark: more and more people seem to be buying huge quantities of specialty items, whole shopping carts full of apri-cot yogurt, frozen tacos, Sprite in liter plastic jugs. She's heard that American families hardly ever sit down to dinner together. So who knows, maybe there are millions of people out there, each eating only one thing. She could tell him how she took Bertie to the park to see some other babies. He'd slept the whole time, leaving her with the other mothers, none of whom even smiled at her. At one point, a little boy threw sand at a little girl. The girls' mother ran over, grabbed the boy's ankles, and turned him upside down. Anita expected coins to rain out of his pockets like in the movies, but none did. After a while, the boy's mother came over, and instead of yelling at the woman who was shaking her upside-down son, said, "I'm glad it's you and not me." Anita felt as if she'd stumbled in on a game already in progress, like polo or a new kind of poker with complicated rules which no one would stop to explain.

But the last thing she wants is to sound like some pitiful housewife drifting back and forth between the supermarket and the play-ground. She wonders what sort of lawyer Lizzie is. Corporate taxes, she hopes, but fears it's probably the most interesting cases: mad bombings, ax murders, billion-dollar swindles.

She's tempted to tell Jamie about her father, how for a week or so last month he'd been instructed by his rebbe: instead of saying grace, he should clap his hands whenever the spirit of thanksgiving moved him. In the hour-and-a-half it took to eat—with her father dropping his silverware, clapping, shutting his eyes as if smelling something sweet—Anita tried to predict these outbursts, but couldn't; she'd thought of the retarded people one heard sometimes in movie theaters, shouting out randomly, for no reason. She could tell Jamie how her father came home in a green velvet Tyrolean hat with a feather; apparently, the rebbe had given out dozens of hats to illustrate his sermon: the righteous man must climb this world like a mountain.

But she knows that telling Jamie would

only make her angry at him for not being around tomorrow when she'll need to tell him the next installment. Nor does it make her happy right now to think that Jamie knows her father well enough to know: in the old days, he wouldn't have been caught dead in a Tyrolean hat.

The obvious subject is Bertie. Everything he does interests her; she thinks he's a genius. Why can't she tell Jamie about his practiced smiles, about his picking up his own Cheerios? Why? Because what could be more pitiful than thinking that anyone cares if your five-month-old can pick up his own Cheerios?

Bertie's victory over Cheerios should be their victory. Instead she can hardly talk about Bertie; it's as if she's accusing Jamie. Bertie should be the mortar cementing them; as it is, he's part of the wall.

When Jamie rings the doorbell, Anita half-hopes that Bertie—who hasn't seen his father for two weeks—will not recognize him and scream. Bertie looks at Jamie, then at Anita, then at Jamie, then smiles a smile which anyone could tell is his real one.

Anita's mother says, "Jamie!" She says, "There's apple cake in the fridge if you kids get hungry." Then she backs out of the room. It's so uncomfortable they could be high schoolers dating—except for the presence of Bertie and the fact that Anita and Jamie didn't know each other in high school.

"Can we go for a walk somewhere?" Jamie is staring to the side of Anita's head at Bertie. Anita feels as if he's asking Bertie out and is one of those guys who's scared to be alone with his date. She's the friend he drags along, the chaperone.

"Sure," says Anita. Bertie's wriggling so hard his feet jam halfway down the legs of his snowsuit and she has to thread them through. She knows she's making herself look incompetent, making the process of dressing Bertie look harder than it is.

On the way to the park she can't think of anything to say. She doesn't want to discuss specialty items at the Pathmark or the upside-down boy. Of course she's done this before, rehearsed whole conversations which turned out to be inappropriate. But never with Jamie.

The playground is chilly, almost deserted. In one corner, two five-year-old boys are playing soccer while their parents—all four of them in ponytails—hunker on the ground, passing a joint. There's a dressed-up Orthodox family sitting in a row on a bench. By the swings, a young mother says to her daughter, "Okay, ten more pushes and we're going home." And finally there are some boys—ten, eleven, twelve—playing very hard and punishingly on the jungle gym and slide, as if it's the playground equipment's fault that they've grown too big for it.

"When is Bertie going to be old enough for the slide?" asks Jamie.

"Tomorrow," says Anita.

The mother by the swings counts to ten, and when the little girl says "Ten more!" grabs her daughter's hand and pulls her out of the park. Jamie sits down on one of the swings and stretches his arms out for Bertie. Holding the baby on his lap, Jamie pushes off. Anita can't look till she reassures herself: she trusts Jamie that much—not to drop Bertie. She sits on the other swing and watches Bertie, who is leaning forward to see where they're going before they get there.

"Look how he holds his head up," says Jamie. "That's my boy."

"He's been doing that for four months," says Anita.

Jamie trails his long legs in the sand and stops with a bump. "Anita," he says, "just what am I supposed to do? What do you want?"

Anita wonders what she does want. She's not sure she wants to be back with Jamie. Bertie or no Bertie, it's too late. Something's happened which can't be fixed. Basically, she

Tompkins Square Park,
Morris Schulman, 1982.
The Jewish Museum, NY/
Art Resource, NY.

wants what her mother wants: for everything to be the way it was before everything changed.

"I want to know one thing," she says, "Remember that garden party at Mel's?"

"What about it?" says Jamie.

Anita remembers a buffet of elegant, salty things—sun-dried tomatoes, smoked salmon—which by then she wasn't allowed to eat. "I want to know if you and Lizzie were already. . . ." She thinks: if a woman could walk clear across a party to feel her lover's wife's belly, her lover's unborn child inside it, well then, you really can't know anything about people.

Jamie says, "Of course not," in a tone which makes Anita suspect it began at that party, or thereabouts. She wonders: did their fingers brush accidentally over a Lebanese olive? A long look near the pesto and sour-cream dip?

"It wasn't Lizzie." Jamie's swinging again, distractedly. "It wasn't you."

"Who was it?" she says. "Don't blame Bertie, he wasn't born yet."

"It wasn't the baby. It was me. Listen." Jamie stops himself by grabbing the chain on her swing together with his. The seats tilt together crazily. "When I was in the seventh grade, there was a kid in my class named Mitchell Pearlman. One day we got to talking about our dads, and Mitchell said that his was a photographer. He'd been everywhere, done everything. Had he fought with the Mau Maus? Sure. Sipped tea with Queen Elizabeth? Of course. Lived with the Eskimos, crossed the Sahara on a camel? You bet.

"Naturally we thought he was lying till we went to his house for his birthday. The minute we met Mitchell Pearlman's father—mustache, jeans, big silver belt buckle—we began to think Mitchell was telling the truth. After the cake and ice cream, his father brought out the pictures of himself in front of the igloo, the camel, arm in arm with Jomo Kenyatta, dandling the baby Prince Charles on his knee. And for months after that, for years, I hated my own father. I wouldn't speak to him."

102

"So?" says Anita. "I don't get it."

"So when Bertie was born, I suddenly thought: in a couple of years, he'll be me in the seventh grade. And I'll be my father. And he'll go out and find his own Mitchell Pearlman's father. And he'll hate me. I thought: we've made a terrible mistake! We should have waited to have Bertie till I *was* Mitchell Pearlman's father! Does this make any sense?" There are tears in Jamie's eyes.

Anita thinks: not much. For one thing, the chronology's wrong. Jamie fell in love *before* Bertie was born. For another, Bertie isn't Jamie and Jamie isn't his father. Jamie's father owns a dry-cleaners, while Jamie is a labor lawyer with interesting cases. She wants to shout at him that exchanging long looks with a lady lawyer over the pesto is nothing—nothing at all—like fighting with the Mau Maus. But she doesn't. She's beginning to see that her sister's right: this is something some men do. Jamie himself doesn't understand, any more than Mitchell Pearlman's father understood why he found it so easy to leave the wife and kids and take off across the Sahara.

She imagines Jamie ten years hence, taking Bertie out for the afternoon. He's one of those weekend fathers she never really noticed till she was pregnant, and then she saw them everywhere. She could always tell how uneasy it made them to take their kids places whole families went. Recently she read in the *Times*: there's a health club in Manhattan which, on Saturdays and Sundays, caters exclusively to single fathers and their children. Ten years from now, there will be hundreds of these places.

She imagines men and children lolling in a steamy pool, pumping exercycles, straining on Nautilus machines. There are no women in her vision, it's as if all the mothers have died of some plague. She hears the cries of the children, sees the shoulders of the fathers rounded as if from the weight of the children tugging their arms.

The only thing she can't picture is how Bertie will look in ten years' time.

For weeks, her father has been asking her to come to a service in his *shul*. "The worst that'll happen is that you'll have fun," he says. It's made Anita a little nervous, like having a Moonie ask her to go away for the weekend. But the day after Jamie's visit, she agrees. There's nothing but football on TV.

"Can me and Bertie sit in the same section?" she asks.

"Don't be smart," says her father.

When she comes downstairs in a turtleneck and good brown corduroy jeans, she sees him really suffering with embarrassment. She goes and changes into a long skirt from the back of her closet, an Indian print from the 60's.

On the drive down Eastern Parkway, Anita and her father don't talk. Again she has the peculiar feeling of being on a date. There's not much traffic on this Sunday, and everything seems so slowed down that she's slow to notice: her father's whole driving style has changed. He used to zip around like a cabbie—teeth-grinding, swerving, cursing. Now he keeps to his lane, he's got all the time in the world. His elbow is out the side window, cold air is rushing into the car.

"Can you shut that?" says Anita. "The baby."

"Sure," says her father. "Sorry."

"What kind of service are we going to?"

"A wedding."

"Turn the car around," says Anita.

"Don't be stupid," says her father. "Would you have preferred a funeral? All right. Next time, a funeral."

"What next time?" says Anita.

"You'll be interested," says her father. "The ceremony is outside under the stars."

"Stars you can see from Crown Heights?" says Anita. "I'll be interested."

In the old days, her father used to start looking for parking places miles in advance. She remembers hours of accelerating, then falling forward as the brakes squealed in the search for a spot in Chinatown. Now as they pull up to the block on which hundreds of Hasidim are milling around, her father cruises smoothly into an empty space.

The short winter afternoon is darkening. The street lights come on. The air is crisp and clear. The men wear nearly identical black coats, the women's are of various subdued hues. Most of the women are in high, good leather boots which remind Anita of the ad on the microfilm. It's easy to spot the converts like her father in his fur-collared car coat, the young men in denim and down; it annoys her that several young women wear paisley skirts much like hers.

The crowd spills off the sidewalk, blocking the northbound lane, but the two cops parked in their squad car ignore it. Leaning on other cars, Puerto Rican kids in sweatshirts and down vests idly stroke their girlfriends as they watch the Hasidim assemble. The wedding canopy is already up, held by four men who keep switching the pole from hand to hand so they can warm the free hand in their pockets.

Suddenly everyone's buzzing like bees. Anita's father leans forward and says, "The rebbe."

Anita stands on tiptoe. But from a quarter-block away, the rebbe looks pretty much like the photo: Mr. Natural. That's another reason she could never join this sect: being female, she'd never get closer to the rebbe than this. She turns to say this to her father, but he's gone—drawn, she imagines, toward his rebbe.

The crowd buzzes again when the bride and groom appear. The bride's leaning on some women, the groom on some men. They both look ready to drop. When Anita gets a good look at the groom—gangly, skin the color of skim milk—she understands why the bride can hardly walk. How could anyone marry *that*?

Nearly rigid in his quilted snowsuit, Bertie's getting heavy. Anita holds him up

though she knows he's too young to focus on the center of attention, too young to know there is a center. To Bertie, everything's the center: the scarf of the woman in front of him, his own inaccessible fist.

Anita thinks: the bride must be freezing. Maybe that's why she's so hunched over as the women lead her in circles around the groom. Under the veil, she could be anything—old, ugly, sick, some covered-up temple idol. No wonder the groom is so panicky!

Even with all the Hebrew prayers, the ceremony is over in no time. They always are, thinks Anita, except when people write their own. Real religions and even the state seem to know: if it drags on too long, somebody *will* faint. Anita and Jamie got married impulsively in a small town on the California-Nevada border. What she mostly remembers is sitting in a diner in Truckee, writing post cards to all their friends saying that she'd just been married in the Donner Pass by a one-armed Justice of the Peace.

Her thoughts are interrupted by cheers; the groom has broken the glass. Then bride and groom and wedding canopy disappear in the crowd bearing them—and Anita and Bertie—into the hall.

Just inside the door, the men and women peel off in opposite directions. Anita follows the women into a large room with a wooden dance floor surrounded by round tables, set with centerpieces of pink carnations in squat crystal vases and groupings of ginger ale and seltzer bottles.

No one's saving places, jockeying to be near friends. The ladies just sit. Anita stands for a minute or so, then sees two women beckoning and patting the chair between them, so she goes and sits down. She soon understands why the women have found places so quickly: it doesn't matter where they sit, no one stays put for more than two seconds. They kiss and gab, then get up, sit next

Women at Prayer in Synagogue,
K. Felsenhardt,
Poland, 1893.
From the HUC Skirball
Cultural Center and
Museum, Los Angeles, CA.
Kirschstein Collection.

RIGHT: *Men at Prayer
in Synagogue,*
K. Felsenhardt,
Poland, 1893.
From the HUC Skirball
Cultural Center and
Museum, Los Angeles, CA.
Kirschstein Collection.

they so interested? But they are, they're full of questions. How old is he? What's his name? Does he sleep through the night? Is he always so good?

Anita feels like Bertie's ventriloquist. She has to make an effort to speak in her normal voice as she says, "His name's Bertie. He's five months old. He can pick up his own Cheerios."

"Cheerios?" cry the women. "At five months? He's a genius!"

The partition separating the men's and the women's section stops a few feet from the ceiling. Anita's facing it when suddenly she sees three furry brown things fly up, then plummet, then fly again. Just as she figures out someone's juggling hats, she hears applause from the other side of the plywood.

With each course, a different woman is making Bertie smile and nibbling from whatever plate the waiter has put down. First comes stuffed derma, then a platter of thick roast beef, little round potatoes, canned peas. Anita picks up a forkful of peas. She isn't very hungry, it isn't very good. No one's eating much: even the fleshiest ladies are just tasting. But every woman who sits down offers to hold Bertie for Anita, or to cut her roast beef. They

to a friend at another table, kiss and gab some more. Meanwhile the waiters are weaving through with bowls of hot soup, shouting to the women to get out of their way. But no one's paying attention.

The woman to Anita's right is middle-aged and kind of pretty. She's Mrs. Lesser. When the waiter brings Anita's soup, Mrs. Lesser pushes it away so Anita won't spill it in her struggle with Bertie's zipper.

"Your first baby?" asks Mrs. Lesser.

"Yes," says Anita.

"I had my first when I was sixteen. Can you believe I'm a grandmother?"

Anita might not have thought it, but she can believe it; she doesn't know quite what to say.

"Can *you* believe it?" Mrs. Lesser puts her big face near Bertie's little one, and Bertie rewards her with his most radiant, sweetest, and most inauthentic social smile.

"Look at this baby smile!" Mrs. Lesser says to the whole table. "Look at this sweetheart!" It's Anita's introduction to the room at large, and all at once it's open season on Bertie. Mrs. Lesser gets up and someone else sits down and starts stroking Bertie's cheek.

These women have children and grandchildren of their own, thinks Anita. Why are

say to Bertie, "Too bad you can't eat roast beef, pussycat," and "Next year at this time you'll be munching little brown potatoes."

Slowly at first, the men begin dancing. Anita feels it through the floor before she hears it. Stamp, stamp. Soon the silverware is rattling, the peas are jumping on her plate. The stamping gets faster, there are shouts. Anita wonders if her father is dancing. Probably he is. The door between the two sections is open, children are running back and forth. No one would stop her from looking. But she doesn't, she just doesn't.

Singing, clapping, the men make their own music. The women have help. Two men come in with an accordion and a mandolin. The women dance sweetly in couples, a dance which seems part waltz, part foxtrot, part polka. Mrs. Lesser reappears, and when a sprightly gray-haired lady to the far side of her makes swaying motions with her arms, Mrs. Lesser says, "If you're asking, I'm dancing," and away they go. A tiny old woman approaches Anita and says, "Would the baby care to dance?"

All the women want to dance with Bertie. Young and old, they keep cutting in, passing him around. Anita catches glimpses of him, first with this one, then with that, sailing, swaying to the music, resting his cheek on their pillowy breasts. When Mrs. Lesser sits back down, she asks where the baby is.

"Dancing," says Anita.

Mrs. Lesser cranes her neck. "He's smiling," she says. "He's the belle of the ball."

Suddenly there's a whoop from the other room, and Anita sees the groom's head and shoulders over the partition. From the angle of his head, the stricken expression, she knows that this is the part where the men hoist the groom up in a chair and dance. Then the women gather and raise the bride's chair. The music gets louder and the women begin circling the bride, dancing with enough intensity that

Anita goes and finds Bertie and takes him back.

At last the bride's chair is nearly touching the ceiling. Above the partition, she and the groom look at each other. Anita wants to study this look. She thinks it's something she should pay close attention to. But she's only half-watching. Mostly she's concentrating on not dropping Bertie, whom she's holding up above her head.

"Look, sweetheart," she's saying. "Look at the lady in the chair."

Bertie sings when he nurses, a sweet satisfied gulping and humming high in his nose. On the night of the wedding, Anita falls asleep while he's nursing, and his song turns into the song in her dream.

In her dream, Bertie's singing "Music, Music, Music" just like Teresa Brewer. He's still baby Bertie, but he's up on stage, smiling one of his phony smiles, making big stagey gestures like Shirley Temple or those awful children in *Annie*. One of these gestures is the "okay" sign, thumb and forefinger joined. The circle his fingers make remind her of the Buddha. It reminds her of a Cheerio.

Anita wakes up laughing, wondering how a little baby could know words like "nickelodeon." She gets up and, without detaching Bertie from her breast, slips a bathrobe over both of them and goes downstairs. Except for her parents' bedroom, where earlier she's heard her mother preparing for sleep, every room is lit up. In the kitchen, light is shining from around the edges of the cellar door. Anita and Bertie go down.

Opening the door to the family room, she sees her father sitting cross-legged on the cork-tiled floor. His eyes are shut and tears are shining on his cheeks. But he's not so out of it that he doesn't hear her come in. Looking up, he seems frail and embarrassed, an old man caught doing something he's not supposed to do.

Anita wants to apologize and leave. Then it dawns on her that she's not down there to bother him. There's something she wants to ask, but she's not sure what it is. She wants to ask why all the lights in the house are always on. She wants to ask who he thinks is paying the electric bills.

Anita's father stands up and dries his eyes with his palm. Then he says, "Hold up your hand."

Anita holds up her hand and he lifts his, palm facing hers, a few inches away. He asks if she feels anything.

She feels something. A pressure.

She remembers how when she was in labor with Bertie, she held Jamie's hand. Just before the nurses let her start pushing, she turned to Jamie and said, "I don't think I can do this." "Sure you can," he said, and squeezed her hand so hard she'd thought it was broken. By the time it stopped hurting, the contraction was over and she knew she could go on. Now she sees that Jamie didn't mean to hurt her. He was scared too.

Her father's hand is still a few inches away, but its hold feels as tight as Jamie's. She can almost feel electrons jumping over the space between them, electricity drawing them as close as she is to Bertie, who just at that moment lets go of her breast and sits up, watching them.

In "Fiddler on the Roof," Tevye the Milkman at one point asks his wife Goldie: "Do you love me?" Exasperated, Goldie quickly straightens out her hopelessly romantic husband, describing for him the real virtues of a good Jewish wife: "For twenty-five years, I've cooked your food, cleaned your house, milked your cow. . . . " Goldie is here drawing upon sound precedent; the biblical book of Proverbs ends with a similar description of an ideal Jewish wife: "Her husband puts his confidence in her, and lacks no good thing. She is good to him, never bad, all the days of her life. . . . She rises while it is still night, and supplies provisions for her household. . . . She sees that her business thrives." Indeed, for centuries, Jewish wives have been prized for their prodigious industry and skill. Significantly, no comparable description exists for a Jewish husband, either in the Bible or in "Fiddler." Therein hangs a tale—or several tales.

MARRIAGE

As in many traditions, the battle of the sexes provides plentiful grist for the Jewish storyteller's mill. In this section we encounter nine courtship and marriage tales from a variety of Jewish communities, each imbued with the special flavor of its indigenous culture. Some of these tales, such as the Sephardic trickster tale "Djuha Seeks a Bride," and "Three Hairs of a Lion," are humorous and earthy, bordering on the vulgar; others, such as "The Most Precious Thing in the World," "The Clever Wife," and "The Mouse Seeks a Wife," are poignant and bittersweet. Still others are bitter, like the sharp, spare dialogue of Grace Paley's "In This Country But in Another Language." And then there are romantic fairy tales, replete with familiar motifs: the princess imprisoned in a tower, rescued by a handsome young adventurer ("The Ruby Serpent"); the beautiful girl with long silken hair, fleeing her monstrous stepmother with the aid of a handsome prince ("Lanjeh"); the young beauty, hated by her jealous stepmother, the wicked queen, who escapes to the woods where she is befriended by a merry band of thieves, almost killed by the queen's treachery, and married by the handsome prince ("The Pomegranate Girl").

Despite the many differences among the Jewish communities represented by these tales, the rituals of wooing, winning, and sustaining love are remarkably similar. In the stories based on conventional motifs, women tend to be the passive objects of men's desire, trophies to be won; in these narratives, romantic love is the engine that drives the plot. Even a modern story such as "Apples from the Desert," by Israeli writer Savyon Liebrecht, dramatizes the triumph of youthful romance over parental design, a fairy tale in a modern key.

Yet not everything in these stories follows a traditional script. Many of these stories show women not only holding their own, but often getting the upper hand. The female protagonists in several of these tales draw upon their wit, guile, courage, and resolve to preserve themselves and their marriages from harm, despite all the forces arrayed against them. Indeed, more than in any other section in this book, these tales celebrate the marvelous resourcefulness of both women and men.

The Walk,
Marc Chagall, 1917.
State Russian Museum,
St. Petersburg/Bridgeman Art
Library, London.
© 1997 Artists Rights
Society, NY/ADAGP, Paris.

THE MOST PRECIOUS THING IN THE WORLD

—TRADITIONAL MIDRASH, adapted by Ellen Frankel

In the Talmud it is taught: If a man has married a wife and lived with her for ten years and she has not borne him children, he is not free to neglect his duty to beget children.

So taught Rabbi Idi: It happened once that a woman in Sidon had lived for ten years with her husband without bearing him a child. They came to Rabbi Simeon bar Yohai and asked for a divorce.

He said to them, "Just as you have always joyously shared festivals together, do not part from one another without a festive meal."

They took his advice and made a great holiday feast and drank very freely. Feeling in a cheerful mood, the husband said to his wife, "My dear, pick out any article you want in my house and take it with you to your father's house."

What did she do? When he was asleep, she ordered her servants and handmaids to lift him up on the bed and carry him to her father's house. At midnight he awoke and when he was recovered from the effects of the wine, he asked his wife, "My dear, where am I?"

She replied, "You are in my father's house."

"And what am I doing in your father's house?"

She replied, "Did you not say to me last night, 'Take any article you like from my house and go to your father's house'? There is nothing in the world I care for more than you."

The couple then returned to Rabbi Simeon bar Yohai and he prayed for them, and they became fertile and gave birth to a child.

Torah Binder for Nehemiah
Halevi (detail),
Germany, 1836.
The Jewish Museum, NY/
Art Resource, NY.

111

DJUHA SEEKS A BRIDE

—SEPHARDIC TRICKSTER TALE, retold by Peninnah Schram

Djuha was a trickster. At times, he was ready to teach someone a lesson in a shrewd and clever way. At other times, he would act in such a stupid way that he duped himself. Sharp and sly or naive and foolish; I'll leave it to you to match the description that fits him better. . . . But going along with Djuha is always an adventure!

Djuha always wanted to get married, but somehow it never happened to him. You see, whenever he met a young woman of marriageable age, he would always manage to do something stupid, and that would be that! It would convince the young woman to look for a different prospect without wasting another moment.

One day, Djuha was walking down the street. Who should be walking toward him but the matchmaker, the *shadkhan*. No sooner had they greeted each other when Djuha began to complain.

"I want to get married, but I can't seem to find anyone who will marry me. Perhaps I am doing something wrong. Can you give me some good advice so that I can find a bride?"

The matchmaker listened, and then suddenly his face brightened. "Listen, Djuha, meet me later this afternoon and come along with me to this certain house where we will meet with a young woman who is ready to be married. The father of this young woman would be delighted that I am bringing an eligible suitor. Now about the advice, listen! When you are sitting with the young woman, you must pay some attention to her. *Lizrok 'ayin*—throw her an eye! Glance at her! Be a gallant! Remember, above all, *lizrok 'ayin!*"

Djuha questioned him more about this, and finally he said, "I understand." And they decided on the time and place to meet later that day. As soon as Djuha left the matchmaker, he went home to change his clothes and then he went directly to the butcher and asked, "Do you have any cow's eyes?"

The butcher answered matter-of-factly. "Yes, as many as you want."

"Good! Give me a dozen and put them in a sack." Djuha took the sack and went to meet the matchmaker. Then they both went to the house where they would meet the young woman.

When the father of the young woman opened the door and saw the matchmaker and a suitor for his daughter, he heartily welcomed them and invited them to sit in the best chairs. He then asked the daughter to bring the guests some drinks.

The young woman came in, bringing a large silver tray with some refreshments, which she put on the table. Then she sat in a chair near her father.

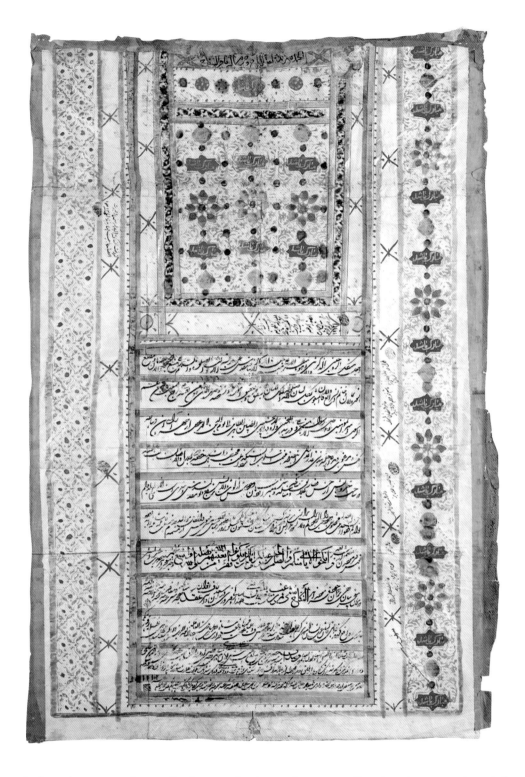

Marriage Contract,
Iran, early 19th century.
Erich Lessing/
Art Resource, NY.

At first there was silence. Djuha was thinking what to say. But then he remembered the matchmaker's advice, *lizrok ayin*, throw her an eye!

Djuha reached into the sack, took out one of the cow's eyes, and threw it at the young woman.

"Ai!" she said, startled.

A short while later, Djuha again remembered the advice. He took out a second cow's eye and threw it at the young woman. "Oi, va voi!" she cried out. And when Djuha threw the third eye, the father stood up, and in a rage shouted, "This man is crazy! Get out of here, both of you!" And Djuha and the matchmaker were chased out the door.

So now perhaps you can understand better why Djuha was never able to find a bride!

THE RUBY SERPENT

—MIDDLE EASTERN FOLKTALE, retold by Ellen Frankel

Solomon knew that he was the wisest king in the world, but he wished to prove it. So he decided to make a test to demonstrate his extraordinary wisdom.

He gave a great banquet to which he invited all the neighboring kings and queens. After they had eaten and drunk their fill, Solomon announced, "I say that there is nothing in the world more powerful than love! Human hands cannot build walls high enough to keep true love out."

His guests laughed gaily at his bold words.

Solomon smiled. "We shall see who has the last laugh." Then he said, "To prove my claim about love, I will command a tower to be built on a faraway island. There I will lock up my beautiful young daughter Keziah. Then we will wait to see what happens."

The guests all looked at each other and shook their heads. Surely Solomon had gone mad!

Over the next few months Solomon's Flying Cloak flew hundreds of workers to a secret island where they built a tall stone tower. Its walls were so smooth that no human hand or foot could ever hope to scale them. Beside the tower grew a great oak tree, whose lowest branches were one hundred feet above the ground and whose massive trunk was as thick as fifty men standing together. At the top of the tower was a room with a single window. There the princess would live—alone. From this window she could see the green forest below and the wide ocean all around.

When the work was completed, the Cloak flew Solomon and Keziah to the room at the top of the tower.

Solomon took his daughter's hand in his and said to her, "Do not fear, my little dove. No harm will come to you here. Each day, my White Eagle will bring you the tastiest foods from the royal table. And a beautiful bird will perch in this oak tree to talk to you and keep you company."

But at his words the princess began to cry.

"Do not be sad," said the king. "I promise you that soon someone will come to rescue you. Then you will leave this tower forever."

Then he flew off upon the Flying Cloak, leaving Keziah all alone.

Far to the north lived a Hebrew merchant who had an only son named Natanyah, a wise and handsome boy. The merchant loved Natanyah and gave him everything he wanted, except for one thing: He would not let his son go to sea. Many years before, the merchant's beautiful young wife had drowned at sea. The merchant was afraid that the same thing would happen to his only son.

But Natanyah wanted to sail in a ship more than anything in the world. Every day he asked his father, "When will you let me go to sea, Father? Please, if you love me, let me go!"

Flying Spice Box,
Yosel Bergner, 1966.
Courtesy of Ein Harod
Museum, Israel.

Finally his father gave in. When the day came for Natanyah to sail, the old merchant gave him a small box. Inside the boy found the largest ruby he had ever seen, so bright he had to shield his eyes with one hand.

"I captured this jewel from a powerful serpent," said the merchant, "and gave it to your mother on her wedding day. May its magic powers protect you in your travels."

Happily, Natanyah grasped the ruby, leapt aboard the ship, and waved good-bye to his father. But the merchant's heart was seized by a terrible fear as he watched the ship sail away.

After a few days a great storm arose at sea. When the ship was about to sink, the merchant's old servant tied Natanyah between two wine sacks and tied a waterskin around his neck. Then Natanyah tied the leather pouch containing the ruby around his waist. A moment later a huge wave swept him overboard into the boiling sea.

For days Natanyah drifted, drinking from the waterskin to quench his terrible thirst. Suddenly he saw above him a great White Eagle, which swooped down and plucked him out of the sea with its powerful claws. The bird carried him to a deserted island and dropped him in the middle of a beautiful forest.

After wandering for many hours, Natanyah saw, on top of the island's only mountain, a tall stone tower standing alone.

"Surely this belongs to pirates or a sorcerer," he thought.

But when he came near the tower, Natanyah saw at the top a young girl talking to a gaily colored bird perched upon her finger. How beautiful she was! She had long, black hair like silk, golden skin, and tiny hands like a kitten's paws. Natanyah instantly fell in love with her.

"But how can I reach her?" he wondered.

Then he remembered the ruby. Hadn't his father said that it had magical powers? Maybe it had brought him here to rescue the princess in the tower. He took it out of its leather pouch and rubbed it between his fingers.

Torah Binder (Wimpel), Germany, 1838. From the HUC Skirball Cultural Center and Museum, Los Angeles, CA. Kirschstein Collection.

Suddenly a giant speckled serpent slithered out of the bushes and seized the gleaming ruby in its mouth. Before Natanyah could stop it, the snake sped to the tall oak tree beside the tower and coiled around it like a giant screw.

Then magically, the tail slithered down and wrapped itself around Natanyah's hands, pulling him up. He scrambled up the serpent's twisted body as though scaling a ladder. When he reached the top of the tree, he saw that the snake's neck had stretched itself out to the window of the tower like a stiff beam. Eagerly Natanyah bounded across it and leapt down.

There on the stone floor lay his ruby, and looking up at him with startled black eyes was the princess in the tower.

"You have come at last!" she cried. "Now we are two!"

The two embraced and told each other all that had happened to them.

The next day Solomon noticed that the White Eagle took two portions from the royal table to bring to the tower. Immediately he ordered his Flying Cloak to fly him and his ministers to the island to see what had become of the lonely princess.

Imagine their amazement to find Princess Keziah sitting together with a handsome young man!

The Cloak then flew them all back to the palace, where Natanyah's old father awaited them, flown there upon the wings of the White Eagle. Soon afterward, the young couple was married amid great festivity.

"And now," said the king to the wedding guests, "do you acknowledge how wise I am? Has not love conquered all?"

All eyes turned toward the young bride and bridegroom who blushed beneath their gaze. Love shone in their eyes as brightly as the brilliant red ruby now sparkling upon Princess Keziah's smooth, honeyed brow.

LANJEH

—*MOROCCAN FOLKTALE*, retold by Barbara Rush

Once there was a monster who, every day, would go off into the forest to hunt for food, and there devour plants, animals, anything it could.

Now, this monster had a home, set deep in the forest near a grazing pasture, as large and luxurious as the home of a wealthy person. It lacked for nothing. And, upon arriving home each day, the monster would chant a certain spell, then be transformed into a beautiful woman, and thus enjoy the luxury of her palatial home, while outside the house, it remained a ferocious beast.

One day, while rummaging about in some ancient ruins hidden in a deep cave in the forest, the monster came upon a cradle, shaped like an egg. From the cradle came a weak, thin voice. "Please, please don't eat me."

Greatly frightened, the monster asked, "Who are you? Where do you come from, the land of demons or the land of humans?"

"From the land of humans," squeaked the voice.

So then the monster slowly opened the cradle, and behold! There within lay a beautiful girl, whom the monster took home and adopted as a daughter. The girl was called Lanjeh.

Now, when the mother went out to hunt, she locked the girl in the last and highest room of the many rooms in that house, so that Lanjeh was out of sight, should anyone by chance come upon that house. And every morning before leaving, the monster would wash and clean the girl's lovely black hair, which seemed to become even more beautiful as she grew. In the evening the mother would check and count the girl's lovely hair to make sure that no one had touched it but she. Thus the days and years passed until the girl reached the age of ten. And her sparkling beauty grew even greater with time.

One day, when the king's shepherd had brought his flock to the pasture to graze, his own horse lifted its head and beheld an amazing sight. There in the window of a huge house was a young girl of radiant beauty. "How can God bestow so much beauty upon one person?" thought the horse. And every day, as it grazed, the horse looked up at that window. Soon it could think of nothing else, not of grass, not of drink, until it became thin and gaunt.

Now it so happened that one day the king himself came to inspect his flock and inquired about the reason for the horse being so thin. "May my soul live, I know only one thing," replied the shepherd. "Every day, when the horse grazes, it lifts its head and stares intensely at a nearby house."

"Silly shepherd," retorted the king, "you too must lift your head and see what the horse sees." The shepherd, greatly embarrassed, begged forgiveness for his foolishness, and did as the king bade. And when he saw the face of the beautiful girl, he too wondered, "How could God bestow so much beauty on one person? Why, she is surely fit for no one other than the prince."

And, before long, the king had received this suggestion, and sent his son to the forest to look upon the girl. The prince stood beside the shepherd's horse, and when the animal lifted its head, the prince did likewise, casting his eyes at the radiant girl. His heart went out to her at once, and, the very next day, determined to speak to her, he approached the walls of the house and whistled—one long, shrill sound.

"What is that?" asked the girl as she looked out the window, and, seeing the face of the youthful prince, she fell in love with him as well.

"Can you, perhaps, give me some water?" asked the prince. "My journey has been a long one and I am quite thirsty."

"Oh, I gladly would," she answered, "but I have no way to get it down to you."

"Well, you have a long braid," advised the prince. "Tie the water bucket to your hair and, in that way, lower it down." This the girl did, but soon afterwards, she became worried. "My monster mother will soon be home. Leave at once, or your end will be bitter." And soon afterward, upon her return, as the monster mother counted the girl's hair, as usual, she did indeed find one missing.

"Who has been here?" she demanded in an angry voice.

"No one, Mother. As I looked out, the passing birds must have plucked one hair from my head." Thus the girl told her mother a lie.

The woman was quiet, but the girl spoke deviously. "Tell me, Mother, how could a person succeed in escaping from an enemy?"

The mother's heart sank. She took these words as a bad omen. "Lanjeh," she asked, "are you planning to leave me?"

"How can you think such a thought? Where would I go, Mother? Who has even seen me here?"

So the monster mother answered the girl's question. "You would take with you a comb, a mirror, and black *kabal* for the eyes. When the enemy approaches, throw down the comb. At once the road will be covered with thorns. As the enemy succeeds again, throw down the mirror. At once the woods will be filled with water. And if the enemy succeeds again, throw down the *kabal*. At once the road will be clouded in darkness, and you will be able to make your escape." The girl listened and remembered the words of her mother in her heart.

The very next morning, after the monster mother had brushed the girl's hair and left on her daily hunt, the prince came for the lovely girl. Lowering herself down on a rope, Lanjeh was sure to take with her a comb, a mirror, and a small quantity of *kabal*. Then the prince mounted his horse and rode off like a thundering storm. But the monster, hearing the great noise, dashed through the forest to overcome them.

"Lanjeh! Lanjeh! Lanjeh!" she called. The girl did not stop. "Lanjeh! Lanjeh! Lanjeh!" the mother begged, cried, pleaded. She almost came upon the horse, when the girl threw down her comb, and, in an instant, the entire road was covered with thorns. The monster, in her anguish, made her way through this obstacle and almost came upon the horse once again, when Lanjeh lifted the mirror and threw it down upon the road. Deep lakes filled the road. But the monster mother made her way through these as well, and just as she was about to overtake the horse, Lanjeh threw down the *kabal*, black as coal. In an instant the fog and darkness blocked her way. The monster mother, unable to continue, cried and wept at the loss of her daughter.

As loudly as she could, she called, "Lanjeh, Lanjeh, listen to my words, which I tell you for your own good. Heed my words and no harm will come to you, I promise. At the crossroads you

OPPOSITE:

Portrait of a Lady in Red, Ben Shahn, 1929. © 1997 Estate of Ben Shahn/ Licensed by VAGA, NY.

will find two spools of thread: one white; the other, black, and where the white spool rolls, take that path. Remember, Lanjeh, don't take the black road. Farewell, Lanjeh, farewell."

Soon Lanjeh and the prince came to the crossroad, and Lanjeh did as her mother's words told her. She prepared to follow the path of the white thread.

"No, no, no," objected the prince, "your mother means only to trick us. If she told us to follow the white path, it is there that she will catch us. It is the other road we must take."

And no amount of the girl's pleading would dissuade the prince. So, putting spurs to the horse, they rode off down the path of black. There, in front of them, swooped a powerful eagle of enormous size, whose feathers were a palette of color as if they were enchanted. "Who wants my special feathers?" it cried. "Come forth and pluck them!" The colors were so beautiful that at first the girl was tempted, but then she thought, "No, no, we don't need them."

But the prince insisted, "I must have those feathers," and so he dismounted and put his hands on the eagle's back. At that moment he felt himself lifted up, up, up as the eagle swept away into the sky. "Lanjeh, Lanjeh, ride to my parents' palace. The horse knows the way," he cried. And so, as her beloved prince was carried away, out of sight, she rode to the palace, where the whinny of the horse brought the king and queen at once. "And where is our son?" they asked, as they recognized the horse. The girl was thrown into a prison room. "This is my punishment," she thought, "for the way I treated my monster mother, who adopted me and cared for me with great love."

That night the eagle descended to the roof of the prison, the prince upon its back.

"Lanjeh, Lanjeh, where did you sleep tonight?" he asked.

"In a warehouse of straw," she replied.

"Lanjeh, Lanjeh, what did you eat tonight?"

"Only water and crusts of bread."

"My God," thought the prince, "this is my bad luck for not heeding your voice."

On the second night the eagle reappeared, the prince again upon its back.

"Lanjeh, Lanjeh, where did you sleep tonight?"

"In a warehouse of animals."

"Lanjeh, Lanjeh, what did you eat tonight?"

"Crusts of bread from dishes filled with dirt."

"My God," thought the prince, "why did I not heed your voice?"

Meanwhile the people of the house were awakened by the voices. "Whom were you speaking to?" they inquired of the girl.

"Only to your son, the prince."

Upon uttering these words, the girl was taken to the palace, there fed and garmented, as befits a royal princess.

That night the eagle and the prince descended again.

"Lanjeh, Lanjeh, where did you sleep tonight?"

"In the palace in a warm bed."

"Lanjeh, Lanjeh, what did you eat tonight?"

"The finest of foods on dishes of gold."

"Be happy, my heart," called the prince, "for at last you are in the trusty hands of my parents."

At all this talk the king and queen were most alarmed, and quickly summoned the most trusted advisors to find a way to rescue the prince.

"Only the rabbi, the teacher of the Jews, can help you," they were told.

And so the rabbi was summoned. "Find a way to save our son or your people will be expelled!" The king's demand was curt and clear.

"The solution is simple," stated the rabbi. "Order your servants to bring forth a wide, deep bowl filled with boiling tar. Spread this on the roof on the very spot where the eagle lands."

And so the rabbi's advice was carried out at once. That night when the eagle landed, its feet indeed stuck to the hot tar, and the prince, weakened and almost dead from thirst and hunger, was rescued.

Of course, he was quickly nursed back to health, after which preparations were made for a wedding feast of great luxury, never before seen in that kingdom.

And the prince and his bride lived together in health and in wealth all the remaining days of their lives.

So may we as well!

Orchard of Lovers,
David Sharir, 1967.
Courtesy of the artist.

THE MOUSE SEEKS A WIFE

—BY BERECHIAH BEN NATRONAI HA-NAKDAN,
retold by Ellen Frankel

I f you run after honor and power, they will quickly run from you.

A mouse wished to marry, but he desired a wife of rare virtue—whose beauty was without equal, whose body required no food, and whose heart would not pursue him when he went wandering.

First he went to the sun and said, "With everlasting love have I loved you. I will betroth you unto me."

The sun replied: "Just hours ago my face was darkened by the night. For the sun forever rises and sets. It is far better that you take a wife from your mother's kin and birthplace."

"No," said the mouse, "it is you I wish to wed."

"Always does the cloud conceal me," said the sun. "Go to her. She will not turn her face from you."

So the mouse went to the cloud. "This day have I labored and found my beloved, my beautiful one, my perfect one," declared the mouse. "By the sun's counsel I take you and will never forsake you."

"The One who watches upon the height of heights placed me in the power of the wind," replied the cloud, "and the wind shifts me east, west, north, and south. If you wed me, you will forever be a wanderer upon the earth. Forsake the handmaiden and take the mistress: Go to the wind."

So the mouse went to the wind in the desert. "Be not ashamed to marry a lowly creature like me," he said. "For you will be mine and I yours."

"Only a fool would marry me," said the wind, "for my breath is powerless against the wall. Go to her, for she will be your fortress in time of distress."

So the mouse went to the wall. "I come to you by the counsel of the Sun and the Cloud and the Wind," said the mouse, "and I will betroth myself to you in loving-kindness and mercy."

"Not out of loving-kindness do you come but out of scorn—to mock me!" lamented the wall. "For although I am a wall and my breasts are like towers, the mice have made a hundred holes in my side! I can no more hold them back than a sieve can hold back water. If you wish to marry a worthy bride, go to the mice and wed one of them!"

So the mouse returned to his mother's birthplace and married one of his own kin. And his heart filled with joy at his good fortune.

Aboard the Ark (detail), David Sharir, 1972. Courtesy of the artist.

THREE HAIRS OF A LION

—MOROCCAN FOLKTALE, retold by Barbara Rush

A married woman was on bad terms with her husband, and often ran to the rabbi to seek advice, as Jews have always done. The rabbi would advise her, to no avail.

But one day the rabbi said to the poor woman, "I have a remedy for you but it's risky, and you have to follow my instructions exactly."

"Rabbi, I will do anything you say. My life is involved and anything you say will be worth trying. There is no other way."

So the rabbi said, "Listen carefully. If you can pluck three hairs from the mane of a lion and bring them to me, I'll give you the remedy."

So, frightened but excited, the woman went to the forest, and there carried on daily observations of the comings and goings of the animals. And one day, as she observed a lion approaching in her direction, she pulled from her bag a big piece of meat she had prepared for him. She threw it on the ground, and ran for her life. But, as the lion slowly ate his meal, she crept back and came closer to the beast. The same thing happened the next day and the day after until the woman became acquainted with the lion, and the lion felt familiar enough to come closer to her. And after the two had achieved this familiarity and while the lion was eating his meat, she gathered up her courage and plucked a handful of hair from the lion's mane. Then she quickly ran to the rabbi, and, with a cry of victory, burst in uninvited. "Rabbi, here they are. Now, where is the remedy?"

The rabbi turned to the woman. "You fool!" he answered. "If you have learned to tame a lion, you can certainly learn to tame your husband."

THE CLEVER WIFE

—IRAQI FOLKTALE, retold by Simah Hagoli,
translated by Gene Baharav

O nce there was a king who was ready to marry, on condition that his wife would break off relations with her parents after marriage and never see them again. Many beautiful girls were eager to marry the king, and time and again he chose from amongst them the one most befitting him.

One, two, and three weeks would pass, while the king was very busy attending receptions and audiences. His wife was always left alone at home, and she had no one to speak

Torah Binder (Wimpel), Germany, 1778. From the HUC Skirball Cultural Center and Museum, Los Angeles, CA.

to. After several months of suffering the wife would pass away. The king used to mourn his wife's death, and then, after a short time, he would proclaim a new contest for a bride.

This went on for a long time. Queen succeeded queen, and not one of them was able to bear up for more than a few months. At last there came a lovely, clever girl who wished to marry the king. Her parents were against the match, especially her mother.

"My beloved only daughter. It is difficult for me to throw you into the fire," she said. "The king is a woman-killer, because of his harsh treatment. At first he buries his wife in the castle and then in a grave. If you marry him, you will bury me together with yourself."

"Do not be afraid, mother," the daughter consoled her. "The king will bury neither you nor me. I will settle everything, if you have patience."

At last the mother gave in. Her daughter was the only one to find favor in the king's eyes, and she won the contest. In due course she married him and was parted from her parents. After two days, however, she became bored, as the king was always preoccupied with his duties. Indeed, it was difficult for her to become accustomed to the silent house without a soul to talk to.

What did she do? She took the skin of a goat, blew it up, dressed it in clothes, drew a face, and put a hat on its head. It looked like a

Milliner,
Raphael Soyer, late 1930s.
Collection of Judge Irving
Hill, Los Angeles, CA.
Courtesy of The Estate
of Raphael Soyer and
Forum Gallery, NY.

man indeed. Afterward she placed the stuffed doll on a chair and began relating to it all that weighed on her heart and troubled her.

One month passed, two months went by, and the woman did not change her habit. When her husband came home, she used to talk to him cheerfully, and while he was away, she used to play with her doll.

The king did not know how his wife managed to bear up for so long. Three months passed, four months went by, and the king decided to look into the matter. What did he do? He bored a small hole in the wall of her room, and lo, what did he see? His wife sitting with a stranger, talking to him. "Unfaithful one!" he said in his heart. "She has been deceiving me all the time."

He decided to take his revenge and afflict her and her lover with severe and terrible sufferings. He behaved as if he knew nothing of the matter, but he gave orders to the watchman to be on the lookout for anyone trying to leave the palace. In the evening the watchman reported that not a single person had left the palace. Then after dinner, the king suggested to his wife, "Come, let us look around the house and inspect your rooms." At last they reached the chamber where the king had watched his wife conversing with a man. Suddenly the king stopped and drew out a dagger. "Where have you hidden your lover?" he asked.

The queen showed him the doll hidden in the cupboard. The king stabbed it with his dagger, whereupon blood poured out.

"What is this?" the king asked. "If it is a doll, where does the blood come from?"

"That is my sorrow and grief, O king I told my doll all that there was in my heart. Otherwise I myself would have burst from suffering."

At last the king understood that he himself had caused the death of his former wives and that his present wife was the cleverest of them all. He decided to revoke his decree and allowed his wife to visit her parents. You can imagine the rejoicing of the mother and her daughter.

THE POMEGRANATE GIRL

—EGYPTIAN FOLKTALE, retold by Barbara Rush

Once upon a time there lived a king and queen who had no children. One day the king announced, "You know, my dear, we have been married for many, many years and still don't have a child." These words hurt the queen very much, and she sat and wept, afraid that the king would marry another in order to bring forth an heir.

As the queen sat thus, crying hysterically, behold! An old woman appeared and asked, "Beautiful queen, why are you crying?" And so the queen told her story, to which the old woman replied, "Don't cry. I will give you a pomegranate. Eat half and give the other half to the king. Soon you will give birth to a daughter, and, when you do, name her Romana." So saying, the old woman disappeared.

Exactly nine months later the queen gave birth to a baby girl, who was so full of joy that she cast light in every place she went. The girl was as beautiful as she was joyous, and her mother named her Romana, as the old woman had instructed.

A few years later the queen died, and the king took a second wife, a woman who was quite pretty but whose beauty could not compare with that of Romana. Because of this, the new queen envied her stepdaughter. Now, the king and queen had a daughter of their own, who was not very pretty at all, and this made the queen even more jealous than before.

Now, the queen had a friend who was a wizard, a man who could perform all sorts of magic— and evil magic at that! One day she invited him to come to live at the palace. And one day, as the two were talking, she asked him, "Tell me, who is more beautiful than I?" The wizard answered:

> I am handsome,
> You are fairer still. But no!
> The girl Romana's beauty
> is a thousand times more so.

OPPOSITE: *Pensive Child*,
Michael Kovner, 1994.
Courtesy of the artist.

The queen glared in envy. "And how can I get rid of Romana?" she asked.

"Take a dirty piece of cotton, call Romana to the cellar, and there bid her knit the cotton into stockings."

So the stepmother did as the wizard advised. And soon the girl sat in the cellar, crying miserably.

But, behold! There appeared before her an old woman, the very same as had appeared before her mother years ago. "And what happened to you, my dear? Why are you crying?" the old one asked, to which Romana told of her sad plight.

"Don't worry. Listen and do as I say," said the old woman. "A stream of red water will pass near you. Ignore it. A stream of black water will appear near you. Do not go near it. Then a stream of white water will flow near you. Into this water dip your cotton and with it wash your face and hands."

So saying, the old woman disappeared.

Romana did as she was told, and when she dipped the cotton into the white water, the cotton at once was transformed into knit stockings. And when the girl washed her hands and face with it, why, she became even more beautiful than before.

Now, when the stepmother saw what had happened, she was quite astonished, and forced Romana to tell her about the appearance of the old woman. And what did she do out of jealousy? The queen took the cotton to the cellar, where she brought her own ugly daughter, and bade her wait for the old woman to appear. And just as the woman had come to Romana, she appeared before this girl as well. But the daughter was not as well-mannered as Romana, and shouted harshly at the old woman. So the old woman instructed her: "A stream of red water will appear before you. Ignore it. A stream of black water will appear near you. Into this water dip your cotton and with it wash your hands and face."

So the girl did as she was told, but no sooner did she wipe her face with the cotton than, behold! She was even uglier than before. Meanwhile the king had gone abroad, and the queen, not knowing what to do to gain revenge against Romana, asked the wizard's advice. "Send the king a letter telling him that his daughter is going out with young men and coming home way into the late hours of the night," he instructed.

This the stepmother did, and when the king read the letter, he became so enraged that he sent his vizier at once to have his daughter slaughtered and to bring him her blood.

So it was that Romana soon found herself in the midst of the forest, understanding full well that she was to be killed. "Oh please," she begged, "have mercy on me and leave me here. Slaughter a dog and give its blood to the king in place of mine." And so, because the vizier was fond of the beautiful girl, he had mercy on her and did as she asked, sending her off into the forest by herself.

The girl wandered until she saw a flickering light in the distance. And as she approached a small hut and entered, she sensed at once that it belonged to thieves.

There on the table she found fresh vegetables, which she washed and cooked and later ate. And when she heard the thieves coming, she hid herself in a corner.

Now, the thieves felt the presence of someone in their house but did nothing. The next day, however, when they left for their daily work, one stayed behind and hid. And when Romana, thinking all the inhabitants had gone, came out of her corner, the thief pounced upon her. "Are you a woman or a girl?"

"I am a girl," she answered.

"Then you will be a sister as well." And so Romana remained with the thieves, forty in all, preparing their food, tidying the house, and receiving a new gift from her "brothers" every day.

Now, one day at the palace the queen happened to ask the wizard, "Tell me, who is more beautiful than I?" to which the wizard answered:

> I am handsome,
> You are fairer still. But no!
> The girl Romana's beauty
> is a thousand times more so.

❖

"Romana?" shrieked the wicked queen. "But she is dead!"

"No," answered the wizard, "she lives in the forest at the home of the forty thieves. If you want to be rid of her, go to her and pretend to be a seller of jewelry. Place this ring on her finger, and she will die."

The queen quickly did as she was told, and the girl fell into a deep sleep. Then the queen returned to the palace, happy to be rid of Romana at last.

When the thieves returned and saw their "sister" dead, they grieved, for they had come to love her very much. Tenderly they placed her in a glass coffin in the forest, so that they could gaze upon her beauty every day.

Now one day a king's son went hunting, and shot a bird, which fell out of the sky right onto the coffin of the sleeping princess. And so it was that the prince cast his eyes upon Romana and fell in love with her at once. He asked permission of the thieves to move the coffin to his home, where she could be properly buried.

Soon people were called to cleanse the body and bury the girl, and, when they began to work, they removed the ring. Then and there the girl came back to life.

The prince, astonished beyond words, confessed his love to the beautiful girl, and asked her to marry him. She agreed at once, upon the condition that the forty thieves, whom she loved like brothers, be invited to the wedding. And so, for seven days and seven nights there was feasting and rejoicing as the couple were wed.

Sometime later the queen found herself again in the company of the wizard. "Tell me, who is more beautiful than I?" she asked. The wizard said:

> I am handsome,
> You are fairer still. But no!
> The girl Romana's beauty
> is a thousand times more so.

"But Romana is dead!" cried the queen.

"No, she is not dead. She has married the prince."

"And what can I do to be rid of her?" asked the queen, her eyes glaring.

"Go to the palace and say that you are the mother of the new princess and you wish to see her. When you are admitted to Romana's room, stick this pin into her head. At once she will become a dove and fly away. Then send your daughter to take Romana's place. Say that she is ill and that you wish to stay and nurse her."

So the stepmother did as she was told. And the moment the pin was stuck into Romana's head, the girl became a dove and flew off into the forest. She flew at once to a favorite orange tree that had grown in the spot where she herself had thrown the pits. Day after day the dove ate the fruit of the tree, for only from this tree did she gain her nourishment. Day after day she would fly near the head of the gardener, chirping, "Water the orange tree! Water the orange tree!"

But one day the gardener fell asleep and did not give the tree its water. For several days the tree was not watered, until at last its roots dried up, and the dove too began to wither.

Marriage Ring,
Italy, 17th century.
Collection Israel Museum,
Jerusalem.

The prince, meanwhile, walking in the forest, found the dove, spread his net over the trees, and caught her. When he saw how weak she was, his heart went out to her. "Oh, you poor dove," he cried. "I will take you home to the palace and nurse you back to health." And so he did.

The next day the queen, visiting her friend, the wizard, asked idly, "Tell me, who is more beautiful than I?" The wizard answered:

I am handsome
You are fairer still. But no!
The girl Romana's beauty
is a thousand times more so.

"How can that be?" shouted the stepmother. "She became a dove."

"Yes, but the prince caught her and nurses her, more than he cares for your own daughter."

"And what can be done?"

"Go to the prince and tell him you dreamed that he caught a white dove and that if he slaughters it and spreads its blood on his sick wife, she will recover."

Once again the queen did as she was told. And so the prince believed her story, went to the dove and lifted it to be slaughtered, but, as he did so, the pin became loose, and, at once, the dove was transformed into his beautiful princess.

Then the prince understood what had happened and thought of a plan to punish the wicked queen. He stuck the pin back into the head of the girl, after which she turned back into a dove. Then he invited the woman—and the king and all the ministers—and the wizard too, to witness the curing of his sick wife. And so, when all were present, he held the dove in one hand and lifted the knife, as if to slaughter it, in the other. Instead, he quickly pulled the pin, and there in front of everyone stood the beautiful young princess, looking radiant, as always. The queen and wizard had no choice but to tell the truth.

Then everyone present took a twig or branch in hand. "Let all who love the king come and add oil," cried the prince. And before long a bonfire blazed high, into which the queen and the scheming wizard were thrown.

After that the king, the prince, and the princess Romana lived together in happiness and health.

The Rothschild Mahzor (detail), Florence, 1492. The Library of The Jewish Theological Seminary of America, NY.

IN THIS COUNTRY BUT IN ANOTHER LANGUAGE...

—BY GRACE PALEY

My grandmother sat in her chair. She said, When I lie down at night I can't rest, my bones push each other. When I wake up in the morning I say to myself, What? Did I sleep? My God, I'm still here. I'll be in this world forever.

My aunt was making the bed. Look, your grandmother, she doesn't sweat. Nothing has to be washed—her stockings, her underwear, the sheets. From this you wouldn't believe what a life she had. It wasn't life. It was torture.

Doesn't she love us? I asked.

Love you? my aunt said. What else is worth it? You children. Your cousin in Connecticut.

So. Doesn't that make her happy?

My aunt said, Ach, what she saw!

What? I asked. What did she see?

Someday I'll tell you. One thing I'll tell you right now. Don't carry the main flag. When you're bigger, you'll be in a demonstration or a strike or something. It doesn't have to be you, let someone else.

Because Russya carried the flag, that's why? I asked.

Because he was a wonderful boy, only seventeen. All by herself, your grandmother picked him up from the street—he was dead—she took him home in the wagon.

What else? I asked.

My father walked into the room. He said, At least *she* lived.

Didn't you live too? I asked my aunt.

Then my grandmother took her hand. Sonia. One reason I don't close my eyes at night is I think about you. You know it. What

Auntie Clara,
Jan Rauchwerger, 1983.
Courtesy of the artist.

will be? You have no life.

Grandmother, I asked, what about us?

My aunt sighed. Little girl. Darling, let's take a nice walk.

At the supper table nobody spoke. So I asked her once more: Sonia, tell me no or yes. Do you have a life?

Ha! she said. If you really want to know, read Dostoevsky. Then they all laughed and laughed.

My mother brought tea and preserves.

My grandmother said to all our faces, Why do you laugh?

But my aunt said, Laugh!

APPLES FROM THE DESERT

—*BY SAVYON LIEBRECHT*, translated by Barbara Harshav

All the way from the Orthodox quarter of Sha'arei Hesed in Jerusalem to the great stretch of sand where the driver called out "Neve Midbar" and looked for her in his rearview mirror, Victoria Abravanel—her heart pounding and her fists clenched—had only one thing on her mind. She took some bread in brown paper and an apple with a rotten core out of her string bag and joined the blessing on the fruit to the prayer for travel, as prescribed. Her eyes were fixed on the yellowing landscape spread out in front of her—and her heart was fixed on her rebellious daughter Rivka who left the Orthodox neighborhood six months ago and went to live on a kibbutz of secular Jews. Now, Victoria had found out from her sister Sara that Rivka was sharing a room with a boy, sleeping in his bed and living as his wife.

All through the eight-hour trip, she pondered how she would act when she was face to face with her daughter: maybe she would cajole her as if she weren't angry with her, teach her about a girl's honor in a man's eyes, explain sensitive issues, one woman to another. Or maybe she would start out with cries of despair, shout out the grief, the disgrace that Rivka had brought down on their noble family, shriek like a funeral mourner until the neighbors heard. Or maybe she would perform her mission stealthily, draw her daughter away from there with false news and then put her in her room under lock and key and obliterate all trace of her. Or maybe she would terrify her, tell her about Flora, Yosef Elalouf's daughter, who fell in love with some boy, gave up her virginity for him and he deserted her; so she lost her mind and wandered around the streets, pulling little children by the ear.

On the road from Beer Sheva, she came up with something new: she would attack the boy with her nails, rip off his skin and poke out his eyes for what he did to this change-of-life daughter of hers. Her daughter would come back to Jerusalem with her. Which was what she promised her sister: "I'll bring her back by the hair."

From her sister Sara, Victoria already knew that her daughter was sixteen when she met him. He was an army officer and was brought in to tell them about military service for Orthodox girls. Later on, there was a fuss about letting people from the army come and poison the girls but the venom had already worked on Rivka. Cunningly, he'd sent her letters, through a friend, even after he went back to his kibbutz. And she, the fool, who was known for neither grace nor beauty—even when she was a baby, people would mistake her for a boy—she fell for it, and when she was eighteen, she picked up and went to him in the desert.

The further Victoria got from Beer Sheva, the more her heroic spirit deserted her and the pictures in her imagination made her sigh: What if Rivka turned her back on her and threw her out? What if the boy raised his hand to hit her? How would she spend the night if they locked her out and the bus doesn't leave till tomorrow morning? What if they didn't get her message?

She didn't know anything about traveling, hadn't been out of the neighborhood since the barren Shifra Ben-Sasson of Tiberias gave birth four years ago.

But when the driver called out "Neve Midbar" again and found her in his mirror, she got off the bus, pulling her basket behind her. She stood there in the sand, the dry wind struck her throat. How could you leave the pure air and beautiful mountains of Jerusalem—and come here?

By the time she came to a path and found a woman to ask about Rivka, drops of sweat were streaming from her kerchief. Coming toward them, on the opposite path, was a girl also wearing pants whose hair was cut short. "Here's Rivka," said the woman. Just as Victoria was about to say: "That's not the one I meant"—she recognized her daughter and burst into a shout which rang like weeping. The girl put down the laundry basket she was carrying and ran to her, her head thrust forward and her eyes weeping.

"What's this . . . what's this. . .?" Victoria scratched her nose. "Where are your braids? And those pants . . . that's how you dress . . . oy vey!" Rivka laughed: "I knew that's what you'd say. I wanted to get dressed but I didn't have time. I thought you'd come on the 4 o'clock bus. When did you leave home? Six? Come on. Enough crying. Here's our room. And here's Dubi."

Stunned by the short hair, the frayed trousers with patches on the back and the shoes spotted with chicken droppings, Victoria found herself squeezed in two big arms, a fair face was close to hers, and a male voice said: "Hello, Mother." Her basket was already in his hand and she—not understanding herself, her hands suddenly light—was drawn after her daughter into a shaded room and seated on a chair. There was a glass of juice in her hand at once; her eyes looked but didn't know what they saw and, later on, she'd remember only the double bed covered with a patchwork quilt and the voice of the giant with golden hair saying "Welcome, Mother." And, as soon as she heard him say "mother" again, very clearly, she swallowed some juice which went down the wrong way and started choking and coughing; the two of them rushed to her and started pounding her on the back like a child.

"Leave me alone," she said weakly and pushed them away. "Let me look at you," she said after a moment. Once again she scolded Rivka: "What is this, those pants? Those are your Sabbath shoes?" Rivka laughed: "I'm working in the chicken coop this week. They brought in new hens. I usually work in the vegetable garden. Just this week in the chicken coop."

Weary from the journey, confused by what she was seeing, shaken by the vicissitudes of the day and straining to repress her rage which was getting away from her in spite of herself, and always remembering her mission, Victoria sat down with her daughter Rivka and talked with her as she had never talked with her children before in her life. She didn't remember what she talked about and she didn't remember when the boy who called her mother left, only her eyes saw and knew: her daughter's face looked good. Not since Rivka was a little girl had she seen her eyes sparkle like that. Even her short hair, Victoria admitted to herself, made her look pretty. Not like when she wore a skirt and stockings, with her broad shoulders, like a man dressed up in women's clothes.

"You don't miss the neighborhood?"

"Sometimes. On holidays. I miss the Shabbat table and the songs and Aunt Sara's laugh. But I like it here. I love working outside with the animals . . . . You too, I miss you a lot."

"And Papa?" Victoria asked in a whisper into the evening light filtering in.

First Fruits,
Reuven Rubin, 1923.
Rubin Museum Collection,
Tel Aviv.

"Papa doesn't care about anybody. Especially not me. All day long in the store and with his books and prayers. Like I'm not his daughter."

"God forbid! Don't say such a thing." Victoria was scared. Of the truth.

"He wanted to marry me off to Yekutiel's son. Like I was a widow or a cripple."

"They talked. You heard. We don't make forced matches. And anyway, Yekutiel's son is a genius."

"A pale, sick genius, like he sits in a pit all day long. And anyway, I don't love him."

"What do you think? You think love is everything?"

"What do you know about love?"

"What does that mean?" Victoria was offended and sat up straight. "This is how you talk to your mother around here?"

"You didn't love Papa and he didn't love you." Rivka ignored her and went on in the silence that descended: "I, at home . . . I wasn't worth much."

"And here?" Victoria asked in a whisper.

"More."

A question began to take shape in Victoria's mind about Dubi, the fair-haired giant but the door opened, a light suddenly came on and he himself said: "Great that you're saving electricity. I brought something to eat. Yogurt and vegetables on a new plastic plate, that's OK, isn't it? Then, Rivka, you should take Mother to Osnat's room. It's empty. She must be tired."

In the room that went out to the darkening fields, Victoria tried to get things straight in her heart. But years of dreariness had dulled her edge and yet she already knew: she wouldn't bring her daughter back to Jerusalem by the hair.

"Why did it take you half a year to come here?" Rivka asked.

"Your Papa didn't want me to come."

"And you, you don't have a will of your own?" And Victoria didn't have an answer.

When Dubi came to take her to the dining hall, she poured all her rage on him and yet she was drawn to him and that only increased her wrath.

"What's this Dubi, what kind of name is that?" Anger pulled words out of her mouth.

"It's Dov, after my mother's father. The Germans killed him in the war."

"That's a good name for a baby, Dov?" She hardened her heart against him.

"I don't mind," he shrugged and then stopped and said with comic seriousness: "But if you do—I'll change it tomorrow." She strained to keep from laughing.

In the evening, the two of them sat at the table with their eyes on Rivka as if she were all alone in the big hall, walking around with a serving cart, asking people what they wanted.

"You want something else to drink, Mother?" she heard him ask and returned the question angrily:

"You call me mother. What kind of mother am I to you?"

"I'm dying for you to be my mother."

"Really? So, who's stopping you?" she asked and her sister Sara's mischievousness crept into her voice.

"Your daughter."

"How is she stopping you?"

"She doesn't want to be my wife."

"My daughter doesn't want to get married. That's what you're telling me?"

"Exactly."

As she was struggling with what he said, he started telling her about the apple orchard he was growing. An American scientist who grew apples in the Nevada desert sent him special seeds. You plant them in tin cans full of organic fertilizer and they grow into trees as high as a baby with little roots and sometimes they produce fruit in the summer like a tree in the Garden of Eden. Apples love the cold, he explained as their eyes wandered after Rivka, and at night, you have to open the plastic sheets and let the desert cold in. At dawn, you have to close the sheets to preserve the cold air and keep the heat out.

"Really," she muttered, hearing these words now and thinking about what he said before. Meanwhile, somebody came to her and said: "You're Rivka's mother? Congratulations on such a daughter." And suddenly her heart swelled in her.

Then she remembered something that came back to her from long ago and far away. She was fifteen years old. On Saturdays in the synagogue, she used to exchange glances with Moshe Elkayam, the goldsmith's son, and then she would lower her eyes to the floor. In the women's section, she would push up to the wooden lattice to see his hands that worked silver and gold and precious stones. Something arose between them without any words and his sister used to smile at her in the street. But when the matchmaker came to talk to her about Shaul Abravanel, she didn't dare hurt her father who wanted a scholar for a son-in-law.

At night, when Rivka took her back to her room, she said: "You came to take me back to Jerusalem, right?"

Her mother chose not to answer. After a pause, she said apropos of nothing: "Don't do anything dumb."

"I know what I want. Don't worry about me."

Victoria plucked up her courage: "Is it true what he told me, that you don't want to marry him?"

"That's what he told you?"

"Yes or no?"

"Yes."

"Why?"

"I'm not sure yet."

"Where did you learn that?"

"From you."

"How?" Victoria was amazed.

"I don't want to live like you and Papa."

"How?"

"Without love."

"Again love!" She beat her thighs until they trembled. A gesture of rage without rage. They reached the door. Victoria thought a moment about the bed with the patchwork quilt and heard herself asking: "And the *Sh'ma* at bedtime, do you say that?"

"No."

"You don't say the *Sh'ma*?"

"Only sometimes, silently. So even I don't hear it myself," said Rivka, laughing, and kissed her mother on the cheek. Then she said: "Don't get scared if you hear jackals. Goodnight." Like a mother soothing her child.

Facing the bare sand dunes stretching soft lines into the frame of her window as into the frame of a picture, Victoria said a fervent prayer, for both of them, her and Rivka. Her heart both heavy and light: ". . . Let not my thoughts trouble me, nor evil dreams, nor evil fancies, but let my rest be perfect before Thee. . . ."

And at night she dreamed.

In the dream a man approaches white curtains and she sees him from behind. The man moves the curtain aside and the trees of the Garden of Eden are in front of him: the tree of life and the tree of knowledge and beautiful trees in cans of organic fertilizer. The man goes to the apple tree, there is a lot of fruit on it, and the fruit drops off and rolls into his hands and, suddenly, the fruit is small and turns into stones. Victoria sees: handfuls of precious stones and gold and silver in his white fingers. Suddenly, the man turns his face, and it's Moshe Elkayam, the goldsmith's son and his hair is flaming.

All the way back to Sha'arei Hesed she sat, her eyes still holding onto their rage but her heart soothed, her basket at her feet and, on her lap, a sack of apples hard as stones that Dubi gave her. She remembered her daughter asking: "You see that everything's fine, right?"—her fingers on her mother's cheek; and Dubi's voice saying: "It'll be fine, Mother."

All the way, she pondered what she would tell her husband and her sister. Maybe she would sit them down and tell exactly what happened to her. When the bus passed the junction, she considered it. How could she describe to her sister, who had never known a man, or to her husband, who had never touched her with love—how could she describe the boy's eyes on her daughter's face? When the mountains of Jerusalem appeared in the distance, she knew what she would do.

From her sister, who could read her mind, she wouldn't keep a secret. She'd pull her kerchief aside, put her mouth up to her ear, like when they were children, and whisper, "Sarike, we've spent our lives alone, you without a husband and me with one. My little daughter taught me something. And us, remember how we thought she was a bit backward, God forbid? How I used to cry over her? No beauty, no grace, no intelligence or talent, and as tall as Og, King of Bashan. We wanted to marry her off to Yekutiel and they were doing us a favor, like Abravanel's daughter wasn't good enough for them. Just look at her now." Here she would turn her face to the side and spit spiritedly against the evil eye. "Milk and honey. Smart too. And laughing all the time. Maybe, with God's help, we'll get pleasure from her."

And to her husband, who never read her heart, she would give apples in honey, put both hands on her hips and say: "We don't have to worry about Rivka. It's good for her there, thank God. We'll hear good things from her soon. Now, taste that and tell me: apples that ripen in summer and they put them in organic fertilizer and their roots are small—did you ever hear of such a thing in your life?"

OPPOSITE:

Girl Holding a Flower,

Reuven Rubin, 1920s.

Rubin Museum Collection,

Tel Aviv.

I F FAMILY IS THE KEYSTONE OF JEWISH CULTURE, THEN COMMUNITY is its foundation. For to live as a Jew requires living in community; in fact, the entire tradition has been

COMMUNITY

structured to ensure that this is so. The Talmud teaches that *kol yisrael arevim zeh-la-zeh* ("All Jews are responsible for each other.") Numerous social mechanisms have evolved over the centuries to compel such communal habits. In ancient times, the entire people of Israel shared in common the experience of three annual pilgrimages to the Temple in Jerusalem. In the Diaspora where social cohesion has been much harder to sustain, Jews have required themselves to live

together within walking distance of their synagogues, to gather themselves into a minimum quorum of ten for prayer, and to limit their interactions with non-Jews. Other social institutions—free loan and burial societies, self-taxation for charitable causes, an elaborate cycle of holiday and community celebrations, and a highly ritualized tradition of grieving—have all contributed to this profound sense of belonging.

When Jews lived in their own sovereign kingdom in ancient Israel, they were proudly self-governing, regulating religious law and observance, maintaining an army, patrolling their own borders, and taking responsibility for the weaker members of their communities—the widow, the orphan, the poor, and the stranger among them. But once in diaspora, they lost most of this autonomy, finding themselves instead at the mercy of other masters. Still, they supported as many communal institutions as they could under these new conditions—aiding the less fortunate in their midst, praying collectively, and maintaining their own synagogues, schools, ritual baths, and cemeteries. They also kept the community together by drawing clear boundaries around themselves, and when necessary, exercising social control over nonconformists through gossip, public censure, and, on occasion, excommunication.

The eight stories in this section explore what it means to live so closely together in a community. In "A Meal for the Poor," for instance, a rich man comes to realize that he depends as much upon the poor as they depend on him. In the German folktale, "The Prince and the White Gazelle," a similar realization dawns upon a gentile prince after he experiences first-hand the bitterness of exile, which shocks him into sympathy with the Jews he has vowed to banish from his kingdom. In both cases, those in power come to recognize that the faces of their social inferiors undeniably mirror their own.

Sometimes communities are bound together not by what they have, but rather by what they lack in common. Thus, in the Yiddish folktale, "*Skotsl Kumt*," a community of Jewish women, disenfranchised from the ritual life of their community, band together to storm the heavens, demanding that they be granted equal rights with their men. Although they fail to achieve their goal, they remain united in their expectations for a better future. In the modern parable, "The Sheep of the Hidden Valley," a community comes to appreciate its blessings only after it has surrendered them to envy and discontent. In the legendary village of Chelm, the foolish citizens owe their solidarity to their common lack of sense. And in two Holocaust stories, "A Cupboard in the Ghetto" and an excerpt from Leslie Epstein's novel of the Lodz Ghetto, "King of the Jews," we witness how Jews managed to sustain each other solely on shreds of hope when all else was taken from them.

At all times the core of community is serving God, as in I. B. Peretz's classic story, "If Not Higher," which transports us to a magical world now buried in the ashes of Eastern Europe. In this story, a Lithuanian rationalist, determined to unmask the hasidic rabbi of the town, secretly follows him when the latter fails to show up in synagogue for penitential prayers. What he learns is that you can sometimes serve God better in secret than by standing in a place of public honor.

CHELM LIGHTS UP THE NIGHT

—CHELM TALE, retold by Beatrice Weinreich, translated by Leonard Wolf

The Chelmites were troubled by the night. When it was dark they often fell and broke their arms and legs. One day they heard a man from Vilna saying that even the nights in Vilna were bright. So they held a meeting at which they formed a fine plan. First they had to wait for a moonlit night. Finally it came—and what a night! A night of nights! The moon shone so brightly that it simply begged to be blessed, so they blessed it in proper form. Then, seeing the moon's reflection in a barrel of water, they took a board and quickly nailed it over the barrel.

Later, when it was the new moon again and the night was pitch-black, they opened the barrel, meaning to take their moon out of storage. But lo and behold, when they looked into the water, there was no moon to be seen. "Alas, alas," they cried, "someone has stolen our moon!"

הגדה לפסח

ברוך אתה ײ אלהינו מלך העולם בורא פְּרִי

הגפן ײ ײ

Skotsl Kumt

—EASTERN EUROPEAN FOLKTALE, retold by Beatrice Weinreich,
translated by Leonard Wolf

You know that among Yiddish speakers, the expression *Skotsl kumt*, "Skotsl's here," is used by women to greet another woman when she comes into the house. Would you like to know its origin? I'll tell you a story that will explain it.

Once upon a time the women complained that everything in the world belonged to men. Men got to perform the *mitsves*, the religious commandments; they got called to read from the Torah. In short, they got to do everything. As for the women, they got nothing. No one paid them any attention at all. So they decided to form a deputation that would take their complaint to the Lord of the Universe.

But how was it to be done? Well, they decided that they would heap women up in a pile, one on top of the other, until the woman at the very tip could pull herself into heaven.

The first thing they did, then, was to dig a pit in which one of the women knelt. Then other women climbed on her, one on top of the other. At the top of the pile was Skotsl. Because she was both very clever and a skillful speaker, she was chosen as the one to talk with the Lord of the Universe.

Everything went well as the women were climbing onto each other. But just as Skotsl reached the top, the hunchbacked woman at the base of the pile twisted about, and the women came tumbling down. Well, of course there was nothing but noise and confusion, with everyone trying to locate everyone else. But Skotsl was nowhere to be found, though they searched for her everywhere.

And so there was no one who could be counted on to talk with God, and the situation of the women remained unchanged. Everything still belonged to the men.

But from that time on, women have not lost their hope that one day Skotsl will come. And that's why, whenever a woman comes into a house, they call out joyfully, "*Skotsl kumt*, Here comes Skotsl," because who knows—one day she might really be there.

OPPOSITE:
Passover Haggadah,
Germany, 1797.
Erich Lessing/
Art Resource, NY.

A MEAL FOR THE POOR

—*BY MORDECAI SPECTOR*, translated by Milton Hindus

I was invited to a wedding.

Not to any of your newfangled weddings where dowagers and pretty young girls in décolleté are surrounded by a halo of powder as they move like goddesses, or where gentlemen in frock coats, white gloves, and waxed black mustaches reek of scented pomade.

Not to a wedding, you understand, where one eats according to a printed timetable—Fish à la Prince So-and-So, Bouillon La Falutin, Meat Diplomatique, Salad Wiltedgreen, Dessert Fifi, Wine Antediluvian—that is to say, served in bottles plentifully smeared with last year's mud!

Not at all. I was invited to an old-fashioned Jewish wedding, a wedding, in other words, where respectable Jewish men and women gather together, dressed in the same holiday attire they use for going to the synagogue every Sabbath. The kind of wedding where the "smorgasbord" consists of home-made honeycake and strudel, followed by gefilte fish, warm fresh rolls, golden-yellow broth, stuffed spring chicken, roast duck, and wine drunk out of large, immaculate white jugs.

A wedding at which every last religious ceremony is observed, including, naturally, the one that commands the host to serve a free meal for the poor.

The host, Reb Yitzchok Berkover, had provided a free meal for the poor at the marriage of each of his children. And now it was the turn of his youngest daughter, his favorite child, and he had invited all the poor folk from the neighboring town of Lipowitz to the village in which he had lived all his life.

It was now the wedding day, two o'clock in the afternoon, and still no sign of the poor, for whom a servant in charge of three huge wagons had been dispatched that morning. Lipowitz was only a few miles away. What could the matter be? All the relatives and wedding guests were waiting impatiently for the ceremony to begin. At last the servant, out of breath and galloping on a horse that had been unhitched from a wagon, arrived by himself.

"What's this? Are you alone?" asked his master.

"They don't want to come," was the answer.

"What do you mean, 'They don't want to come'?" we asked in astonishment.

"They say that unless each one is promised a ruble, under no circumstances are they coming to the wedding."

We all burst into laughter, but the servant continued with his story.

"You see, there's already been one wedding in Lipowitz today, complete with a free meal for the poor. So they're all full. Naturally they're in rebellion. If they're not given a ruble each they won't budge. The ringleaders you all know—there's that cripple with the crutches, and the lanky beggar, also Feitel Dragfoot, and Flatnose Jake. The rest would probably come, but these four won't let them. I wasn't sure what to do. After debating with them for an hour and coming to no conclusion, I took one of the horses and have come back for more instructions."

We roared with laughter at the thought of this bizarre uprising, but Reb Yitzchok went into a rage. "You bargained with them? They won't take any less?" he screamed at the messenger.

"Bargained, of course. They won't take a kopeck less."

"Their stock of merchandise must have gone up in price lately," snapped Reb Yitzchok with an angry laugh. "Then why did you leave the wagons behind? We'll do without the paupers."

"I wasn't sure what to do. I was afraid you would be angry. I'll run back this instant and bring the wagons."

"Wait a while. Don't be in such a hurry." And Reb Yitzchok began to discuss this unlooked-for problem with his guests and also with himself.

"Who ever heard of such a thing? Those ragamuffins are going to dictate what I should do? Bargain with me? Just because I want them to have a good free meal and a little donation besides. I must give each one precisely a ruble, they say! If I gave them a quarter of a ruble each, they couldn't afford to take it, of course! Their overhead is too high. The nerve of the beggars! I'll get along without them, they'll see. Fiddlers, strike up the tune! Where's the sexton? You can start the final preparations."

But immediately he changed his mind and waved his hands. "Wait a while. It's still early. What did I do to deserve such a fate? Is my whole enjoyment to be spoiled? Why shouldn't I have the pleasure of giving a free meal to the poor at the wedding of my youngest child? I'd be willing to give them half a ruble. Money's not the question. It's the principle. The nerve of them! To haggle with me! Well, let it go. I've done my share. If they don't want to come, that's their business. They'll be sorry later. Weddings such as this don't come every day. We'll get along without them!"

"Shall I prepare the bride?" asked the sexton.

"Yes, let them—no! Wait!"

The guests were unanimously in favor of forgetting the beggars, but Reb Yitzchok's face suddenly underwent a profound change. His rage subsided and he came to ask me and a few others to do him a favor. He requested us to go to the town and see if we couldn't manage to win over the poor. "He hasn't any sense. There's no use depending on him," he said, nodding at the servant.

They made another horse and wagon ready for us, and we rode away. The servant on his horse lagged behind us.

"A mutiny, a strike of the poor—how do you like that?" That's the tone we talked in the whole way. "I've heard of strikes by workingmen. They refuse to work. They demand higher pay. But a strike, an ultimatum by paupers—paupers demanding a higher scale of pay for coming to eat a free meal! That's something new."

Twenty minutes later we entered the town of Lipowitz. In the main square of the town, in the market place, stood three great peasant wagons filled with straw; the small horses were unharnessed and eating their bags of oats. Around the wagons were at least a hundred people— the lame, the halt, and the blind, and in addition half the loafers and urchins in town. They were making a terrific noise.

The cripple who had been described as one of the chief ringleaders was sitting in the driver's seat of one of the wagons and banging his crutches on the wood. The lanky beggar with a red plaster on his neck stood near him. The two were haranguing the crowd.

"Look," cried the lanky one triumphantly as soon as he caught sight of us, "they've come to beg."

"Beg!" called out the cripple, bringing his crutches down with a crash.

"Why aren't you at the wedding?" we asked them. "There'll be a good meal, and each of you will get some money to take home with him too."

"How much?" asked a chorus of voices.

"We can't tell exactly. But you'll take what you can get."

"A ruble maybe? If not, we stay put."

"The sky will fall in if you don't go!" mocked some loafers in the crowd.

The beggars raised their sticks and ran at their tormentors. For a minute it looked like a real riot, but the lanky one on the wagon stretched himself to his full height and thundered at them, "Quiet! Quiet, you miserable beggars! It's impossible to hear what these gentlefolk are saying to us. Listen to them!" He then turned to us. "Please realize, brothers, that unless we get a ruble each we don't move from here. We've no fear that Reb Yitzchok will marry off his favorite daughter without us. Where can he get another gang of paupers on the spur of the moment? Is he going to send to the next town for them? It'll be a lot more expensive for the wagons, and besides the wedding will have to be postponed."

"Do you think that just because we're poor they can do as they like with us?" cried one of the rebels perched on top of a wheel; he was completely blind in one eye, and he had a rag tied around his jaw as if to keep his teeth from falling out. "Nobody can force us to go. Even the chief of police and the governor general himself can't do anything to us. A ruble each or we don't go!"

"R-r-r-ub-bles," stuttered a beggar.

"Rubles," screamed the one with the flattened nose.

Marriage Contract of Yosef,
son of Moshe Tarica and Rivka,
daughter of Moshe Soriano,
Rhodes, 1830.
The Jewish Museum, NY/
Art Resource, NY.

"Rubles," sang out two merry beggars, doing a dance.

"Rubles! Rubles!" screamed all the poor together.

All their lives they had been condemned to silence, forced to swallow with their spittle every insult anyone cared to offer them, anyone who had given them a kopeck or thrown them a crust of dry bread or a gnawed bone. Now for the first time they were tasting the same pleasure as the well-to-do. For the first time these beggars felt that the well-fed people needed them, and they were determined to gain their point. And sure enough, even as we were arguing with them, there came another messenger from Reb Yitzchok with word for the poor to set out at once and each would receive his ruble.

Bedlam broke loose, pandemonium. The three large wagons filled up in a twinkling. One pauper cried, "Oh, my broken back!" Another, "Oh, my arm!" A third, "My leg, my leg!" The merry beggars seated in the wagons started to jig with their feet. The horses were harnessed, and with much laughter the procession got under way. An escort of urchins accompanied us some distance, crying loudly, "Hooray!" Some of the hecklers fired a few rocks after the wagons amid hoots and whistles and catcalls. But to the beggars it was as if they were being pelted with flowers and accompanied by bursts of triumphant song, so happy were they over their victory.

For the first time and perhaps the last, they had spoken out in loud voices and succeeded in getting their way. They had done exactly as they wanted.

After the bridal ceremony, after the golden-yellow broth, the feast was served to the wedding guests and to the poor, seated at separate tables. Reb Yitzchok and his closest relatives observed the commandment to wait on the poor with their own hands and to anticipate whatever their hearts desired in the way of food or drink.

"Your health, Reb Yitzchok. We wish you long life, happiness from your children, and even greater wealth!" The poor men kept drinking toasts to him.

"And your health, your health too, brothers. Drink hearty. Long life to you. May God help the whole congregation of Israel, and you among the rest," Reb Yitzchok responded.

After the meal the musicians began to play again, and the poor danced around in a great ring, holding Reb Yitzchok by the hands. Reb Yitzchok danced out into the very center of the ring made by the poor. His satin coat tails flew like the wings of an eagle. His eyes, from which tears of joy were freely running, seemed to be staring straight upward, while his thoughts soared higher than the Seventh Heaven. He laughed and he cried at the same time, like a child. And all the while he kept embracing the poor, each in turn. He hugged them affectionately and kissed their cheeks.

"Brothers!" he cried out to them, dancing. "We must be merry! Let us be merry as only Jews know how to be merry! Fiddlers! Play something a little faster, louder, livelier, stronger!"

That is how a Jew is happy.

That is how a real Jewish wedding ought to be.

The poor, as well as the rest of the wedding guests, clapped their hands in time to the music.

In short, as I have already said, dear reader, I've been to a Jewish wedding.

THE PRINCE AND THE WHITE GAZELLE

—GERMAN FOLKTALE, retold by Judith Ish-Kishor

A small German state, at some time during the Middle Ages, was ruled by a wise and beneficent prince. He remained at peace with neighboring rulers, for he had no other ambition than to see his country well governed, with justice and understanding of its people's needs. To this task he devoted his life. The land flourished. The inhabitants were prosperous and content. Even the Jews found a peaceful refuge here, for the Prince would not allow them to be taxed beyond reason, or molested, or victimized in any way. It was even known that a Jewish merchant, Meyer Rothfels, had on occasion been his trusted adviser.

But the good Prince could not live forever. As he felt himself failing in strength he began to give his eldest son charge over the country's affairs. Especially, Prince Gottfried recommended his Jewish counselor, Meyer Rothfels. "When you are not content with the advice of other men, that is the time to send for Rothfels," the old Prince said. "He is deeply sagacious. He will find a way out of your difficulty."

Prince Erhard thanked his father respectfully; but to himself he said: "May I never be so poor in wisdom as to ask advice of a Jew!"

The old Prince died and the young man ruled in his stead. In most respects he did justice to his father's training. The people were pleased with him.

However, there was one change noticed by those whom it concerned. Rothfels was never called to the palace; and one day the Prince declared to his councilors that he would issue a decree giving the Jews of his country one month in which to gather their belongings and prepare for banishment. They would be allowed to remain if they became Christians. The most influential of his advisers agreed in praising Prince Erhard's "wise severity."

On the following morning Meyer Rothfels, who seemed to know about every contingency before it arose, gained admission to the Prince's chambers. Erhard had just awakened. As his attendant helped him dress, he listened unconcernedly to the old man's pleadings that the decree should not be made public—that there be further consideration of the possible results to the country's well-being—that the young Prince should remember his father's friendship to a hunted people. . . .

"All this we have considered," said the Prince. "It pleased my father to indulge you. Under God, I shall be a stricter friend. The decree stands."

Leaving the old man red-eyed and shuddering, Prince Erhard strode into the morning room. He began on his breakfast, which was served before a window opening on the park of the palace grounds. As he ate, there crossed his line of vision a white gazelle, limping as though it were hurt. What a lovely little creature! he thought. Wounded, too. I can easily catch it.

Door for the Torah Ark (detail),
17th century.
Giraudon/Art Resource, NY.

He rose from the table and taking the bow and quiverful of arrows from a man-at-arms on guard, he leaped over the low windowsill into the park. As if the gazelle knew of his coming, she quickened her pace a little, but could not go fast enough to escape him. Feeling sure of her, he followed in leisurely fashion. Near the fence separating the park from the forest, she seemed to gather her strength. She leaped across the paling and spurted up a narrow path between the fir trees.

The Prince set an arrow to the bow and drew the string. But before he could let fly, the little creature turned its head and gazed at

him. The big brown eyes shone with a human entreaty. They were full of tears.

He lowered the arrow. "I could as soon slay a beautiful woman," he murmured. "No, I shall take it alive. It will be pleasant to keep it as a pet." He opened the gate and quickened his pace. The gazelle began to run, too. It led him a long chase, farther and farther into the forest.

He flung himself down, panting. Then the pretty creature came near and lingered so close that he could almost reach up and put an arm around her neck. When he made the attempt, however, she moved off, just beyond him, and he started after her again.

So it went the entire day. The Prince was so absorbed in the chase, and always so near winning, that he could not give up.

All at once he realized that the sun was setting. A last red ray lit up the forest path. At the same moment, the white gazelle sprang into a thicket and disappeared. Cursing with rage, the Prince scrambled after her but succeeded only in losing the cleared pathway.

Before nightfall he found some nuts and berries that somewhat satisfied his hunger; and since he had left the palace without a cloak, he was obliged to burrow among the dead leaves for cover against the chill of autumn.

By the first light of morning he tried to retrace his steps. But he could find no landmark. Though he had often gone hunting among these oaks and hemlocks, he had been attended by experienced foresters and had not troubled himself to learn his way about. The thought that by this time his followers would be searching for him, gave him hope. But he walked all that day without sight or sound of a human being. On the following day he set out in the opposite direction, with no better success.

For sixty days the Prince wandered about in the forest. His velvet doublet was muddy and full of holes. His hose had long ago been torn to shreds by thorns and briars. His shoes were broken and let in the rain. He was bearded now, and his hair was long and ragged.

Woods,
Michael Kovner, 1994.
Courtesy of the artist.

Apart from his present plight, the thought of what must be happening at the palace tormented him with anxiety and useless speculations. What were his ministers doing? What did his people think? Did they give him up for dead?

One day the snow began to fall, whitening all the forest. The Prince looked up at a strip of gray sky and despair overwhelmed him. His time had come. He would surely freeze, ill-clad and shivering as he was.

The deep silence was broken by the sound of cracking branches as some creature pushed its way through the underbrush. The Prince turned his weather-stained face with little expectation of good. But it was not an animal that approached.

The Prince saw before him a charcoal-burner—a big, rough man, warmly dressed except for his red hands which he clapped from time to time, and breathed on, against the cold. "Who is this? What have we here?"

152

the man exclaimed. It was German, but in an accent so different that the Prince, at first, understood the tone of his voice, rather than the words.

"I am Prince Erhard," he burst out. "You shall be well rewarded if you bring word to the palace that you have found me!"

The man's mocking expression reminded the Prince of what he himself had seen in a forest pool a few days earlier. The charcoal-burner clearly thought him drunk or demented. Besides, the forest was so extensive he must have wandered from his own state. Collecting his wits, the Prince said slowly and clearly: "I am a poor wayfarer. Lost in the forest."

"Wayfarer?" the man grunted. He touched the Prince's sleeve. Stained and ragged, still it was velvet. "Some clown or mountebank," he said. "A lazy fellow, hiding himself when there is work to be done, and food and shelter to be honestly earned."

"I would gladly work, friend," the Prince rejoined. "I should be grateful to the saints for a human shelter."

"Good. Prove your words," said the charcoal-burner. "I need a helper." And he led the way to his clean, warm hut, where his wife was setting out supper, and three small children—two boys and a girl—made a merry noise that fell gratefully on the Prince's ear.

Wild and unkempt as he seemed in the glow from the hearth fire, there was something so chastened in his manner that the charcoal-burner and his wife felt compassion for him. After the filling meal, they made him a bed of clean straw in the shed behind the hut; and the woman gave him a hot brick wrapped in a rag to lay against his feet. He thanked them and lay down to a sound sleep.

He awoke at daybreak. The charcoal-burner fitted him out warmly with some old clothes of his own, gave him an axe and after a plain but plentiful breakfast, they went to his furnace in the woods. Here they worked together, day in and day out, returning only at

dusk to the shelter of the hut. The Prince toiled willingly. He was glad of human company, and while he worked he was able to forget his anxieties and all that he had lost. In the evenings, the liveliness of the children and their affection kept him from relapsing into melancholy; and at night he fell into deep, dreamless sleep.

Two months passed in this way. The charcoal-burner came to like and trust him, despite his reserve and the refinement of his manners. Once or twice the Prince was sent a day's journey to the nearest village, with a load of charcoal to sell. Before returning, he walked about among the villagers and country folk, asking a question here and there, in the hope of hearing news of his own domain. But those who had even heard of such a state and city, knew it only as "far away."

At last he was driven to question the charcoal-burner. Lifting his smoke-blackened face from the pile of ash he was shoveling, he asked: "How far might it be to the principality of ———?"

The charcoal-burner wiped the sweat from his forehead with a rag of sacking and said: "Over a hundred leagues. Why, have you kinsfolk there?"

"An old aunt . . ." said the Prince hesitantly. "She was good to me."

"Is it your wish to visit her, then?"

"Yes. In the spring," said the Prince, catching at a plan of action. "I will leave you in the spring."

"Good," said the charcoal-burner. "It's wise to wait until the roads are clear."

When the bright spring weather set in, the charcoal-burner gave the Prince a purse with ten pieces of silver. The wife gave him food for the day, to carry with him. The children kissed him and waved to him until he was out of sight.

The Prince felt that his journey was well begun. No matter what bad news might be awaiting him in his own country, he was alive and well despite his strange misfortunes. He bought himself a leather jerkin, good strong shoes, and a dagger for self-defense. The money remaining would last until he could reach his own people. Eagerly he trudged along the highway.

On the fourth night of his journey, robbers raided the wayside inn where he was staying, stripped him and the other guests of all their belongings and when he fought back, beat him unconscious. Bruised and aching, he came to himself. He was penniless and still eighteen days' journey from home. But at least he was not in the depths of the forest. What he had done once, he could do again.

So he set out along the road. Wherever he found work he remained for a few days; when he had money enough to pay for food and lodging along the way, he continued his travels. The journey that should have taken not more than three weeks, lengthened itself to another two months.

At last he came to his own country, and to its capital, the seat of his court. It shocked him that he could move about unnoticed among his own people, until he came to understand that his poverty, his ragged beard and haggard face were a total disguise. Who would believe him if he were to proclaim himself?

But, being unrecognized, he could ask the questions that a stranger might naturally ask—about the former Prince, about the present ruler. . . . To his secret horror, there was no news whatever! Nothing exceptional had happened during the past year.

He had not been missed. There was some imposture. Incredibly, someone was taking his place. Who might it be? Who resembled him? His cousin? His cousin was too much older. One thing was clear, his disappearance had been kept from his people.

After a night without sleep he came early to the palace and entered that part of the grounds that was open to the public. He went as far as he might, and posted himself near the great gate leading to the private garden and park.

His heart swelled with bitter longing at the familiar sights. He could see the little summerhouse near which, under a marble slab, his old hound lay buried. He could see into the courtyard where, as a child newly able to walk, he had ridden his first pony. And there was the window through which he had gone so lightly, in pursuit of the white gazelle over six months ago.

He could see among the guardsmen on duty one or two with whom he had practiced fencing. But now he knew that he must not reveal himself too soon. Who were his friends at the palace, who might be on his side against the usurper?

He was sifting his memories of the more influential courtiers, when his thoughts were arrested at sight of an old man in a dark gabardine and somber hood. The Jew, Meyer Rothfels, was slowly, as if reluctantly, leaving the palace grounds. Erhard suddenly remembered his father's words: "When you are not content with the advice of other men . . . send for Rothfels. . . . He will find a way out of your difficulty."

The Prince met him at the gate. He drew the old man aside. "As you were my father's friend, Meyer Rothfels," he said, "will you aid me now in my need?"

The old man's discerning ear and shrewd eye unraveled the disguises. "What masquerade is this?" he muttered. "What has befallen you, my Prince? But come with me. It is better that we talk privately."

Rothfels brought him to his house in the *Judengasse*, gave him a velvet suit and helped him to remove the beard and cut his neglected hair. "Now you are yourself again," the old man said, "what do you require of me?"

The Prince stared at him, astonished. "You ask me that?" he cried. "I have but one wish. Bring me into the palace that I may face the usurper and unmask him!"

Meyer Rothfels studied the Prince's face in silence for some time. Then, "Tell me what troubles you?" he said.

"Am I of such small account that since I left my palace more than six months ago, no word of my disappearance has reached my people?" And he told about that evil hour when he had started after the white gazelle and the long trail of loneliness and hardship and misfortune he had followed from that day to this.

As he mentioned his lighthearted sally after the limping doe, his hearer's eyes widened in amazement; but the old man made no comment, though his fervent interest never slackened throughout the story.

"Now will you bring me to my successor?" the Prince demanded, rising to his feet.

"I will bring you to him."

Through a little door the Prince had never known, Meyer Rothfels led the way amid winding corridors. As they came to the part of the palace familiar to him, the Prince strode ahead to his own apartments. He hurried from one chamber to another, but found nobody except his servants. He entered his bedroom. That also was empty.

"Where is he? Where is the new Prince? Summon him here before me!" he exclaimed, as the old Jew followed at a more leisurely pace.

"This is he." Meyer Rothfels brought him to face a mirror. "You have no successor. You left the palace but an hour ago."

The Prince seated himself, for his strength failed him.

"It is a miracle! A miracle from the hand of God Himself. Blessed be

He, and blessed be His name!" The old man's voice quivered like a harp string. "I saw you— I, myself—saw you leap from the window an hour ago, and follow the gazelle." He drew back the coverlets. "See, my lord, your bed is still warm."

A servant entered and, bowing, patiently asked: "Will it please the Prince to finish his breakfast?"

"How long is it—When did I leave the table?" the Prince asked carefully.

"It is more than an hour since—" The Prince dismissed him.

"Is it not written in the Psalms," Meyer Rothfels went on: "'For a thousand years in Thy sight are but as yesterday when it is past, and as a watch in the night'? And in your own prayer, the *Magnificat*, you say: 'He hath put down the mighty from his seat, and hath exalted those of low degree.' Glory be to God, who preserved you unharmed!"

Silently the Prince reflected on the anguish, the vicissitudes of those vanished months. His heart filled with an enduring wonder. "By His Grace," he murmured at length, "I have learned enough for a lifetime." With fond appreciation his eyes wandered about the rich, comfortable chambers, in gratitude for all that he had not lost. On the mantel he saw the writing that would exile the Jews.

His mind returned to Meyer Rothfels. Answering the look in the old man's eloquent eyes, he rose and threw the document into the fire. "I know now what it is, to be homeless and a stranger," he said.

From then on the Prince had a friend from whom nothing need be hidden, and the people had a wise and merciful prince.

THE BIRD'S NEST

—BY MARTIN BUBER, translated by Olga Marx

Once the Baal Shem stood in the House of Prayer and prayed for a very long time. All his disciples had finished praying, but he continued without paying any attention to them. They waited for him a good while, and then they went home. After several hours when they had attended to their various duties, they returned to the House of Prayer and found him still deep in prayer. Later he said to them: "By going away and leaving me alone, you dealt me a painful separation. I shall tell you a parable.

You know that there are birds of passage who fly to warm countries in the autumn. Well, the people in one of those lands once saw a glorious many-colored bird in the midst of a flock which was journeying through the sky. The eyes of man had never seen a bird so beautiful. He alighted in the top of the tallest tree and nested in the leaves.

When the king of the country heard of it, he bade them fetch down the bird with his nest. He ordered a number of men to make a ladder up the tree. One was to stand on the other's shoulders until it was possible to reach up high enough to take the nest. It took a long time to build this living ladder. Those who stood nearest the ground lost patience, shook themselves free, and everything collapsed."

SHEEP OF THE HIDDEN VALLEY

—BY TSVI BLANCHARD

There was once a tailor in a valley so small, and so far away, that you have probably never heard of it. The tailor was a man of great skill. His excellent material, perfect stitching and precision in fitting assured that his customers were always satisfied. When the clothes became torn, the tailor could mend them so that they were almost like new. Despite his great skill, the tailor was a troubled man. Even when he used the best of materials his clothes did not last forever.

They sometimes lasted out the life of a customer, but rarely was a suit passed down from father to son.

One night the tailor dreamt that he was wandering about the surrounding towns. Suddenly he found a valley hidden away from the eyes of the world. In this valley were sheep with thick coats of beautiful wool. In his dream, he spoke to a man who confided to him the many intricate details of raising sheep whose wool was fine as golden thread,

Go Forth,
Michal Meron, 1996.
Courtesy The Studio,
Old Jaffa, Israel.

soft as baby's skin, as shining as a star, and as firm when woven as the resolve of a wise man. The tailor awoke from his dream determined to seek out the valley and its sheep. For many years he traveled the countryside without success.

At last behind a waterfall at which he had stopped to refresh himself, the tailor found a hidden valley in which grazed sheep with marvelous wool. In the real valley, unlike the one of his dream, there was no shepherd to guide him in raising the sheep. In moments of deep concentration, the tailor was able to remember the special rules communicated to him in his dream. He dedicated himself to raising these sheep, and followed the rules for their care scrupulously.

Skull Cap, Eastern Europe, 18th century. The Jewish Museum, NY/ Art Resource, NY.

Wishing to share his discovery with the villagers, his beloved friends, the tailor announced that he would sew new clothes for all adults in the village. He sheared his sheep, wove their wool into cloth, and began to sew the new garments. The tailor found to his surprise that he had just enough cloth to make clothes for every man and woman in his village. Although the tailor guarded them well, the sheep somehow disappeared within a week of their shearing, and no more clothing could be sewn from their splendid wool.

The new garments were a delight to the village. The people discovered that this clothing, so warm and snug in winter, was never uncomfortable even in the hottest heat of summer. The rain did not ruin these fine clothes nor did the years wear them thin. When they were torn through carelessness, it needed but a stitch to restore them. These were charmed garments, and the villagers of that generation counted themselves blessed.

A boy reaching the age of manhood approached his father in secret. He asked his father to acquire for him a fine suit of clothes like the ones owned by the adults in the village. He too would soon be a full member of his village, and, he argued, he should have as splendid a garment as anyone else. When the father explained that there were no more miraculous garments, the boy cried bitterly. Finally the father, out of his great love for the boy, took off his own coat and gave it to his son. A great miracle followed. Having put on his father's coat over his own garments, the boy found that his clothing was transformed into the material of his father's garments. Soon it was discovered that whenever a child near the age of adulthood put on his parent's cloak, the child's own clothing turned to the cloth woven from the marvelous wool of the sheep of the hidden valley.

As the young people grew, they found the clothes changing to fit them. Arms lengthened, chests filled out, and at the same time the garments had longer sleeves and fuller breadth. However a person changed, if he became fatter or thinner, wider or narrower, straighter or more bent with age, the miraculous clothing fit exactly.

The village became famous throughout the area and many envied the fine garments. People in the surrounding towns began to gossip, and they whispered that wearing the same clothes continually showed the backwardness of the villagers. They said that it made the villagers boring. Believing the garments worn by the young to be those of their parents, they bitingly asked: who wears the clothes of dead people? They did not know the secret of the garments or their source, so they did not understand.

After many years, some say generations, the trust of the village itself was undermined and many came to doubt what their own eyes had seen. The village became divided. Some sold or gave away their old garments, preferring to wear the stylish new clothing they found in the surrounding towns. These who bought new clothes found that they soon wore out. When they tore they could not be restored and had to be discarded. Their ancestral garments, when worn by others, lost their special properties. The garments, once the pride of the town, became rags for the poor in the neighboring towns.

Others in the village tried refashioning the old garments. They dyed them new colors, lengthened and shortened hems, and restitched the seams to fit the newer fashions. Their newly restyled clothes did not wear well and, as with the others, were discarded. Still others in the village desperately tried to prevent the slightest change in the clothing. They refused to allow the alteration of the garments even a stitch. But their clothes grew stiff about them, losing their ability to fit throughout the whole of a person's life. Finally, these garments too were discarded.

Fewer and fewer of the original coats were to be found. As the years passed many in the village began to doubt that there ever were such marvelous clothes. They could not believe in the funny story about the tailor, his dream and his hidden valley. Where was this valley? What proof was there that such a tailor had ever existed? Who trusts dreams? And most of all, where were these so-called magic garments?

The few who claimed to own original coats were regarded as half-crazy or deluded, or at the least as very poorly dressed. Among those who still wore the old coats there was a desire, born from the love of their neighbors, to restore the miracle of their special clothing. They alone knew the value of the clothing. They alone knew how much superior were the original garments to the new ones. There arose among them a question: will we, they asked, need once again a tailor who dreams of wondrous sheep, and can then find them? Or, they wondered, do we simply need to collect the worn rags and reweave them into the fine garments? They have not yet answered this question.

The Wanderers, Peter Krasnow, 1927. From the HUC Skirball Cultural Center and Museum, Los Angeles, CA. Gift of Mr. and Mrs. Peter Krasnow.

IF NOT HIGHER

—BY ISAAC LEIB PERETZ, translated by Marie Syrkin

Early every Friday morning, at the time of the Penitential Prayers, the Rabbi of Nemirov would vanish.

He was nowhere to be seen—neither in the synagogue nor in the two Houses of Study nor at a *minyan*. And he was certainly not at home. His door stood open; whoever wished could go in and out; no one would steal from the rabbi. But not a living creature was within.

Where could the rabbi be? Where should he be? In heaven, no doubt. A rabbi has plenty of business to take care of just before the Days of Awe. Jews, God bless them, need livelihood, peace, health, and good matches. They want to be pious and good, but our sins are so great, and Satan of the thousand eyes watches the whole earth from one end to the other. What he sees he reports; he denounces, informs. Who can help us if not the rabbi!

That's what the people thought.

But once a Litvak came, and he laughed. You know the Litvaks. They think little of the Holy Books but stuff themselves with Talmud and law. So this Litvak points to a passage in the *Gemarah*—it sticks in your eyes—where it is written that even Moses, our Teacher, did not ascend to heaven during his lifetime but remained suspended two and a half feet below. Go argue with a Litvak!

So where can the rabbi be?

"That's not my business," said the Litvak, shrugging. Yet all the while—what a Litvak can do!—he is scheming to find out.

That same night, right after the evening prayers, the Litvak steals into the rabbi's room, slides under the rabbi's bed, and waits. He'll watch all night and discover where the rabbi vanishes and what he does during the Penitential Prayers.

Someone else might have got drowsy and fallen asleep, but a Litvak is never at a loss; he recites a whole tractate of the Talmud by heart.

At dawn he hears the call to prayers.

The rabbi has already been awake for a long time. The Litvak has heard him groaning for a whole hour.

Whoever has heard the Rabbi of Nemirov groan knows how much sorrow for all Israel, how much suffering, lies in each groan. A man's heart might break, hearing it. But a Litvak is made of iron; he listens and remains where he is. The rabbi, long life to him, lies on the bed, and the Litvak under the bed.

Then the Litvak hears the beds in the house begin to creak; he hears people jumping out of their beds, mumbling a few Jewish words, pouring water on their fingernails, banging doors. Everyone has left. It is again quiet and dark; a bit of light from the moon shines through the shutters.

(Afterward the Litvak admitted that when he found himself alone with the rabbi a great fear took hold of him. Goose pimples spread across his skin, and the roots of his earlocks pricked him like needles. A trifle: to be alone with the rabbi at the time of the Penitential Prayers! But a Litvak is stubborn. So he quivered like a fish in water and remained where he was.)

Finally the rabbi, long life to him, arises. First he does what befits a Jew. Then he goes to the clothes closet and takes out a bundle of peasant clothes: linen trousers, high boots, a coat, a big felt hat, and a long wide leather belt studded with brass nails. The rabbi gets dressed. From his coat pocket dangles the end of a heavy peasant rope.

The rabbi goes out, and the Litvak follows him.

On the way the rabbi stops in the kitchen, bends down, takes an ax from under the bed, puts it in his belt, and leaves the house. The Litvak trembles but continues to follow.

The hushed dread of the Days of Awe hangs over the dark streets. Every once in a while a cry rises from some *minyan* reciting the Penitential Prayers, or from a sickbed. The rabbi hugs the sides of the streets, keeping to the shade of the houses. He glides from house to house, and the Litvak after him. The Litvak hears the sound of his heartbeats mingling with the sound of the rabbi's heavy steps. But he keeps on going and follows the rabbi to the outskirts of the town.

A small wood stands behind the town.

The rabbi, long life to him, enters the wood. He takes thirty or forty steps and stops by a small tree. The Litvak, overcome with amazement, watches the rabbi take the ax out of his belt and strike the tree. He hears the tree creak and fall. The rabbi chops the tree into logs and the logs into sticks. Then he makes a bundle of the wood and ties it with the rope in his pocket. He puts the bundle of wood on his back, shoves the ax back into his belt, and returns to the town.

He stops at a back street beside a small broken-down shack and knocks at the window.

"Who is there?" asks a frightened voice. The Litvak recognizes it as the voice of a sick Jewish woman.

"I," answers the rabbi in the accent of a peasant.

"Who is I?"

Again the rabbi answers in Russian. "Vassil."

"Who is Vassil, and what do you want?"

"I have wood to sell, very cheap." And, not waiting for the woman's reply, he goes into the house.

The Litvak steals in after him. In the gray light of early morning he sees a poor room with broken, miserable furnishings. A sick woman, wrapped in rags, lies on the bed. She complains bitterly, "Buy? How can I buy? Where will a poor widow get money?"

"I'll lend it to you," answers the supposed Vassil. "It's only six cents."

"And how will I ever pay you back?" said the poor woman, groaning.

"Foolish one," says the rabbi reproachfully. "See, you are a poor sick Jew, and I am ready to trust you with a little wood. I am sure you'll pay. While you, you have such a great and mighty God and you don't trust him for six cents."

"And who will kindle the fire?" said the widow. "Have I the strength to get up? My son is at work."

"I'll kindle the fire," answers the rabbi.

As the rabbi put the wood into the oven he recited, in a groan, the first portion of the Penitential Prayers.

As he kindled the fire and the wood burned brightly, he recited, a bit more joyously, the second portion of the Penitential Prayers. When the fire was set he recited the third portion, and then he shut the stove.

The Litvak who saw all this became a disciple of the rabbi.

And ever after, when another disciple tells how the Rabbi of Nemirov ascends to heaven at the time of the Penitential Prayers, the Litvak does not laugh. He only adds quietly, "If not higher."

Silent Prayer, Reuven Rubin, 1942. Rubin Museum Collection, Tel Aviv.

A Cupboard in the Ghetto

—*BY RACHMIL BRYKS*, translated by S. Morris Engel

Hershel Zeif was an emaciated man with a pale, peaked face and lusterless eyes. A native of Kalisz, he had been married in Lodz just before the war. He and his wife, luckily, were able to bring with them into the ghetto their entire wedding outfit, all their clothes, as well as twin beds, a table, several chairs and a clothes cupboard.

For a long time Hershel Zeif ran to the Civil Administration every day looking for work. After a while he became exasperated with the false promises of the officials and decided that if you had no "shoulders" (protection) you couldn't get anything. Now he and his wife spent most of the day in bed—he in one of the twin beds, she in the other—writhing from hunger and cold, like all their neighbors.

Mrs. Zeif was small and thin, with hollow cheeks and big black eyes. She was a quiet woman who never raised her voice. Silently, within herself, she endured the grief and agony of hunger and cold. Both she and her husband were positive that the war would end any day.

When the sun rose higher and lavished its rays, also brightening their window, Hershel and his wife hung their wedding clothes out to air. There was Zeif's black winter coat with a velvet collar; a blue capote with a vent in back; trousers with a crease and cuffs; a pair of boots and a pair of shoes; a half-dozen white shirts; undershirts; a pair of soft leather bedroom slippers and a hard black hat, round as a coin, with a crescent brim like a new moon.

Mrs. Zeif had a black winter coat; a light summer coat; a suit; several dresses; a plush hat and a hand-knitted hat; underclothes; linens and four pairs of shoes.

All these things were brand new, they had never been worn. They were coated with green mildew. After several days in the sun the mildew whitened and then vanished. But after a few days in the house the green mildew appeared again. They decided to air their wedding clothes every day, sunny or not, just as long as it didn't rain. They made a pact: one day he hung his clothes outside the sunny window for several hours—the next day she hung hers. The sun never reached the other window, because it was in a corner opposite a high wall.

When Zeif saw that the mildew was gone a smile of pleasure lit up his haggard face: "Yes, the war might end any minute. God can do anything, and we'll go home in our new clothes. Yes, yes, my dear Henye." His wife nodded in agreement: "That's right."

Hershel Zeif invited his neighbor Bluestein into his house. "Guess how my wife cooked supper today," he said in his weak voice, looking into Bluestein's eyes with a mischievous smile, like a schoolboy trying to confuse a friend with a difficult riddle.

Bluestein looked around, in all the corners, and saw that all was as before: the mouldings of the door and windows and floor had long ago been swallowed up by the tiny kitchen stove. The floor itself could not be ripped up, because it was the second story and they would fall through. Besides, one of "Emperor" Rumkowski's men came by every few days to inspect the floor. Bluestein also saw that the beds, the clothes cupboard, the table and chairs were all there. The beds, by the way, were new and modern. The Zeifs had gotten them in exchange for their old oak beds, and were even paid for the difference in weight.

Bluestein wracked his brain. He wanted to guess the answer, he didn't want to be fooled.

"Come on, guess! You can't guess, can you?" Zeif teased him.

"I know!" Bluestein cried confidently. "With the board you got from the tinsmith."

"Ha-ha! A likely story! Why don't you say with last year's snow? That board was used up long ago—even the ashes are gone," Zeif shouted triumphantly.

This was what had happened. It had rained in, and Zeif had to put pans on the beds. After much pleading, the administrator of the buildings in the neighborhood sent him a tinsmith to fix the roof. The tinsmith climbed into the attic, and immediately Zeif heard boards being pried loose over his head. Soon the tinsmith climbed down calmly, with a pile of boards under his arm. Zeif started to shout: "You're a robber! You've ruined me! I almost died until you finally got here! Instead of fixing the roof so it shouldn't rain in on me, you destroyed it and are taking home the wood!? You've made it worse! Don't you have any feelings?"

"Oh, come on now," the tinsmith replied calmly, "why should you eat your heart out over such a little thing? The house isn't even yours. Until it rains again the war might end. Look how hot it is. You know it rains very seldom in the summer, and when it does, it's hardly more than a drizzle. The roof doesn't even get wet. Anyway, we are having a dry summer, and by the fall we'll all have forgotten that there was ever a war, with a ghetto, with an 'Emperor' Rumkowski."

"God forbid that the war should last until the fall," Zeif interrupted him. "It's lasted almost two years already."

"Of course. Now take a board for yourself for fuel and it'll bring you luck—you'll see the end of the war," and he thrust a board under Zeif's arms.

Zeif thought: "As I live and breathe, the man is right." Aloud, he said: "What can I do with you? Shall I report you to the 'Emperor's' police? How can I?" He seized the board with both hands and pointed to Bluestein: "But *he's* the one you have to watch out for. He sees that nobody steals any wood."

The tinsmith grew a little frightened, but Bluestein looked at him pityingly and he felt better. Zeif added: "Don't be afraid. I should live so long what a nice man he is, huh, Mr. Bluestein? I swear he would never hurt anyone."

Cooking Pot,
Frankfurt, 1580.
The Jewish Museum, NY/
Art Resource, NY.

165

The tinsmith left quickly with his bundle and Zeif went into the house with the board and broke it into small pieces for several days' fuel.

"Mr. Bluestein, can you guess what my wife used for fuel when she cooked supper tonight? You can't guess, can you?"

"No," said Bluestein firmly.

Zeif opened the clothes cupboard with the expression of an inventor demonstrating his work. Bluestein saw that everything was ship-shape. The glassware, the china; even the paper shelving lay flat and smooth, and the linens were arranged in neat piles. Bluestein wondered: "What is he trying to show me?"

Zeif could no longer refrain from boasting. Quickly he lifted up the paper shelving and pointed: "See? Why do I need whole boards on the shelves? The wooden strips are enough." He cut an arc through the air with his thumb, chanting in talmudic fashion: "So I removed the boards. I chopped up three boards, split two of them into strips, put four strips on each level, laid out the shelving paper with the clothes and all the rest of the things and there are my shelves. Can you tell the difference? Now my wife will be able to cook and cook for a long time." He pointed to the bunches of wood which he had divided into four tiny strips each. "More than that isn't necessary. I'm like 'Emperor' Rumkowski with his rations. I dole out rations to my wife. And, thank God, we have what to cook." He showed Bluestein a big heap of cabbage roots.

Not far from Zeif's house there was a large field which the Agriculture Division had rented to one of Rumkowski's officials—formerly a rich man. After the cabbage was picked, Zeif dug out the roots, which were hard and bitter, and also took home the wild cabbage leaves that grew near the roots.

Two weeks later Zeif called Bluestein again and said: "Well, be smart and guess with what my wife cooked her cabbage stew today."

The same game was reenacted. Bluestein pondered, searched, examined every corner of the house and couldn't find any clues to the riddle. Finally Zeif solved it for him. He flung open the door of the cupboard. "Why does a cupboard need a back wall when it stands against a wall? I removed the rest of the wall and now I'll have fuel for a long time."

From the roots and wild leaves Mrs. Zeif prepared appetizers, fish, meat, soups, tsimmes. She let the cabbage cook a while and then put in a lot of bicarbonate of soda, because soda boils up in hot water. She thought: "It is cooking and at the same time the soda draws out the poisons." (The cabbage roots don't get soft even over the biggest fire.)

From the poison Zeif made "marinated herring" (his own invention). He removed the bulbs from the roots, salted them heavily and let them stand. Then he mixed a little vinegar and water, added some paprika ersatz and saccharin. Into this mixture Zeif dipped his scrap of ersatz bread and sighed with pleasure: "Ah—ah—delicious," smacking his lips as in the good old days over a savory roast. He hummed a hasidic tune, drumming his fingers on the table in rhythm. "Oh, a delicious marinated herring! Henye, our enemies should never enjoy it!" And his wife nodded in agreement as they ate with relish.

Two weeks later Zeif called in Bluestein again and asked: "Well, guess how my wife cooked today? This time you must guess!" and he pointed to the cupboard that was covered with a blanket. "See? Today I got still smarter! Why does a cupboard need a door? What's bad about this? Anything wrong? With the door my wife will be able to cook for a long time, and the cupboard is still a cupboard!"

Bluestein touched the cupboard with one finger and it began to sway back and forth.

Zeif defended the dignity of the cupboard: "That's nothing! Who's going to fight with it? A cupboard doesn't have to be strong, man!"

Bluestein's heart ached because of Zeif's

decency—and he agreed that Zeif was a smart, practical man, a real inventor. Zeif tried to smile, but a grimace distorted his face.

The next day Mrs. Zeif, sobbing with terror, called in Bluestein: "Mr. Bluestein, look what's happened to my husband!"

Zeif lay in bed, unable to move. Overnight he had grown so swollen and his head and face so huge, that it covered the entire pillow. The bed was too narrow for his body.

Zeif said in a weak voice: "Look what happened to me! And all because I have no 'shoulders!'"

Bluestein tried to console him: "Don't worry, Mr. Zeif, the war will end any day now, and we'll go home together."

"Yes, Mr. Bluestein, my wife and I haven't even used up our wedding outfit."

"Listen to me, Mr. Zeif, sell some of your wedding clothes and buy yourself some bread and a bit of meat. When you go back to the city you'll get new clothes, maybe even better ones."

"We'll never sell anything from our wedding outfit. I just told you, we didn't even replace any of it. To spite the Germans we'll go home in those clothes!"

Bluestein didn't urge him, because he didn't want Zeif to doubt that the war would end any day. He said lightly:

"Don't worry about the swelling, it's nothing," but he was sure that Zeif would soon lose the battle with his hunger. At the door he said: "Mr. Zeif, in the middle of the night I'll come running in to tell you that the war is over!" and he left the house. He recalled that he had read in the forbidden *Deutsche Zeitung* the speech which Hans Greizer, may his name be blotted out, delivered to the Hitler youth on May 1, 1940, the day when the ghetto was sealed off with barbed wire:

"The Jews are finished," Greizer said. "Hunger will turn them into mad dogs. They will bite chunks of flesh from each other.

They will devour themselves!"

"It's true, we are dying out because of hunger," Bluestein thought, "but we have not become wild beasts. Not only are we not biting chunks of flesh from each other, but we don't even want to exchange a single garment from our wedding outfits for a piece of bread and meat. We don't steal and we don't kill. No, he will not turn us into mad dogs! On the outside we look like corpses, but inside we have preserved the image of God."

Early next morning Bluestein went to see how Hershel Zeif was feeling. He was afraid that Zeif had not lasted the night, or that he had taken his own life because of his suffering and despair.

But Bluestein was surprised! Overnight Zeif had grown as thin as a rail, and his skin was like that of a corpse. He couldn't get off the bed. Again Bluestein consoled him: "See, the swelling is gone! That's a good sign. You're getting better, you'll soon be well. Be patient, Mr. Zeif, we'll go home together."

"Oh, I haven't lost faith yet! What's this nonsense about my getting well soon? I'm not sick! I was never sick in my life! I'm just a little weak from hunger. I have pain—but that's nothing. The hell with 'them!' Do you remember what Greizer, may his name be blotted out, said in those days? You should remember. He said: 'The Jews are finished.' Believe me, Mr. Bluestein, 'They are finished!' Last night I had a wonderful dream. I saw my father, of blessed memory, and—the war was over and I was beating up the Germans and 'Emperor' Rumkowski and his henchmen. How I took revenge! How I cooled my heart! I should be as sure of meeting my family again as I am sure that 'they' will die an unnatural death!" Zeif ranted in his weak voice.

"It's good, Mr. Zeif, good that you haven't lost faith! I admire you. You'll see, we'll go home together!"

Bluestein walked down the stairs with an

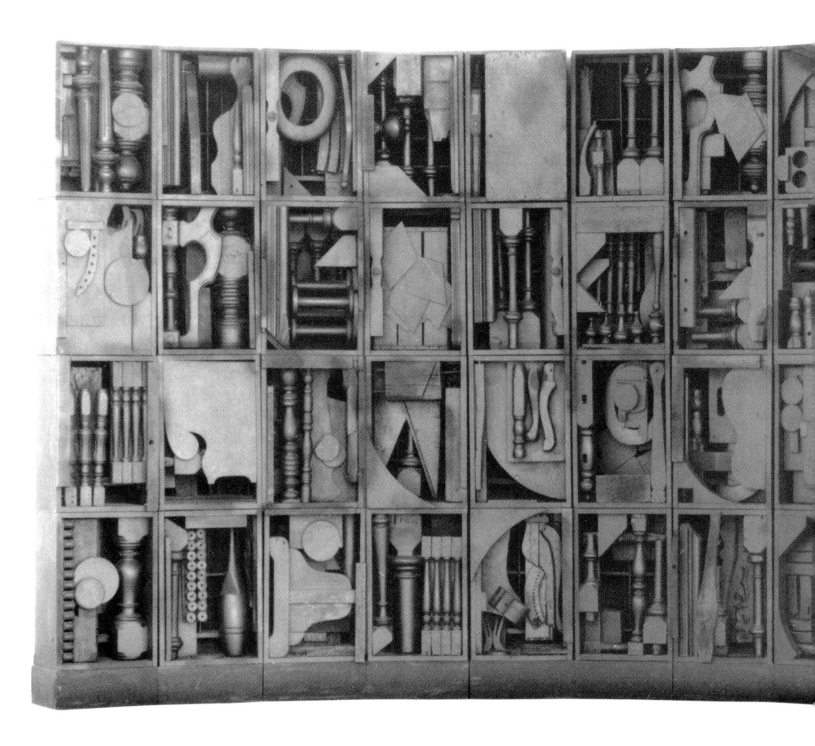

aching heart, thinking: "Who knows what will happen to him? Hunger has already turned him into an obituary. The Angel of Death has placed his mark on him."

A little later Bluestein received the new ration which contained two kilos of potatoes. He brought one kilo to the Zeifs: "Mrs. Zeif, I'm lending you a kilo of potatoes. When you get your ration you'll give it back. Cook the potatoes right away. They'll be a good medicine for Zeif."

Husband and wife didn't know how to thank Bluestein. They showered blessings on him. With several slivers of wood Mr. Zeif boiled the potatoes half-raw in their skins. When they were eating, Henye tried to give

the larger portion to Zeif and he tried to give the larger portion to her. After eating a few potatoes Zeif felt better: "See, Henye, all we need is faith. With God's help we'll survive the war. Do you have any wood left for cooking?"

"Yes, for a few more times," she replied with satisfaction.

"See, Henye, the cupboard is still a cupboard," he smiled.

And they dipped the unpeeled potatoes in salt and ate. Because the ghetto Jews said: "The peel is healthy. In the peel there is iron and under it there is sugar, and that's why cattle are so healthy and strong—because they eat the peel."

FROM KING OF THE JEWS

—BY LESLIE EPSTEIN

The children in the orphanage thought their leader was a giant, a hero, bigger than life. So did the adults in the ghetto. That was not only because he rode around in a carriage with a white horse and had a cape on his shoulders and a mane of hair on his head like a lion; it was also because, unlike any of the other Elders in any of the other ghettos, he had kept them alive. But on one afternoon, when I. C. Trumpelman returned to the orphanage, he was not the same man who had left in the morning. For one thing, he'd learned that the children were about to be taken away. For another, he'd been beaten by the Lords and Masters when he'd tried to protest. Now he could hardly walk. His clothes were ripped, his cloak gone. There was only one lens left in his frame. He did not go into the mansion, but around it, to the gardens in back. Though early in springtime, the fresh green stems of garlic were pushing out of the ground. Trumpelman sank down among them; wearily, he shut his eyes.

No telling how long he might have stayed there if Bettsack, the schoolmaster, had not walked by carrying what looked like a gigantic squash. *Smuggling!* said the Elder to himself, and keeping low, keeping hidden, he followed the young teacher to the edge of the plowed-up field. There the orphans—both the old-timers and the ones who had joined the Asylum in the last years before the move to the Balut—were waiting. They all had caps on, and coats, and were holding such things as nuts, the head of a cabbage, and a pink India-rubber ball. The sun had dropped well down in the sky, and the air was chilly now. Bettsack was a thin fellow, poorly whiskered, with threads that stuck up from his collar. He made his way to the center of the field, set down the gourd—it was as big as a washbasin, really—and began to call through his hands.

"Stations, children! Positions, if you please! You! Shifter! Leibel Shifter! Further back. Further back! Tushnet! You go back, too!"

The children began to scatter over the field. Shifter, the mad boy, the dog, kept going backward. Every minute or so he would stop, but Bettsack waved him farther on, until he was practically out of sight. "Stop!" the schoolmaster shouted. But Shifter still backpedaled, and the message to him had to be passed from orphan to orphan, from Krystal to Atlas to Tushnet, across the length of the field.

Finally they all held still. Bettsack bent down and picked up the dried squash; he just had the strength to lift it over his head. The next thing you knew the schoolmaster, a grown-up, responsible person, was rapidly spinning around. "Flicker!" he gasped to the boy who was nearest. "Citron!" he called, to the lad next farthest out. "Begin rotation!"

Trumpelman could hardly believe what he saw: both boys, and then Gutta Blit, and then all the others began to spin on the spot. It was like madness. Round and round they went, stepping all over their shadows. "West to east, Miss Atlas! Not like a clock!" Rose Atlas stopped; she reversed direction. The rest kept going, holding their little spheres. Bettsack had begun to stagger a little. The breath came visibly from his mouth.

"Now! Revolutions!"

Little Usher Flicker—between his fingers he had a pea from a pod—began to trip around the teacher, in a circle more or less. A bit farther out Citron was doing the same. The amazing thing was that as both boys went in this circular orbit, they did not stop whirling about. Gutta Blit, with the pink rubber ball, was spinning like a dervish too, and also Krystal, and so was everyone soon. Even Leibel Shifter, way out on the edge of the field, a half kilometer off, had started to run. However, because of the distance between him and Bettsack, he hardly seemed to be moving. Flicker, for instance, had run three times about the center, before Shifter, his legs thrashing, covered any noticeable ground. It would take him forever to complete a revolution.

"Attention! Moons!" Bettsack, with red patches that showed through his beard, with his necktie coming undone, practically shrieked this.

From behind the hill that led to the cemetery grounds fifteen, twenty, more than twenty children came pouring. What they did, with a whoop, with a shout, was to pick out some of the whirling orphans—Gutta, Rose Atlas, the puffing Mann Lifshits—and then begin to race as fast as they could around them. For a time the whole field was covered with these whizzing children, making circles inside of circles, curves within curves.

Then Trumpelman stood up in the dimming light; he walked into their midst. Through his split, puffy lips, he demanded of the reeling Bettsack, "What is the meaning of this? Speak!"

The schoolmaster dropped his squash. He started screaming. "It's the whole solar system! Including the new planet of Pluto! In correct proportions! According to the system of Sir J. Frederick Herschel!" Then he threw his arms around the Asylum Director, clinging to him the way a drunkard does to a post. Just then Nathan Hobnover, an eight-year-old boy, came roaring over the hilltop, making a sizzling sound: zzzzzzz!

"Comet," said Bettsack, and sank down about Trumpelman's ankles.

The exhausted children saw the old man in tatters; they wobbled to a halt. Mann Lifshits, whose heavy cabbage represented Jupiter, simply dropped, as did his eleven moons. One by one the others collapsed. They lay on their backs, with their coats spread, their breath coming up in a mist. Only the man from Vilna, for all his scratches and bruises, remained on his feet. Then he sat down, too. Tushnet caught his breath before anyone else and addressed the schoolmaster.

"Sir, what will happen when the sun goes out?" He was some way off, but it was so still you could easily hear him.

Bettsack said, "What do you mean, Tushnet? It goes *down*. It does not go *out*."

"I mean, when it burns up. Will we burn up, too?"

A high voice broke in. "It can't just go on forever. Sometime it has to run out of fuel."

"That is only a theory, Flicker. It has not been proved."

"But what if it's true? What then? Everything will be dark. It makes me nervous." That was Rose Atlas.

"I don't think it will burn up," said Mann Lifshits, from his spot on the ground. "It'll just get colder and colder. Everything on earth will get colder, too. It will be like the ice age. Nothing but ice."

"But it scares me," Rose replied.

"Listen," said Bettsack. "This is speculation. In any case, it won't happen for thousands of years."

"See? You said it was going to happen! It's going to happen!"

"We'll all be frozen to death!"

"Please!" their instructor said. "Why do you worry? In a thousand years none of us will be alive."

"I don't care! I don't want it to go out! I hate the idea of the cold!"

"I do, too!"

"No one alive! No one! There won't even be animals on the earth. It's terrible!"

"Don't talk about it! Don't think about it!"

Stars of Twilight,
Samuel Bak, 1995.
Courtesy of Pucker
Gallery, Boston, MA.

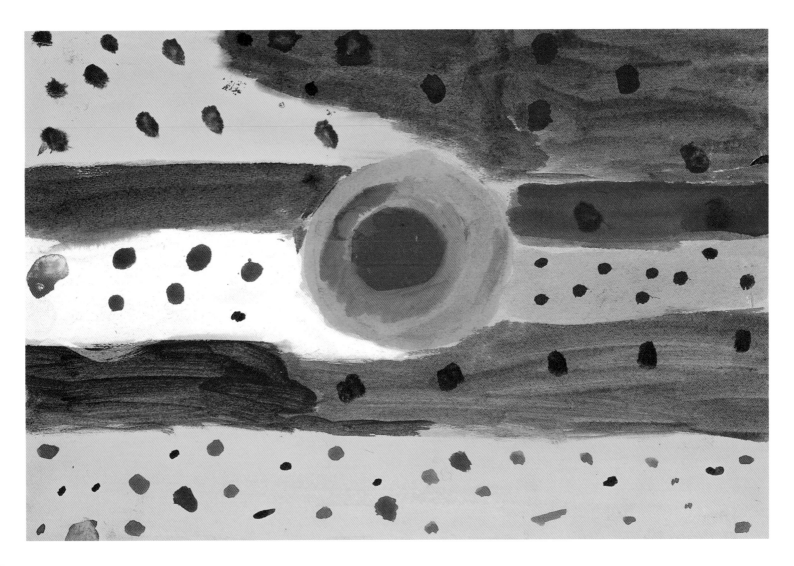

Fantasy,
Nely Silvínová,
Terezín, 1944.
Courtesy of The Jewish
Museum in Prague.

The children began to whimper and moan. So Bettsack spoke in a loud, firm voice. "Pay attention, if you please. The sun is not going to stop burning. It is made in a certain way. And even if it should go out after all, by then men will have invented spaceships, and they will fly off to live somewhere else. To other planets, to other worlds. There is nothing that science cannot achieve. Perhaps in the universe we shall meet other forms of life. Perhaps even people just like ourselves. Think of that! What a wonderful day that will be! How much we shall learn!"

The moaning had completely stopped. Everything was quiet. Then, so that everyone's heart leaped and pounded, there was an awful wail from Leibel Shifter. "Help! I'm so far away! Help! I'm afraid!"

Trumpelman, sitting upright, answered. "Come. All of you. Come closer,"

Silently, on all fours, the boys and girls began to crawl toward the center. They drew near to Trumpelman, who, through his swollen eyes, his single lens, was staring off to the west. They looked, too.

There, on the horizon, the real sun was leaking something. Red stuff, like jam, came out of it and spread over the nearby sky. "Like a raspberry drop," said Usher Flicker. He took the Elder's hand. Citron, a new boy, had curly blond hair coming from under his cap. He laid his head across the Elder's knees. Dark Gutta Blit leaned on his shoulder.

"It's beautiful," she whispered, gazing off to where the sun, cut by the earth's edge, still pumped the sweet-looking syrup from its center. All the children—the planets, the satellites, Hobnover the comet, and at last even Shifter—pressed close to Trumpelman, and to each other. They were like his missing cape.

"THE SPAN OF OUR LIFE IS SEVENTY YEARS, or, given strength, eighty years; but the best of them are trouble and sorrow. Therefore," the biblical author of Psalm 90 entreats God, "teach us to number our days so that we may obtain a heart of wisdom."

The teachings of Jewish tradition offer an abundance of perennial wisdom. In the biblical books of Job and Ecclesiastes (aptly known as wisdom literature), in much talmudic reasoning, and in the speculative writings of thinkers such as Philo, Maimonides, Spinoza, and Rosenzweig, we find the wisdom of the philosophers. In Proverbs, in the popular rabbinic anthology known as "Ethics of the Fathers" (*Pirke Avot*), in medieval piety manuals, in much Torah commentary, and in modern Jewish "how-to"

IN THE HEART
OF WISDOM

books, we find the ethical wisdom called *musar* (from the same Hebrew root as "tradition"). From the Psalms, from kabbalistic and hasidic writings, and from spiritual masters of our own day, we learn spiritual wisdom. And embedded in the proverbs, tales, home remedies, and homespun rules of "kitchen-table" Judaism, we find the practical wisdom of folk Torah, the unacknowledged bedrock of faith.

The stories in this section dip into all these wells. The first two tales demonstrate just how transient are all those things that we hold dear—happiness, material comfort, power, and fame. In "King Solomon's Ring," for instance, a mighty king discovers that he has no power to hold still the ever-spinning wheel of fortune. Similarly, Alexander the Great, the ruler of the world, discovers that no amount of wealth can buy a reprieve from the Angel of Death.

A related theme is the limit of human understanding. For so eager are we to reduce the world's complexities to fit our need for certainty that we often sacrifice truth in the process. In S. Y. Agnon's poignant "Fable of a Goat," a father and son lose their chance to share in redemption because they leap to conclusions too quickly. The eager young seeker in Jiri Langer's "Why Naftali of Ropschitz Wore White Trousers" learns to his embarrassment that great sages share more in common with the rest of us than we think. Ironically, it is Gimpel the Fool, in I. B. Singer's story, who demonstrates to us that ignorance is sometimes bliss, especially if knowledge is pressed into the service of spite.

Finally, we encounter three stories that share a common message: It could always be worse. For a people long subjected to homelessness, persecution, and slander, this motto has proven invaluable. In fact, it may be the key to Jewish survival and is one of the cornerstones of Jewish humor. The Yiddish story that takes its title from this axiom demonstrates that everything, even the peace and quiet of our own home, is relative. In the 18th century memoirs addressed to her own children, Glückel of Hameln teaches us to measure our own dissatisfactions against the collective weight of the world's miseries. And finally, simple Eisik the son of Yekel reminds us that the treasure for which we so avidly seek is often remarkably close to home.

KING SOLOMON'S RING

—MIDDLE EASTERN FOLKTALE, retold by Judith Ish-Kishor

O f all King Solomon's servants, the bravest and most faithful was Benaiah, the captain of the guard. He had been the King's companion in the fabulous adventures of his earlier days and more than once had saved his master's life. He had never failed in any task that Solomon had set him.

This, indeed, was his only boast; for Benaiah was a man of action, not fond of talking. When he was not on duty guarding the King, he would sit among the courtiers so silent that they made the mistake of thinking him dull. They would tease him; but Benaiah, sure of his place with the King, paid no attention to them.

Once, however, Solomon himself took part in a mischievous trick they were playing on his faithful follower. "Benaiah," he said one Sabbath evening early in spring, "you are fond of saying that you have never failed in any task for me."

Benaiah bowed respectfully. "That is my only boast, O King."

"Then let me put you to one more test. I want you to find me a certain wonderful ring, so that I can wear it at the Sukkot festival. That will give you six months for the search."

"If the ring exists under Heaven, my lord, you shall have it! But tell me, I pray, what makes it so precious?"

"It has magic powers," said the King. "If a happy man looks at it, he at once becomes downcast and gloomy; but if a person in misery or mourning beholds it, hope rises in his heart and he is comforted." Now King Solomon knew that there was no such ring. But he met Benaiah's eager gaze with a smile of encouragement.

"You shall wear it at the Sukkot feast," Benaiah exclaimed, "if there be any strength left in me!"

He could hardly wait for the Sabbath to be over, so that he could start on his quest.

First he went to the finest jewelers and goldsmiths and silversmiths in Jerusalem, for he didn't know whether the ring was of silver or gold, set with precious stones or plain. To each man he described its magic qualities, but no one knew anything about it. They had not even heard of such a ring. Benaiah also tried the smaller shops and less prosperous dealers. Always he met with the same raised eyebrows, the same shake of the head.

Ah, this ring must be treasured in some far-off city, thought Benaiah.

When the great caravans came southward from Babylon and Damascus and Tyre, he was the first to meet them, and he spoke to the traders in precious gems, and said: "I am seeking a ring with this magic quality: When a happy person looks at it, he becomes sad; and when a wretched man beholds it, he ceases to grieve and is comforted. Do you have it? I will pay any price. It is for my lord, King Solomon."

These widely traveled merchants also shook their heads. Each told him, "I regret, Captain, that I have no such ring. It may not even exist, for I have never heard of it. I have other rare jewels that will surely please—"

"Look for this ring, I pray you," said Benaiah firmly. "If you have it for me on your return journey, you may name your own price."

He went to Beersheba in the south, to meet the caravans that came up from the cities of Egypt, and from Yemen, the land of perfumes. He asked the jewel merchants: "Can you find me a ring which has the wonderful power of changing a man's grief to joy when he beholds it? Also, it changes happiness to sorrow at a glance."

"Wonderful, indeed!" they answered, "if such a ring exists. But we have not heard of it."

"It exists," said Benaiah. "My lord, King Solomon wishes for it. You shall have any price you ask if you bring me that ring on your return."

He went down to Jaffa, where the ships came in from the Great Sea and the Ocean of Darkness, in the west, and the Spice Islands and the Land of Ophir, to the east and south. To each merchant he said, "I seek a magic ring. It makes a mourner forget his grief, when he looks at it; but when a happy man sees it, his heart sinks and there is no joy in him. I will pay a great price for it."

And each one answered him, "I know of no such ring. You are the first to tell me of it."

"Then seek it, in all lands where you travel. For if you bring it to me on your return, you may ask what you wish in payment."

Benaiah thought, How wise is my lord, the King! He knows the things hidden from other men, even at the ends of the earth!

Meanwhile weeks, then months, went by. It was summer. The caravans returned from the north. None of the merchants brought him the ring, or even any word of where it might be found. The caravans came again from the south. "We would gladly help you," the dealers said, "but in all the cities and the markets where we sought it, we have seen no such ring. Nor have we heard tell of it."

Summer was over. One by one the ships returned from prosperous voyages over calm waters, and each of the sea captains and the merchant-adventurers told Benaiah the same disheartening tale. They had not seen such a ring. No one had heard of it.

The last harvest of the year, and with it the Sukkot festival, was approaching. Every time King Solomon saw Benaiah, he would say: "Well, how goes the search, Benaiah? Have you found the ring?" And when Benaiah shook his head, Solomon said with a pleasant smile, "Search diligently, Benaiah. You will surely find it."

"With God's help!" Benaiah said.

But as the days went by and brought no good news, he began to avoid the places where he might meet the King.

Now it was only a week before Sukkot. There was no more hope in Benaiah's heart. He could not eat and his nights were sleepless. He dreaded the moment when he must tell the King he had failed. He did not mind so much that the clever young courtiers would laugh at him. But he could not bear to have the King's trust in him shaken.

It was the last night before Sukkot Eve. Benaiah lay restless on his bed for several hours; then he rose and dressed and walked about the silent city, hardly knowing where he went. He wandered away from the palace, and the fine houses of the courtiers and those who served the King, through the neighborhoods where the plain people lived.

Night faded from the sky and the east brightened with the rosy fire of dawn as Benaiah went downward from street to street, until he reached the bottom of the valley between the two hills on which Jerusalem was built.

Benaiah looked about him. It was a poor street, with small shabby houses. As the sun rose, people in patched and faded garments came out of their dwellings and set about the morning's business.

Benaiah saw a young man spread a mat upon the moss-grown paving-stones in front of his home, and arrange on it some baskets of silver and turquoise trinkets and mother-of-pearl beads such as people without much money could afford.

Shall I ask here? thought Benaiah. What use, when even the most famous travelers have never heard of the ring?—Still, it will only mean another No.

He approached the jeweler. "I want a ring," he said, repeating words that had lost their meaning for him. "A wonderful ring. It has magic powers. When a happy man looks at it, he becomes sad. When a grieving person sees it, he becomes joyful. Do you have it?"

The young man shook his head. "This is a poor little place, O Captain, and we know nothing of such marvels. . . ."

Benaiah walked away.

But meanwhile the jeweler's old grandfather had come out to sit by the doorway in the early sunshine. He beckoned the young man to him and whispered in his ear.

"Wait, Captain!" the jeweler called out, "I think we can serve you." Hardly able to believe his ears, Benaiah turned back.

The young man took from one of the baskets a plain gold ring, such as is used for weddings. With a sharp tool he engraved something on it and laid it in the captain's hand.

Benaiah looked at it, then he laughed aloud. His heart filled with joy. He had not been so happy since the day he had first started the search. "This is the ring!" he cried, and gave the young jeweler all the money in his purse. "Come to the palace and you shall have more," he added, "for I cannot thank you enough."

He hurried back to his house but was too impatient to sleep. However, he kept out of the King's sight, not to betray his happy secret until the right time should come. He bathed and made ready for the festival. Then in his finest holiday attire he took his place at the banquet table.

He enjoyed the feast, for now that his duty was done he could pay attention to such matters as food and drink. He laughed at every joke, and thought kindly of

Wedding Ring,
Italy, 17th–18th century.
Collection Israel Museum,
Jerusalem.

the clever young courtiers.

When the merriment was at its height, King Solomon turned to Benaiah. A hush spread around the table. "Now, my faithful Captain," the King exclaimed mirthfully, "where is the famous ring?" Of course, after he and the courtiers had laughed for a while at Benaiah's simplicity, Solomon meant to tell him that he had not failed, for no such ring existed.

But to Solomon's astonishment, Benaiah cried: "I have it, O King! It is here." And, almost stumbling in his haste to reach the King's side, he placed it on Solomon's hand.

As the King looked at it, the teasing laughter faded from his face. He became silent and thoughtful, for the magic of the ring was working. The jeweler had engraved on it three Hebrew letters, *Gimmel, Zayin, Yud,* standing for the words *Gam zeh ya'avor*—"This, too, shall pass." Thus King Solomon was sharply reminded that all his glory, and the beauty and splendor with which he was surrounded, must crumble away into dust, leaving at last nothing but an old memory and a tale that is told.

When he raised his eyes again, they met Benaiah's with a humbled, grateful look. He was ashamed of the trick he had played on his loyal follower.

"Benaiah," he said, "you are not only as faithful, but wiser than I thought you. This is a wonderful gift. I shall wear it on the same finger as my signet." He drew from his hand a ring with a precious ruby. "And you, in return, must wear this ruby, so that all men may know you as the King's friend."

ALEXANDER AND THE EYEBALL

—BY GLÜCKEL OF HAMELN, translated by Marvin Lowenthal

As it is told of Alexander the Macedon who, as everyone knows, traveled and conquered the whole wide world: Whereat he thought to himself, "I am such a mighty man and I have traveled so far, I must be near to the Garden of Eden." For he stood by the river Gihon, which is one of the four rivers that flow from the Garden.

So he built himself stout ships, boarded them with all his men, and through his great wisdom reached the fork where you enter towards Eden. When he neared the Garden itself, a fire came and consumed all the ships and men, save Alexander's own ship and its crew.

He now strode to the gate of the Garden and begged to enter, for he wanted to see all the wonders of the world. And a voice answered him and bade him depart, for through this gate "only the righteous may come in."

After Alexander had pleaded some while in vain, he finally asked that something be tossed him from over the wall, that he might show it as a token to prove that he had at last reached the gate of Eden.

Bar Kokhba Coin, Ancient Israel, 133–34 C.E. The Jewish Museum, NY/ Art Resource, NY.

Whereat an eye fell at his feet. He picked it up, without well knowing what to do with it. And a voice told him to heap together all his gold and silver and other goodly possessions and pile them in one scale of a balance, and then lay the eye in the other scale, and the eye would outweigh all the rest.

King Alexander was, it is well known, a great philosopher and a wise man, as his teacher Aristotle had trained him to be, and he sought to master all manner of wisdom. He was loath to believe that a little thing like an eye could outweigh so much heavy gold and silver and other goodly possessions, and he set about to see if it were true.

He brought him a great and mighty pair of balances, and placed the eye in one of its enormous scales. And in the other he poured hundreds and hundreds of gold and silver coins, but the more he poured the higher rose the scale and the eye proved heavier and heavier. And in wonderment he asked the reason.

Then he was told to put the tiniest speck of earth over the eye. He did so, and at once

Ship/Map (No.1),
Joshua Borkovsky, 1990.
The Jewish Museum/
Art Resource, NY.

has the more he wants. And therefore the eye outweighs all your silver and gold.

"But once a man dies and a speck of earth is laid over his eye, the eye is satisfied.

"Behold, you may see it, Alexander, in your own life. You were not satisfied with your kingdom and needs must travel and conquer the whole world, till you have come to the place where are the servants and children of God.

"So long, then, as you live you will never be satisfied, and you will always want and take more and more, till you will go and die in a strange land, and not so long now either.

"And once you are placed in the earth, you will be content with six feet of ground, you for whom the whole world was too small.

"Go at once, and speak nor ask no more, for you will not be answered."

So Alexander sailed with his ship to the land of Hodu, where he presently met a terrible and bitter death. For he died of poisoning, as his teacher Aristotle tells us in his history.

A penny honestly earned is hard to part with. But man must learn to control his greed. For 'tis a universal proverb, "Stinginess never enriches and measured generosity never makes one poor." To everything there is a time—a time to get money and a time to give. And the Dutch say, *Gelt autzugeben in siner tid, dat makt profit.* There are many Gentile sages who have written very wondrously of these things.

the eye rose as though it weighed a feather, and the scale with the gold and silver came tumbling to the ground.

In greater wonderment than ever, he asked how this came about. And the voice replied:

"Hearken, Alexander! The eye of man, so long as he lives, is never full. The more a man

WHY NAFTALI OF ROPSCHITZ WORE WHITE TROUSERS

—*BY JIRI LANGER*, translated by Stephen Jolly

Reb Naftali liked witty people, but he was not over-fond of busybodies. Here is a story of how he got his own back on such a person.

A young man insisted on knowing why Reb Naftali always wore trousers of white cloth.

"I can't tell you that," said the saint, "it's a secret."

When the nosy fellow heard the word "secret," his curiosity increased and he pestered the saint all the more.

"It's a secret I can only confide to somebody who has first fasted for six days."

The young fellow was so anxious to know that he really succeeded in enduring a six-day fast. Then he turned up again.

"So now I'll tell you, but promise me you won't betray the secret to anybody so long as you live."

The fellow solemnly swore not to.

Reb Naftali then led him off into a room, and from that room to a second room, and from the second to a third. Then he went back again to make sure that all the doors were well closed so that no unauthorized person should hear the secret. The young fellow was on tenterhooks.

Reb Naftali grew serious. Then he bent down to the student of mysteries and whispered in his ear:

"Know then that I wear white cloth trousers because they're the cheapest."

Dancing Figure,
Abraham Walkowitz,
1903.
The Jewish Museum, NY/
Art Resource, NY.

"So that's all it is!" exclaimed the disappointed nosy-parker. "Is that what I had to fast six days

for? Why make such a secret of it?"

Reb Naftali smiled a mischievous smile.

"Because if people got to know of it, they'd want this sort of trousers too, and in no time

they'd be more expensive. I shouldn't get them so cheap anymore. . . . Now don't forget your

promise, and don't tell anyone, so long as you live!"

FABLE OF THE GOAT

—*BY S. Y. AGNON*, translated by Barney Rubin

The tale is told of an old man who groaned from his heart. The doctors were sent for, and they advised him to drink goat's milk. He went out and bought a she-goat and brought her into his home. Not many days passed before the goat disappeared. They went out to search for her but did not find her. She was not in the yard and not in the garden, not on the roof of the house of study and not by the spring, not in the hills and not in the fields. She tarried several days and then returned by herself; and when she returned, her udder was full of a great deal of milk, the taste of which was as the taste of Eden. Not just once, but many times she disappeared from the house. They would go out in search for her and would not find her until she returned by herself with her udder full of milk that was sweeter than honey and whose taste was the taste of Eden.

One time the old man said to his son, "My son, I desire to know where she goes and whence she brings this milk which is sweet to my palate and a balm to all my bones."

His son said to him, "Father, I have a plan."

He said to him, "What is it?"

The son got up and brought a length of cord. He tied it to the goat's tail.

His father said to him, "What are you doing, my son?"

OPPOSITE: *Illustration from Had Gadya (Tale of a Goat)*, El Lissitzky, 1919. The Jewish Museum, NY/ Art Resource, NY.

He said to him, "I am tying a cord to the goat's tail, so that when I feel a pull on it I will know that she has decided to leave, and I can catch the end of the cord and follow her on her way."

The old man nodded his head and said to him, "My son, if your heart is wise, my heart too will rejoice."

The youth tied the cord to the goat's tail and minded it carefully. When the goat set off, he held the cord in his hand and did not let it slacken until the goat was well on her way and he was following her. He was dragged along behind her until he came to a cave. The goat went into the cave, and the youth followed her, holding the cord. They walked thus for an hour or two, or maybe even a day or two. The goat wagged her tail and bleated, and the cave came to an end.

Whey they emerged from the cave, the youth saw lofty mountains, and hills full of the choicest fruit, and a fountain of living waters that flowed down from the mountains; and the wind wafted all manner of perfumes. The goat climbed up a tree by clutching at the ribbed leaves. Carob fruits full of honey dropped from the tree, and she ate of the carobs and drank of the garden's fountain.

Landscape,
Israel Paldi, 1928.
Collection Israel Museum,
Jerusalem.

The youth stood and called to the wayfarers: "I adjure you, good people, tell me where I am, and what is the name of this place?"

They answered him, "You are in the Land of Israel, and you are close by Safed."

The youth lifted up his eyes to the heavens and said, "Blessed be the Omnipresent, blessed be He who has brought me to the Land of Israel." He kissed the soil and sat down under the tree.

He said, "Until the day breathe and the shadows flee away, I shall sit on the hill under this tree. Then I shall go home and bring my father and mother to the Land of Israel."

186

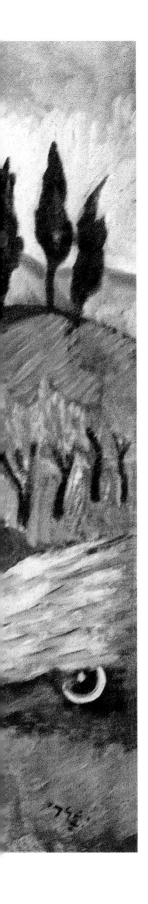

As he was sitting thus and feasting his eyes on the holiness of the Land of Israel, he heard a voice proclaiming:

"Come, let us go out to greet the Sabbath Queen."

And he saw men like angels, wrapped in white shawls, with boughs of myrtle in their hands, and all the houses were lit with a great many candles. He perceived that the eve of Sabbath would arrive with the darkening, and that he would not be able to return. He uprooted a reed and dipped it in gallnuts, from which the ink for the writing of Torah scrolls is made. He took a piece of paper and wrote a letter to his father:

"From the ends of the earth I lift up my voice in song to tell you that I have come in peace to the Land of Israel. Here I sit, close by Safed, the holy city, and I imbibe its sanctity. Do not inquire how I arrived here but hold onto this cord which is tied to the goat's tail and follow the footsteps of the goat; then your journey will be secure, and you will enter the Land of Israel."

The youth rolled up the note and placed it in the goat's ear. He said to himself: When she arrives at Father's house, Father will pat her on the head, and she will flick her ears. The note will fall out, Father will pick it up and read what is written on it. Then he will take up the cord and follow the goat to the Land of Israel.

❖

The goat returned to the old man, but she did not flick her ears, and the note did not fall. When the old man saw that the goat had returned without his son, he clapped his hands to his head and began to cry and weep and wail, "My son, my son, where are you? My son, would that I might die in your stead, my son, my son!"

So he went, weeping and mourning over his son, for he said, "An evil beast has devoured him, my son is assuredly rent in pieces!"

And he refused to be comforted, saying, "I will go down to my grave in mourning for my son."

And whenever he saw the goat, he would say, "Woe to the father who banished his son, and woe to her who drove him from the world!"

The old man's mind would not be at peace until he sent for the butcher to slaughter the goat. The butcher came and slaughtered the goat. As they were skinning her, the note fell out of her ear. The old man picked up the note and said, "My son's handwriting!"

When he had read all that his son had written, he clapped his hands to his head and cried, "*Vay! Vay!* Woe to the man who robs himself of his own good fortune, and woe to the man who requites good with evil!"

He mourned over the goat many days and refused to be comforted, saying, "Woe to me, for I could have gone up to the Land of Israel in one bound, and now I must suffer out my days in this exile!"

Since that time the mouth of the cave has been hidden from the eye, and there is no longer a short way. And that youth, if he has not died, shall bear fruit in his old age, full of sap and richness, calm and peaceful in the Land of the Living.

A HOUSE WITHOUT SUFFERING

—*BY GLÜCKEL OF HAMELN*, translated by Marvin Lowenthal

(The world is one long groan,
Which each man calls his own.)

Aphilosopher was once walking along the street, and meeting an old friend, asked him how things were going. Thanking him, the friend replied, "Badly. No one in the world has more sorrows and troubles than I." Whereupon the philosopher said, "Good friend, come with me to my roof-top. I will point you every house in the whole city, and tell you the misfortunes and miseries they one and all conceal. Then, if you will, you may cast your own sorrow in with the rest and draw out any other you choose in its stead. Perhaps you will find one more to your liking."

Together they climbed to the roof, and the philosopher showed his friend the unhappiness that darkened one house after the other. And he said, "Do now as I told you." But the friend replied, "In truth, I see that every house hides as much woe and hardship as my own, and perhaps more. I think I'll keep what I have."

So run the thoughts of men: each thinks his own burden to be the heaviest. Wherefore naught is better than patience. For if it pleases God Almighty, He can lift our burden in a trice.

Fiddler on the Roof: Anatevka (Set Design), Boris Aronson, 1964. Courtesy of the artist.

189

GIMPEL THE FOOL

—*BY I. B. SINGER*, translated by Saul Bellow

1.

I am Gimpel the Fool. I don't think myself a fool. On the contrary. But that's what folks call me. They gave me the name while I was still in school. I had seven names in all: imbecile, donkey, flax-head, dope, glump, ninny, and fool. The last name stuck. What did my foolishness consist of? I was easy to take in. They said, "Gimpel, you know the rabbi's wife has been brought to childbed?" So I skipped school. Well, it turned out to be a lie. How was I supposed to know? She hadn't had a big belly. But I never looked at her belly. Was that really so foolish? The gang laughed and hee-hawed, stomped and danced and chanted a good-night prayer. And instead of the raisins they give when a woman's lying in, they stuffed my hand full of goat turds. I was no weakling. If I slapped someone he'd see all the way to Cracow. But I'm really not a slugger by nature. I think to myself, Let it pass. So they take advantage of me.

I was coming home from school and heard a dog barking. I'm not afraid of dogs, but of course I never want to start up with them. One of them may be mad, and if he bites there's not a Tartar in the world who can help you. So I made tracks. Then I looked around and saw the whole market place wild with laughter. It was no dog at all but Wolf-Leib the thief. How was I supposed to know it was he? It sounded like a howling bitch.

When the pranksters and leg-pullers found that I was easy to fool, every one of them tried his luck with me. "Gimpel, the Czar is coming to Frampol; Gimpel, the moon fell down in Turbeen; Gimpel, little Hodel Furpiece found a treasure behind the bathhouse." And I like a *golem* believed everyone. In the first place, everything is possible, as it is written in the Wisdom of the Fathers, I've forgotten just how. Second, I had to believe when the whole town came down on me! If I ever dared to say, "Ah, you're kidding!" there was trouble. People got angry. "What do you mean! You want to call everyone a liar?" What was I to do? I believed them, and I hope at least that did them some good.

I was an orphan. My grandfather who brought me up was already bent toward the grave. So they turned me over to a baker, and what a time they gave me there! Every woman or girl who came to bake a pan of cookies or dry a batch of noodles had to fool me at least once. "Gimpel, there's a fair in heaven; Gimpel, the rabbi gave birth to a calf in the seventh month; Gimpel, a cow flew over the roof and laid brass eggs." A student from the yeshiva came once to buy a roll, and he said, "You, Gimpel, while you stand here scraping with your baker's shovel the Messiah has come. The dead have risen." "What do you mean?" I said. "I heard no one blowing the ram's horn!" He said, "Are you deaf?" And all began to cry, "We heard it, we heard!" Then in came Reitze the candle-dipper and called out in her hoarse voice, "Gimpel, your father and mother have stood up from the grave. They're looking for you."

To tell the truth, I knew very well that nothing of the sort had happened, but all the same, as folks were talking, I threw on my wool vest and went out. Maybe something had happened. What did I stand to lose by looking? Well, what a cat music went up! And then I took a vow to believe nothing more. But that was no go either. They confused me so that I didn't know the big end from the small.

I went to the rabbi to get some advice. He said, "It is written, better to be a fool all your days than for one hour to be evil. You are not a fool. They are the fools. For he who causes his neighbor to feel shame loses Paradise himself." Nevertheless the rabbi's daughter took me in. As I left the rabbinical court she said, "Have you kissed the wall yet?" I said, "No, what for?" She answered, "It's a law; you've got to do it after every visit." Well, there didn't seem to be any harm in it. And she burst out laughing. It was a fine trick. She put one over on me, all right.

I wanted to go off to another town, but then everyone got busy matchmaking, and they were after me so they nearly tore my coat tails off. They talked at me and talked until I got water on the ear. She was no chaste maiden, but they told me she was virgin pure. She had a limp, and they said it was deliberate, from coyness. She had a bastard, and they told me the child was her little brother. I cried, "You're wasting your time. I'll never marry that whore." But they said indignantly, "What a way to talk! Aren't you ashamed of yourself? We can take you to the rabbi and have you fined for giving her a bad name." I saw then that I wouldn't escape them so easily and I thought, They're set on making me their butt. But when you're married the husband's the master, and if that's all right with her it's agreeable to me too. Besides, you can't pass through life unscathed, nor expect to.

I went to her clay house, which was built on the sand, and the whole gang, hollering and chorusing, came after me. They acted like bear-baiters. When we came to the well they stopped all the same. They were afraid to start anything with Elka. Her mouth would open as if it were on a hinge, and she had a fierce tongue. I entered the house. Lines were strung from wall to wall and clothes were drying. Barefoot she stood by the tub, doing the wash. She was dressed in a worn hand-me-down gown of plush. She had her hair put up in braids and pinned across her head. It took my breath away, almost, the reek of it all.

Evidently she knew who I was. She took a look at me and said, "Look who's here! He's come, the drip. Grab a seat."

I told her all; I denied nothing. "Tell me the truth," I said, "are you really a virgin, and is that mischievous Yechiel actually your little brother? Don't be deceitful with me, for I'm an orphan."

"I'm an orphan myself," she answered, "and whoever tries to twist you up, may the end of his nose take a twist. But don't let them think they can take advantage of me. I want a dowry of fifty guilders, and let them take up a collection besides. Otherwise they can kiss my you-know-what." She was very plain-spoken. I said, "It's the bride and not the groom who gives a dowry." Then she said, "Don't bargain with me. Either a flat 'yes' or a flat 'no'—go back where you came from."

I thought, No bread will ever be baked from *this* dough. But ours is not a poor town. They consented to everything and proceeded with the wedding. It so happened that there was a dysentery epidemic at the time. The ceremony was held at the cemetery gates, near the little corpse-washing hut. The fellows got drunk. While the marriage contract was being drawn up I heard the most pious high rabbi ask, "Is the bride a widow or a divorced woman?" And the sexton's wife answered for her, "Both a widow and divorced." It was a black moment for me. But what was I to do, run away from under the marriage canopy?

There was singing and dancing. An old granny danced opposite me, hugging a braided white *chalah*. The master of revels made a "God 'a mercy" in memory of the bride's parents. The schoolboys threw burrs, as on *Tishe b'Av* fast day. There were a lot of gifts after the sermon: a noodle board, a kneading trough, a bucket, brooms, ladles, household articles galore. Then I took a look and saw two strapping young men carrying a crib. "What do we need this for?" I asked. So they said, "Don't rack your brains about it. It's all right, it'll come in handy." I realized I was going to be rooked. Take it another way though, what did I stand to lose? I reflected, I'll see what comes of it. A whole town can't go altogether crazy.

2.

The Jewish Marriage, Ilex Bellers, 20th century. Private Collection/ Bridgeman Art Library, London.

At night I came where my wife lay, but she wouldn't let me in. "Say, look here, is this what they married us for?" I said. And she said, "My monthly has come." "But yesterday they took you to the ritual bath, and that's afterward, isn't it supposed to be?" "Today isn't yesterday," said she, "and yesterday's not today. You can beat it if you don't like it." In short, I waited.

Not four months later she was in childbed. The townsfolk hid their laughter with their knuckles. But what could I do? She

suffered intolerable pains and clawed at the walls. "Gimpel," she cried, "I'm going. Forgive me!" The house filled with women. They were boiling pans of water. The screams rose to the welkin.

The thing to do was to go to the House of Prayer to repeat Psalms, and that was what I did.

The townsfolk liked that, all right. I stood in a corner saying Psalms and prayers, and they shook their heads at me. "Pray, pray!" they told me. "Prayer never made any woman pregnant." One of the congregation put a straw to my mouth and said, "Hay for the cows." There was something to that too, by God!

She gave birth to a boy. Friday at the synagogue the sexton stood up before the Ark, pounded on the reading table, and announced, "The wealthy Reb Gimpel invites the congregation to a feast in honor of the birth of a son." The whole House of Prayer rang with laughter. My face was flaming. But there was nothing I could do. After all, I *was* the one responsible for the circumcision honors and rituals.

Half the town came running. You couldn't wedge another soul in. Women brought peppered chick-peas, and there was a keg of beer from the tavern. I ate and drank as much as anyone, and they all congratulated me. Then there was a circumcision, and I named the boy after my father, may he rest in peace. When all were gone and I was left with my wife alone, she thrust her head through the bed-curtain and called me to her.

"Gimpel," said she, "why are you silent? Has your ship gone and sunk?"

"What shall I say?" I answered. "A fine thing you've done to me! If my mother had known of it she'd have died a second time."

She said, "Are you crazy, or what?"

"How can you make such a fool," I said, "of one who should be the lord and master?"

"What's the matter with you?" she said. "What have you taken it into your head to imagine?"

I saw that I must speak bluntly and openly. "Do you think this is the way to use an orphan?" I said. "You have borne a bastard."

She answered, "Drive this foolishness out of your head. The child is yours."

"How can he be mine?" I argued. "He was born seventeen weeks after the wedding."

She told me then that he was premature. I said, "Isn't he a little too premature?" She said she had had a grandmother who carried just as short a time and she resembled this grandmother of hers as one drop of water does another. She swore to it with such oaths that you would have believed a peasant at the fair if he had used them. To tell the plain truth, I didn't believe her; but when I talked it over next day with the schoolmaster he told me that the very same thing had happened to Adam and Eve. Two they went up to bed, and four they descended.

"There isn't a woman in the world who is not the granddaughter of Eve," he said.

That was how it was—they argued me dumb. But then, who really knows how such things are?

I began to forget my sorrow. I loved the child madly, and he loved me too. As soon as he saw me he'd wave his little hands and want me to pick him up, and when he was colicky I was the only one who could pacify him. I bought him a little bone teething ring and a little gilded cap. He was forever catching the evil eye from someone, and then I had to run to get one of those abracadabras for him that would get him out of it. I worked like an ox. You know how expenses go up when there's an infant in the house. I don't want to lie about it; I didn't dislike Elka either, for that matter. She swore at me and cursed, and I couldn't get enough of her. What strength she had! One of her looks could rob you of the power of speech. And her orations! Pitch and sulphur, that's what they were full of, and yet somehow also full of charm. I adored her every word. She gave me bloody wounds though.

In the evening I brought her a white loaf as well as a dark one, and also poppyseed rolls I baked myself. I thieved because of her and swiped everything I could lay hands on, macaroons, raisins, almonds, cakes. I hope I may be forgiven for stealing from the Saturday pots the women left to warm in the baker's oven. I would take out scraps of meat, a chunk of pudding, a chicken leg or head, a piece of tripe, whatever I could nip quickly. She ate and became fat and handsome.

I had to sleep away from home all during the week, at the bakery. On Friday nights when I got home she always made an excuse of some sort. Either she had heartburn, or a stitch in the side, or hiccups, or headaches. You know what women's excuses are. I had a bitter time of it. It was rough. To add to it, this little brother of hers, the bastard, was growing bigger. He'd put lumps on me, and when I wanted to hit back she'd open her mouth and curse so powerfully I saw a green haze floating before my eyes. Ten times a day she threatened to divorce me. Another man in my place would have taken French leave and disappeared. But I'm the type that bears it and says nothing. What's one to do? Shoulders are from God, and burdens too.

One night there was a calamity in the bakery; the oven burst, and we almost had a fire. There was nothing to do but go home, so I went home. Let me, I thought, also taste the joy of sleeping in bed in mid-week. I didn't want to wake the sleeping mite and tiptoed into the house. Coming in, it seemed to me that I heard not the snoring of one but, as it were, a double snore, one a thin enough snore and the other like the snoring of a slaughtered ox. Oh, I didn't like that! I didn't like it at all. I went up to the bed, and things suddenly turned black. Next to Elka lay a man's form. Another in my place would have made an uproar, and enough noise to rouse the whole town, but the thought occurred to me that I might wake the child. A little thing like

that—why frighten a little swallow like that, I thought. All right then, I went back to the bakery and stretched out on a sack of flour, and till morning I never shut an eye. I shivered as if I had had malaria. "Enough of being a donkey," I said to myself. "Gimpel isn't going to be a sucker all his life. There's a limit even to the foolishness of a fool like Gimpel."

In the morning I went to the rabbi to get advice, and it made a great commotion in the town. They sent the beadle for Elka right away. She came, carrying the child. And what do you think she did? She denied it, denied everything, bone and stone! "He's out of his head," she said. "I know nothing of dreams or divinations." They yelled at her, warned her, hammered on the table, but she stuck to her guns: it was a false accusation, she said.

The butchers and the horse-traders took her part. One of the lads from the slaughterhouse came by and said to me, "We've got our eye on you, you're a marked man." Meanwhile the child started to bear down and soiled itself. In the rabbinical court there was an Ark of the Covenant, and they couldn't allow that, so they sent Elka away.

I said to the rabbi, "What shall I do?"

"You must divorce her at once," said he.

"And what if she refuses?" I asked.

He said, "You must serve the divorce, that's all you'll have to do."

I said, "Well, all right, Rabbi. Let me think about it."

"There's nothing to think about," said he. "You mustn't remain under the same roof with her."

"And if I want to see the child?" I asked.

"Let her go, the harlot," said he, "and her brood of bastards with her."

The verdict he gave was that I mustn't even cross her threshold—never again, as long as I should live.

During the day it didn't bother me so much. I thought, It was bound to happen, the abcess had to burst. But at night when I stretched out upon the sacks I felt it all very bitterly. A longing took me, for her and for the child. I wanted to be angry, but that's my misfortune exactly, I don't have it in me to be really angry. In the first place—this was how my thoughts went—there's bound to be a slip sometimes. You can't live without errors. Probably that lad who was with her led her on and gave her presents and what not, and women are often long on hair and short on sense, and so he got around her. And then since she denies it so, maybe I was only seeing things? Hallucinations do happen. You see a figure or a mannikin or something, but when you come up closer it's nothing, there's not a thing there. And if that's so, I'm doing her an

injustice. And when I got so far in my thoughts I started to weep. I sobbed so that I wet the flour where I lay. In the morning I went to the rabbi and told him that I had made a mistake. The rabbi wrote on with his quill, and he said that if that were so he would have to reconsider the whole case. Until he had finished I wasn't to go near my wife, but I might send her bread and money by messenger.

3.

Nine months passed before all the rabbis could come to an agreement. Letters went back and forth. I hadn't realized that there could be so much erudition about a matter like this.

Meantime Elka gave birth to still another child, a girl this time. On the Sabbath I went to the synagogue and invoked a blessing on her. They called me up to the Torah, and I named the child for my mother-in-law, may she rest in peace. The louts and loudmouths of the town who came into the bakery gave me a going over. All Frampol refreshed its spirits because of my trouble and grief. However, I resolved that I would always believe what I was told. What's the good of *not* believing? Today it's your wife you don't believe; tomorrow it's God Himself you won't take stock in.

By an apprentice who was her neighbor I sent her daily a corn or a wheat loaf, or a piece of pastry, rolls or bagels, or, when I got the chance, a slab of pudding, a slice of honeycake, or wedding strudel—whatever came my way. The apprentice was a goodhearted lad, and more than once he added something on his own. He had formerly annoyed me a lot, plucking my nose and digging me in the ribs, but when he started to be a visitor to my house he became kind and friendly. "Hey, you, Gimpel," he said to me, "you have a very decent little wife and two fine kids. You don't deserve them."

"But the things people say about her," I said.

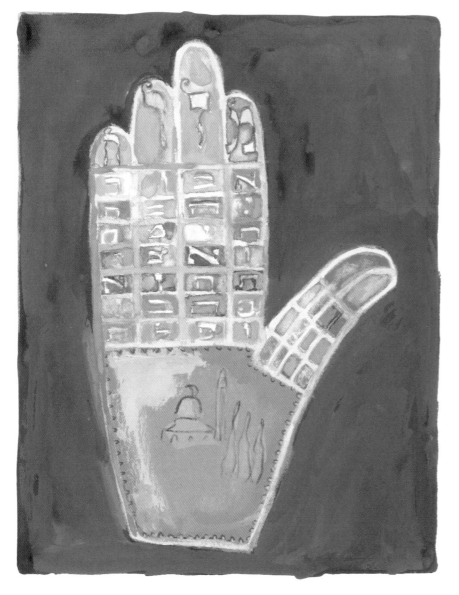

Amulet,
Mark Podwal, 1996.
Collection of Dr. A.
Bernard Ackerman.
Courtesy of Forum
Gallery, NY.

"Well, they have long tongues," he said, "and nothing to do with them but babble. Ignore it as you ignore the cold of last winter."

One day the rabbi sent for me and said, "Are you certain, Gimpel, that you were wrong about your wife?"

I said, "I'm certain."

"Why, but look here! You yourself saw it."

"It must have been a shadow," I said.

"The shadow of what?"

"Just of one of the beams, I think."

"You can go home then. You owe thanks to the Yanover rabbi. He found an obscure reference in Maimonides that favored you."

I seized the rabbi's hand and kissed it.

I wanted to run home immediately. It's no small thing to be separated for so long a time from wife and child. Then I reflected, I'd better go back to work now, and go home in the evening. I said nothing to anyone, although as far as my heart was concerned it was like one of the Holy Days. The women teased and twitted me as they did every day, but my thought was, Go on, with your loose talk. The truth is out, like the oil upon the water. Maimonides says it's right, and therefore it is right!

At night, when I had covered the dough to let it rise, I took my share of bread and a little sack of flour and started homeward. The moon was full and the stars were glistening, something to terrify the soul. I hurried onward, and before me darted a long shadow. It was winter, and a fresh snow had fallen. I had a mind to sing, but it was growing late and I didn't want to wake the householders. Then I felt like whistling, but remembered that you don't whistle at night because it brings the demons out. So I was silent and walked as fast as I could.

Dogs in the Christian yards barked at me when I passed, but I thought, Bark your teeth out! What are you but mere dogs? Whereas I am a man, the husband of a fine wife, the father of promising children.

As I approached the house my heart started to pound as though it were the heart of a criminal. I felt no fear, but my heart went thump! thump! Well, no drawing back. I quietly lifted the latch and went in. Elka was asleep. I looked at the infant's cradle. The shutter was closed, but the moon forced its way through the cracks. I saw the newborn child's face and loved it as soon as I saw it—immediately—each tiny bone.

Then I came nearer to the bed. And what did I see but the apprentice lying there beside Elka. The moon went out all at once. It was utterly black, and I trembled. My teeth chattered. The bread fell from my hands and my wife waked and said, "Who is that, ah?"

I muttered, "It's me."

"Gimpel?" she asked. "How come you're here? I thought it was forbidden."

"The rabbi said," I answered and shook as with a fever.

"Listen to me, Gimpel," she said, "go out to the shed and see if the goat's all right. It seems she's been sick." I have forgotten to say that we had a goat. When I heard she was unwell I went into the yard. The nannygoat was a good little creature. I had a nearly human feeling for her.

With hesitant steps I went up to the shed and opened the door. The goat stood there on her four feet. I felt her everywhere, drew her by the horns, examined her udders, and found nothing wrong. She had probably eaten too much bark. "Good night, little goat," I said. "Keep well." And the little beast answered with a "Maa" as though to thank me for the good will.

I went back. The apprentice had vanished.

"Where," I asked, "is the lad?"

"What lad?" my wife answered.

"What do you mean?" I said. "The apprentice. You were sleeping with him."

"The things I have dreamed this night and the night before," she said, "may they come true and lay you low, body and soul! An evil spirit has taken root in you and dazzles your sight." She screamed out, "You hateful creature! You moon calf! You spook! You uncouth mane! Get out, or I'll scream all Frampol out of bed!"

Before I could move, her brother sprang out from behind the oven and struck me a blow on the back of the head. I thought he had broken my neck. I felt that something about me was deeply wrong, and I said, "Don't make a scandal. All that's needed now is that people should accuse me of raising spooks and *dybbuks*." For that was what she had meant. "No one will touch bread of my baking."

In short, I somehow calmed her.

"Well," she said, "that's enough. Lie down, and be shattered by wheels."

Next morning I called the apprentice aside. "Listen here, brother!" I said. And so on and so forth. "What do you say?" He stared at me as though I had dropped from the roof or something.

"I swear," he said, "you'd better go to an herb doctor or some healer. I'm afraid you have a screw loose, but I'll hush it up for you." And that's how the thing stood.

To make a long story short, I lived twenty years with my wife. She bore me six children, four daughters and two sons. All kinds of things happened, but I neither saw nor heard. I believed, and that's all. The rabbi recently said to me, "Belief in itself is beneficial. It is written that a good man lives by his faith."

Suddenly my wife took sick. It began with a trifle, a little growth upon the breast. But she evidently was not destined to live long; she had no years. I spent a fortune on her. I have forgotten to say that by this time I had a bakery of my own and in Frampol was considered to be something of a rich man. Daily the healer came, and every witch doctor in the neighborhood was brought. They decided to use leeches, and after that to try cupping. They even called a doctor from Lublin, but it

was too late. Before she died she called me to her bed and said, "Forgive me, Gimpel."

I said, "What is there to forgive? You have been a good and faithful wife."

"Woe, Gimpel!" she said. "It was ugly how I deceived you all these years. I want to go clean to my Maker, and so I have to tell you that the children are not yours."

If I had been clouted on the head with a piece of wood it couldn't have bewildered me more.

"Whose are they?" I asked.

"I don't know," she said, "there were a lot. . . . But they're not yours." And as she spoke she tossed her head to the side, her eyes turned glassy, and it was all up with Elka. On her whitened lips there remained a smile.

I imagined that, dead as she was, she was saying, "I deceived Gimpel. That was the meaning of my brief life. . . ."

One night, when the period of mourning was done, as I lay dreaming on the flour sacks, there came the Spirit of Evil himself and said to me, "Gimpel, why do you sleep?"

I said, "What should I be doing? Eating *kreplach*?"

"The whole world deceives you," he said, "and you ought to deceive the world in your turn."

"How can I deceive all the world?" I asked him.

He answered, "You might accumulate a bucket of urine every day and at night pour it into the dough. Let the sages of Frampol eat filth."

"What about judgment in the world to come?" I said.

"There is no world to come," he said. "They've sold you a bill of goods and talked you into believing you carried a cat in your belly. What nonsense!"

"Well then," I said, "and is there a God?"

He answered, "There is no God either."

"What," I said, "is there, then?"

"A thick mire."

He stood before my eyes with a goatish beard and horns, long-toothed, and with a tail. Hearing such words, I wanted to snatch him by the tail, but I tumbled from the flour sacks and nearly broke a rib. Then it happened that I had to answer the call of nature, and, passing, I saw the risen dough, which seemed to say to me, "Do it!" In brief, I let myself be persuaded.

At dawn the apprentice came. We kneaded the bread, scattered caraway seeds on it, and set it to bake. Then the apprentice went away, and I was left sitting in the little trench by the oven, on a pile of rags. Well, Gimpel, I thought, you've revenged yourself on them for all the shame they've put on you. Outside the frost glittered, but it was

warm beside the oven. The flames heated my face. I bent my head and fell into a doze.

I saw in a dream, at once, Elka in her shroud. She called to me, "What have you done, Gimpel?"

I said to her, "It's all your fault," and started to cry.

"You fool!" she said. "You fool! Because I was false is everything false too? I never deceived anyone but myself. I'm paying for it all, Gimpel. They spare you nothing here."

I looked at her face. It was black. I was startled and waked, and remained sitting dumb. I sensed that everything hung in the balance. A false step now and I'd lose Eternal Life. But God gave me His help. I seized the long shovel and took out the loaves, carried them into the yard, and started to dig a hole in the frozen earth.

My apprentice came back as I was doing it. "What are you doing, boss?" he said, and grew pale as a corpse.

"I know what I'm doing," I said, and I buried it all before his very eyes.

Then I went home, took my hoard from its hiding place, and divided it among the children. "I saw your mother tonight," I said. "She's turning black, poor thing."

They were so astounded they couldn't speak a word.

"Be well," I said, "and forget that such a one as Gimpel ever existed." I put on my short coat, a pair of boots, took the bag that held my prayer shawl in one hand, my stick in the other, and kissed the *mezzuzah*. When people saw me in the street they were greatly surprised.

"Where are you going?" they said.

I answered, "Into the world." And so I departed from Frampol.

I wandered over the land, and good people did not neglect me. After many years I became old and white; I heard a great deal, many lies and falsehoods, but the longer I lived the more I understood that there were really no lies. Whatever doesn't really happen is dreamed at night. It happens to one if it doesn't happen to another, tomorrow if not today, or a century hence if not next year. What difference can it make? Often I heard tales of which I said, "Now this is a thing that cannot happen." But before a year had elapsed I heard that it actually had come to pass somewhere.

Going from place to place, eating at strange tables, it often happens that I spin yarns—improbable things that could never have happened—about devils, magicians, windmills, and the like. The children run after

Torah Finial (Rimmonim), Johann Jacob Leschhorn, Frankfurt, 1769–87. From the HUC Skirball Cultural Center and Museum, Los Angeles, CA. Gift of the Jewish Cultural Reconstruction, Inc.

me, calling, "Grandfather, tell us a story." Sometimes they ask for particular stories, and I try to please them. A fat young boy once said to me, "Grandfather, it's the same story you told us before." The little rogue, he was right.

So it is with dreams too. It is many years since I left Frampol, but as soon as I shut my eyes I am there again. And whom do you think I see? Elka. She is standing by the wash-tub, as at our first encounter, but her face is shining and her eyes are as radiant as the eyes of a saint, and she speaks outlandish words to me, strange things. When I wake I have forgotten it all. But while the dream lasts I am comforted. She answers all my queries, and what comes out is that all is right. I weep and implore, "Let me be with you." And she consoles me and tells me to be patient. The time is nearer than it is far. Sometimes she strokes and kisses me and weeps upon my face. When I awaken I feel her lips and taste the salt of her tears.

No doubt the world is entirely an imaginary world, but it is only once removed from the true world. At the door of the hovel where I lie, there stands the plank on which the dead are taken away. The gravedigger Jew has his spade ready. The grave waits and the worms are hungry; the shrouds are prepared—I carry them in my beggar's sack. Another *shnorrer* is waiting to inherit my bed of straw. When the time comes I will go joyfully. Whatever may be there, it will be real, without complication, without ridicule, without deception. God be praised: there even Gimpel cannot be deceived.

REB EISIK'S TREASURE

—*BY JIRI LANGER*, translated by Stephen Jolly

Long, long ago—Reb Simche Binem related—there lived at Cracow a devout scholar, Reb Eisik Yekls by name. Reb Eisik Yekls lived in direst poverty and was totally unable to better his lot. "Only a miracle can help me," he used to say. One night he heard a mysterious voice in his dream: "Eisik! Eisik! An infinitely precious treasure is destined to be yours. Go to the city of the Kings of the Czech Lands, which is called Prague. When you are there, look under the Stone Bridge which arches over the River Vltava!" Eisik Yekls was not a superstitious person. He was familiar with the Talmud and had learnt from it that what a person thought about for days on end he would also dream about at night. But his dream returned a second night and then a third. So Reb Eisik knew that his dream was no ordinary dream and that the voice he had heard was inspired by the Angel of Dreams. He therefore took his stick and set out on his journey.

In the Jewish Quarter Kazimlesz in Cracow, c. 1800. Erich Lessing/ Art Resource, NY.

My Village,
Issachar Ryback, 1917.
The Ryback Museum,
Bat-Yam, Israel.

In those days the road from Cracow to Prague was a bad and dangerous one. But it was worse still if a man's conscience was burdened by the thought that he was leaving his dear ones in hunger and misery and going after a dream.

But when after his long and arduous pilgrimage he stood on a hill, covered with green trees, and saw in front of him a glorious castle on a high mountain and under the castle a town spread out on both banks of a wide river, and when he glimpsed a mighty bridge, built throughout of stone, Eisik's heart thumped with joy. He felt that he had reached his goal and that what he saw was Prague: "*Prag hamaatyro, Ir ve-Em be-Yisroel*, Prague, Crown of the World, City and Mother in Israel." It was a city in all respects like that with which the Angel of Dreams had fired his imagination. And Eisik recognized the river as the River Vltava and the stone bridge as that which arched over the treasure of pearls and silver. Indeed he was not mistaken. There were no other bridges over the Vltava in those days.

But the bridge was guarded by soldiers. Eisik Yekls stepped back a little, but after a short while he returned to the bridge and started looking underneath it, seeking a place where he could search for his treasure unnoticed.

The gendarmes caught sight of him. He was seized and led before the commander. When questioned Reb Eisik Yekls held nothing back and informed the guard commander of the secret of his dream. He was not asked his name nor where he came from.

"You fool," exclaimed the officer with a sneer when he heard Eisik's explanation. "I was really unaware that there are such madmen as you among the Jews, who would go wandering off after dreams. If I were to believe in dreams, I should have to go all the way to *Cracow*. I had a dream that there is some wonderful treasure there hidden near the fireplace in a room occupied by a Jew. The name of this Jew was declared to me in my dream. In fact I remember it very well! His name was . . . *Eisik Yekls*. . . . Do you think I'd want to drag my weary body all the way to Cracow to go scratching for treasure near the fireplace of some confounded Jew?! Dreams are lies and deception. Only old women believe in them!"

When the gendarmes released him Reb Eisik gave thanks to the Lord. The matter was settled in a blast of mocking laughter. Eisik returned home without delay and found the treasure near his fireplace.

To this day the synagogue which he subsequently founded at Cracow bears his name. Everybody knows the "Reb Eisik Yekls-Shil (Schule)" at Cracow. The caretaker there will tell you its story.

But Reb Simche Binem, who used to relate the story to every novice who came to study with him, would always add:

"So you see, my boy, there is something of inestimable value which you will always be seeking as in a dream, and which you will probably never find in the whole wide world. Very likely you will not even find it here with me, and yet there is one place where you could find it. . . ."

IT COULD ALWAYS BE WORSE

—EASTERN EUROPEAN FOLKTALE, retold by Nathan Ausubel

The poor Jew had come to the end of his rope. So he went to his rabbi for advice.

"Holy Rabbi!" he cried. "Things are in a bad way with me, and are getting worse all the time! We are poor, so poor, that my wife, my six children, my in-laws and I have to live in a one-room hut. We get in each other's way all the time. Our nerves are frayed and, because we have plenty of troubles, we quarrel. Believe me—my home is a hell and I'd sooner die than continue living this way!"

The rabbi pondered the matter gravely. "My son," he said, "promise to do as I tell you and your condition will improve."

"I promise, Rabbi," answered the troubled man. "I'll do anything you say."

"Tell me—what animals do you own?"

"I have a cow, a goat and some chickens."

"Very well! Go home now and take all these animals into your house to live with you."

The poor man was dumbfounded, but since he had

Seder Towel (Sederzwehl), Alsace, 1821. From the HUC Skirball Cultural Center and Museum, Los Angeles, CA. Gift of Rabbi Folkman.

promised the rabbi, he went home and brought all the animals into his house.

The following day the poor man returned to the rabbi and cried, "Rabbi, what misfortune have you brought upon me! I did as you told me and brought the animals into the house. And now what have I got? Things are worse than ever! My life is a perfect hell—the house is turned into a barn! Save me, Rabbi—help me!"

"My son," replied the rabbi serenely, "go home and take the chickens out of your house. God will help you!"

So the poor man went home and took the chickens out of his house. But it was not long before he again came running to the rabbi.

"Holy Rabbi!" he wailed. "Help me, save me! The goat is smashing everything in the house—she's turning my life into a nightmare."

"Go home," said the rabbi gently, "and take the goat out of the house. God will help you!"

The poor man returned to his house and removed the goat. But it wasn't long before he again came running to the rabbi, lamenting loudly, "What a misfortune you've brought upon my head, Rabbi! The cow has turned my house into a stable! How can you expect a human being to live side by side with an animal?"

"You're right—a hundred times right!" agreed the rabbi. "Go straight home and take the cow out of your house!"

And the poor unfortunate hastened home and took the cow out of his house.

Not a day had passed before he came running again to the rabbi. "Rabbi!" cried the poor man, his face beaming. "You've made life sweet again for me. With all the animals out, the house is so quiet, so roomy, and so clean! What a pleasure!"

D ESPITE THE FAMILIAR CLAIM THAT JUDAISM IS A WORLDLY RELIGION largely uninterested in the afterlife, we get quite a different impression when we turn to Jewish stories. For many ancient Jewish narratives focus on the World to Come, paradise, hell, the Messiah, the End of Days, and resurrection. And in many folk-tales, including those still told in certain contemporary Jewish communities, the Angel of Death is a favorite character. Much of this otherworldly material was originally imported into Judaism from foreign sources—Egyptian, Mesopotamian, and Asian mythology, gnosticism, hellenis-

THE END OF DAYS

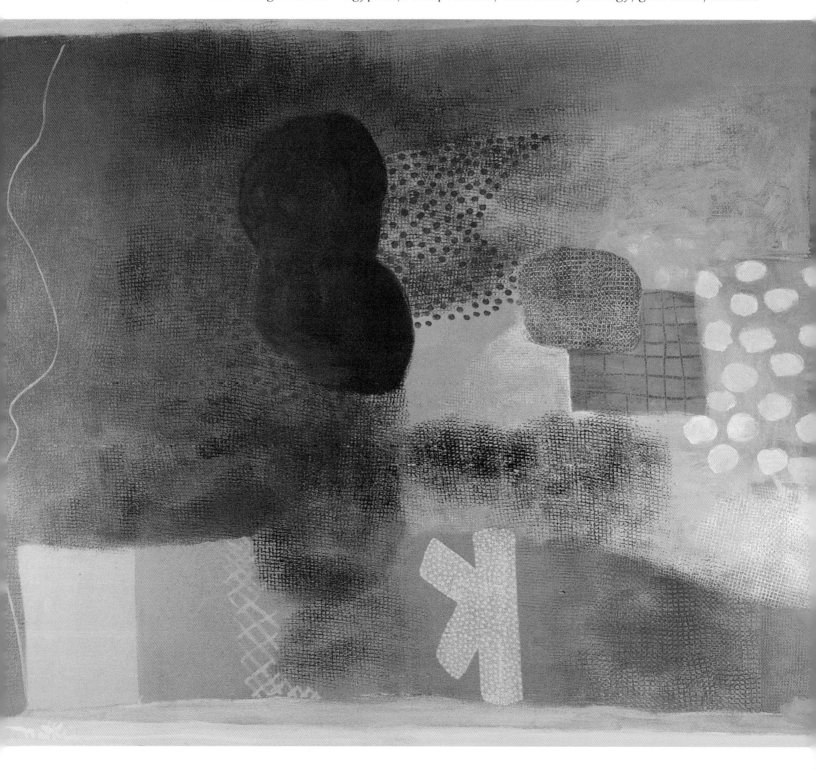

tic philosophy and traditions, and Christian belief—whose cultures were fascinated with death; others focused more on what comes after. Indeed, in a world beset by scarcity, war, disease, and natural disaster, death was a highly respected if not welcome visitor.

But even more dreaded than the end of life was what came after the breath ceased. And it was this universal anxiety that helped religions resolve their greatest difficulty: Why do bad things happen to good people, and good things to bad ones? Religion's answer to this question is known as theodicy, literally, the vindication of God's justice. In many traditions, including Judaism, *theodicy* gives rise to an otherworldly theory of reward and punishment: If the righteous in this world seem to suffer and the wicked to prosper, that is only an illusion, for the scales of justice properly balance out in the next world. Although this notion and the complementary belief that our imperfect world will ulti-

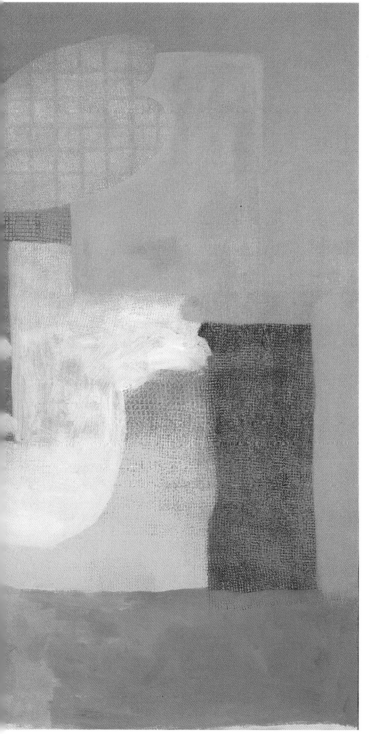

Kaddish,
Robert Natkin, 1992.
Courtesy of the artist.

mately be redeemed in the future have failed to win adherents among most modern Jews, these ideas have succored the faithful for centuries and still remain at the heart of many Jewish tales.

This final section presents eight tales about death and the afterlife. The first two stories, the German folktale "The Bride Who Saved Her Husband from the Angel of Death," and Hayyim Nachman Bialik's version of an ancient Solomon legend, "The Mysterious Palace," transport us to a world where people encounter death in person and even manage to get the upper hand. But in the remaining six stories, set closer to our own day, death is a more elusive presence, sometimes cheating us or changing the familiar rules. Thus, in Kafka's sardonic fable "Before the Law," the long-suffering petitioner at the palace gate only discovers his power to direct his own destiny after he has surrendered that power for good. And in the two Holocaust stories—Elie Wiesel's memoir of his ride in "The Death Train" to Buchenwald and Anna's uncanny encounter with her father's grave in "A Hill in Bergen Belsen"—the young victims have trouble differentiating between the Angel of Death and the Angel of Mercy, because their faces are so much alike. Similarly, in Joseph Opatoshu's "Eternal Wedding Gown," the old woman who has given away her own shroud to bury her cousin rejoices when her friends come to sew her a new one in which to marry her eternal suitor, Death.

Indeed, death has been a constant companion for the "ever-dying Jewish people," as they have been astutely dubbed. Perhaps that is one of the most jealously guarded secrets of their survival. In the final story of this collection, when the Chelm watchman appointed to announce the messiah complains about his inadequate salary, the rabbi explains, "True enough . . . but one must take into account that this is a permanent job."

THE BRIDE WHO SAVED HER HUSBAND FROM THE ANGEL OF DEATH

—GERMAN FOLKTALE, retold by Moses Gaster

Once upon a time there lived a man called Rabbi Reuben. He was a very good and learned man. He studied day and night and the Lord received his prayers with favor, for whenever great danger threatened the people, he averted it by his devout prayer. He had an only son who was a very fine lad. One day the Angel of Death came to Rabbi Reuben and said: "I have been sent by the Lord, blessed be He, to tell you that the time for your son's death has come." He replied: "What God does no man can prevent, but I pray you, let me first marry my son, and then you can do what you have been commanded, but I wish first to have the joy of leading my son under the wedding canopy." The Angel of Death replied: "Your wish is granted to marry your son first." The father went home in sorrow, betrothed his son and fixed the wedding to take place in four weeks. The people wondered at his having fixed the marriage to take place so soon.

Then he sent his son to invite a few people to the wedding ceremony. On his way the son met the Prophet Elijah, who said: "My dear son, where are you going?" He replied: "I am going to invite people to my wedding." The Prophet Elijah said: "Do you not know that you are to die before your wedding and that the Lord wishes to take your soul away, for the time of your death has arrived?" The bridegroom replied: "If that is the will of the Lord, I will submit to it willingly, for I am no better than our fathers Abraham, Isaac and Jacob, who also died." The Prophet Elijah said: "I will give you good advice which you should follow. When the time comes for the blessing and the people are seated round the table, sit down with them, but do not eat or drink, and keep your eyes downcast. A man will come with uncovered head and disheveled hair, and his garments will be torn. As soon as you see him enter the room, get up from the table, go and bow down before him, bid him welcome and invite him to sit at the head of the table among the distinguished guests. And if he refuses to sit at the head of the table, then sit down next to him and show him great honor. Take care to fulfill my instructions." The young man promised to follow his advice and the Prophet Elijah went his way.

The young man invited the people to his wedding and behaved as if nothing had happened. He then returned home to his father and said to him: "I have carried out all your instructions." The father made all the preparations for the wedding, and both father and son behaved as if nothing had happened. People came to the blessing, and sat round the table eating and drinking. The bridegroom sat with them, looking very sad, but no one knew the cause of his sadness. After they had been eating a while, there came into the room a man in tattered garments and bareheaded, looking like a poor man. It was the Angel of Death, who had disguised himself as a poor man, as the Prophet Elijah had foretold the young man. As soon as the bridegroom saw him,

OPPOSITE:

Alefbet-Lexicon, no.6 (detail),

Grisha Bruskin, 1989.

© 1997 Grisha Bruskin/

Licensed by VAGA, NY/

Courtesy of Marlborough

Gallery, NY.

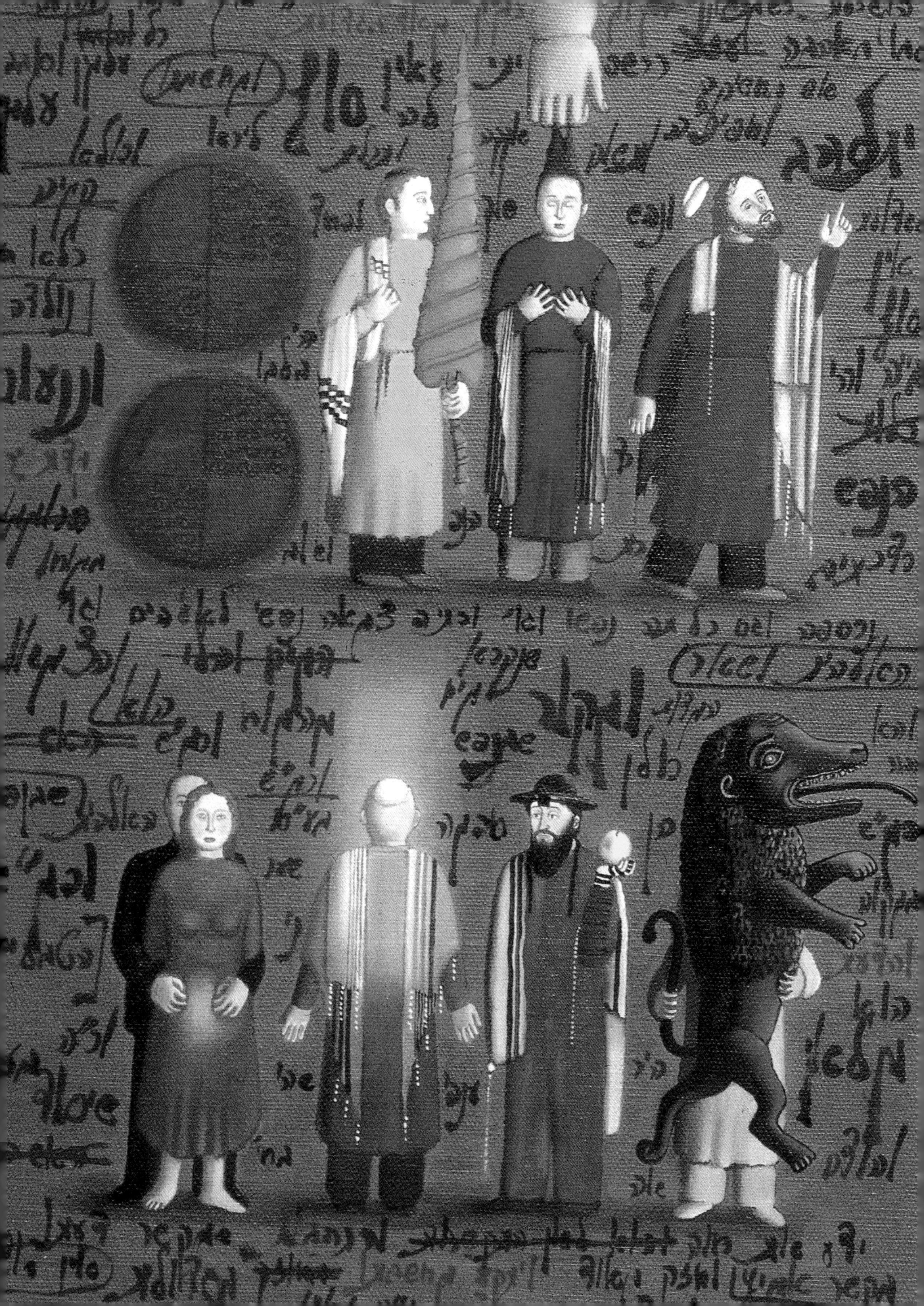

he at once knew who he was. Accordingly he rose from his seat, went up to the old man, took him by the hand and said: "Come with me and sit at the head of the table." The old man refused. So the bridegroom took the shabby old man by the hand, placed him by his own side at the table and brought all kinds of good food, which the old man pretended to eat. The bridegroom did exactly as the Prophet Elijah had told him. The people who were sitting at the table were greatly surprised at the honor the bridegroom paid to the poor man. The bridegroom, on the other hand, was so frightened that he could scarcely speak.

Then the poor man said to the bridegroom: "My dear son, I wish to ask you a question. If you are building a house and are in need of straw to mix with the clay, whence do you get the straw?" The young man replied: "I go to the man in the barn and buy the straw from him, for he makes the straw." Then the old man said: "But suppose after you have made use of the straw, the man came from the barn and asked to have the straw back, what would you do?" The bridegroom replied: "I would pay him for the straw, or I would give him other straw instead." The old man continued: "But suppose the man insisted on having his own straw and refused to accept any other, what would you do?" The young man replied: "I would break up the clay and take out the straw and give it back to him." Then the old man said: "The Lord, blessed be He, is the master of the barn. The straw is the soul of man, and I am the Angel of Death. The Lord is asking for the straw which He gave you and refuses to accept any other straw. Therefore I am here to take your soul."

When the people heard this, they were all very much frightened, but the young man recovered from his fright and said to him: "If it is the will of God that I should die, then pray allow me first to see my father and my mother and my dear bride, and bid them farewell, then I shall willingly die." The Angel of Death said: "Very well, go." The young man went to his father and mother and to the bride and took leave of them amid great weeping. The father began to pray. Meanwhile the bridegroom went to the bride to bid her farewell, and she said to him: "Who is it that wants to take your soul?" The bridegroom replied: "The Angel of Death is here and wants to take my life." And he kissed her and wept. Then the bride said: "Stay here, and I will go to the Angel of Death." She went to him and said: "Are you the man who wants to take my bridegroom's soul?" He replied: "Yes, I am the man." Then the bride said: "Then I ask you to go back to God and say to Him: 'Is it not written in the Holy Law that a man who takes a wife shall be free for a whole year to rejoice with the wife he has taken' (Deut. 24:5), and now will the Lord, blessed be He, violate His own law?" When the Angel of Death heard this, he felt pity for them and went before the Lord and begged for his life, and the other angels joined in the prayer, and the father also prayed fervently. The Lord took pity on him and prolonged his life seven years, corresponding to the seven days of the wedding festivity. This is the meaning of the verse: "The Lord does the will of them who fear Him and call on Him with their whole heart" (Ps. 145:19). God saves them from all pain.

Cup of Elijah for the Tarnov Burial Society, Berlin, 18th century. The Jewish Museum, NY/ Art Resource, NY.

THE MYSTERIOUS PALACE

—*BY HAYYIM NACHMAN BIALIK*, translated by Herbert Danby

King Solomon ruled over the whole earth— over the dry land and over the sea and over the wings of the wind. And God gave to Solomon a magic cloak. On this he could rise up on the wings of the wind and roam to and fro like a bird whithersoever he would. And the cloak was very large. It was forty miles long and forty miles wide. It was made of green silk interwoven with gold, and pictures of everything in the world were embroidered upon it—the plants of the field and the beasts of the earth, the fowls of the air and the fishes of the sea. Four captains were appointed to keep watch over the cloak at its four corners: Asaph son of Berechiah was captain over the sons of men, Remirat was captain over the demons, the lion was captain over the beasts of the field, and the eagle was captain over all winged creatures.

And Solomon went up into the cloak and sat upon his throne, and all his captains and his servants and his mighty men went up with him, a very great multitude, and they stood in their places before the King, according to their custom.

Then would Solomon command the wind, saying,

Come, O wind, and bear us away!

And the cloak, together with all its burden was lifted up by the wind, and it floated in the firmament whithersoever the King desired. It

Planning King Solomon's Temple, Jack Levine, 1940. Collection Israel Museum, Jerusalem. © 1997 Jack Levine/ Licensed by VAGA, NY.

flew over countries and seas, soaring over forests and deserts, and the King could turn it in whatsoever direction he pleased. His morning meal he could eat in Damascus, at one end of the earth, and his evening meal in Media, at the other end of the earth.

One day it happened that the King with all his captains and his servants was journeying on the cloak which, like an eagle, was lifted up into the high places of the firmament. And the sun shone upon it in all its splendor and its glory. And Solomon bent down to see, and lo, the earth beneath was growing smaller and smaller, until it seemed to him no bigger than a pumpkin.

And his pride grew very great, and he said, "Can there be in all the world a king as wise and clever as I!"

Scarce had the word left his mouth when the wind veered, and many of the King's servants were shaken off the cloak. And the King was very wroth, and he called out in his anger,

Return, O wind!

But the wind answered, "Nay! Do thou, rather, return unto thy God, and let not thy heart grow so proud!"

And Solomon was put to shame by the words of the wind, and he bowed his head and was dumb. . . .

The cloak sped onwards and passed over lands and seas and for ten days and ten nights it soared between earth and sky. One day King Solomon looked down upon the earth and, behold, a high palace loomed up from the earth. Now the palace was very magnificent: it was built all of gold and its pillars and its walls and its roof were all of pure gold.

Solomon gazed on the glory of the palace and longed to look within it. And he said to the wind,

Descend, O wind!

Illustration from a Haggadah, Moravia, 1729. Scala/Art Resource, NY.

And the cloak came down to the ground. Then King Solomon turned aside to see the palace; and the captain, Asaph, son of Berechiah, went with him. They looked at the palace from round about, and lo, it was desolate, overgrown with grass and bushes and tall weeds, without any road or pathway. Yet the scent of the grass was in their nostrils like the sweet-smelling savor of the Garden of Eden, exceedingly pleasant. They continued to walk round about the palace seeking some door or entrance, but none could anywhere be found. And they were amazed and mystified.

While they were gazing at the palace, the captain of the demons went up to the roof. There he found a large and very old eagle, crouching over its nestlings. He came back to declare the matter to the King. And the King commanded the chief captain that was over the birds to bring down the old eagle and to set it before him. The eagle opened its mouth and sang a song of praise to God, and then it bowed down before the King, and greeted him and wished him well.

The King sought to know its name and the number of its years.

"My name is Alanad," the eagle answered, "and my years are seven hundred years."

And the King said,

"Perchance thou knowest or hast heard: if there is a way into this palace tell me where it is."

"As my soul liveth and as the soul of my lord the King liveth, I surely do not know," the eagle answered. "But I have an elder brother who is two hundred years older than I, and his name is Alof. Ask him: it may be that he knoweth. Lo, he sitteth on the roof, on the second pinnacle."

So the eagle returned to its own place and its elder brother was brought in its stead.

And the King asked,

"Perchance thou knowest or hast heard: where is the entrance to the palace?"

The second eagle also answered according to the words of the first, and said,

"As my soul liveth and as thy soul liveth, my lord the King, I surely do not know. But I have an elder brother who is four hundred years older than I, and his name is Altaamar. Ask him, and he will tell thee; for he is wise and knoweth all things. Lo, he sitteth on the roof, on the third pinnacle."

And this eagle likewise returned to its own place, and the captain that was over all winged creatures went to fetch the third eagle. It was the most ancient of them all and exceedingly heavy, and by reason of its

age it could not fly. And the captain of the birds bore it on his wings and brought it before Solomon.

And the King asked,

"Dost thou know, or hast thou heard, where is the entrance to this palace?"

And in a quavering voice the aged eagle answered and said,

"As my soul liveth and as the soul of my lord the King liveth, never in my life have I known or seen any entrance. But my grandfather told me that there assuredly was a way into the palace, and that it was in a cave below the ground on the western side. But in the course of many years earth had covered it and blocked it up. Let the King dig there: it may be that he will find it."

And the King commanded the spirits and the demons and they dug near to the palace in the place whereof the aged eagle had spoken. There they found an iron door, eaten away by the rust of years. On the door was a heavy lock and on it these words were inscribed:

Know, ye sons of men, that for many years we dwelt in this palace, and it was well with us and we sated ourselves with pleasure. But famine came upon us and though we ground up precious stones like wheat it availed us naught. So we abandoned our wealth to the eagles and commanded them saying, If any man ask you concerning this palace ye shall say, We found it built. Then lay we down on the ground and died.

And Solomon and his men lifted up their eyes above the door and there they found written:

Let none enter hither save a Prophet or a King.

To the right of the door in a hole in the wall Solomon found a crystal casket and in it

was a bundle of keys, four in number: one was of iron, another of brass, another of silver, and another of gold.

Then Solomon opened the gate of iron and he found a gate of brass. He opened this also and he found another gate of silver; and, after that, a gate of gold.

And it was so that when he had opened the gate of gold, he came into a lofty and spacious hall whose walls were of crystal, its pillars of gold, and its pavements mosaic work in alabaster and marble. Its vaulted ceiling was made from plates of sapphire, pure as the very sky, and set therein were precious stones, rubies and onyx and jasper, shining like stars.

Hanging on the wall he saw a cluster of jewels, carnelian and chrysolite and emerald, as large as eggs, whose like could not be found in the crown of any king. Moreover in the middle of the hall he beheld a small dome encrusted with jewels and overlaid with all kinds of precious pearls, most delicate and graceful in appearance, like the edges of small clouds when they grow pale at sunset.

He entered a second chamber wherein was no window or outlet, and no lamp or light; fiery stones alone lightened the darkness, suffusing it with numerous and variegated glints—shades of red and green and white and blue and amber. In the corners of the chamber lay precious stones like heaps of coals, glowing and flaming in the deep darkness.

Solomon entered yet a third chamber, and there he saw a pool, wholly paved with pure crystal, sparkling as though it were ripples of pure water, with small golden fishes darting to and fro. The rim of the pool was encrusted with precious stones and pearls.

Then he came to chambers of silver, chambers of gold, and chambers of most fine gold. And as he went from one chamber to another his eyes could not grow weary from the sight.

And it came to pass that when he entered into a certain chamber he saw a silver scorpion crouching on the pavement. He kicked it to thrust it aside. Straightway the pavement heaved—and Solomon found himself in a region below the palace.

Here were secret chambers of quite other shape and form, perfect in beauty and majestic in appearance.

Finally in the farthest parts he reached a great chamber, the most magnificent and beautiful of them all. And Solomon stood at the entrance and felt that he was in a dream. Lifting up his eyes he looked, and, behold, before him, sitting on an ivory throne, was a lifelike human statue. Over its breast, hanging from its neck by a golden chain, was a tablet made of silver. Solomon was about to draw near to it when, of a sudden, the image shook and from its nostrils came out smoke and fire.

Solomon called out the Sacred Name of God . . . and the statue fell to the ground, broken and motionless.

Then Solomon came near and took off the tablet from the statue. On it he found writing in some strange language. He could not read it. He was much distressed for he saw that for all his great wisdom there was still something too wonderful for him. And he could have died by reason of his vexation.

But while he was yet vexed and grieving, behold, a hidden door in the wall suddenly opened and a comely youth appeared. He drew near quietly. His steps gave out no

sound. In silence he took the tablet in his hand. Then with an exceedingly mournful voice he read these words:

I am Shedad, the son of Adar.
Supreme was I among kings of the earth.
Lions and bears were in dread of me.
The world was filled with my majesty and
   my glory.
I ruled over millions of princes;
On millions of horses I rode;
Millions of warriors I slew,
But over the Angel of Death I could not
   prevail.

When the youth had made an end of reading he gave a quiet sigh and tears glistened in his eyes. He turned away and, going silently to the door by which he had entered, he disappeared.

To Solomon it was all like a waking dream. He remained standing there, dumbfounded, for his heart was sorely perturbed and words failed him.

So Solomon returned to his own home. His head was bowed down and his heart subdued and broken. And ever after that day the spirit of pain and desolation brooded over him, and in bitterness of soul he cried,

     Vanity of vanities, all is vanity!

Torah Crown,
Germany, 1771.
From the HUC Skirball
Cultural Center and
Museum, Los Angeles, CA.

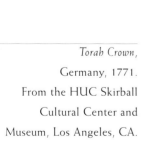

216

THE ETERNAL WEDDING GOWN

—*BY JOSEPH OPATOSHU*, translated by Bernard Guilbert Guerney

D awn was already breaking when the eighty-year-old Glikche Schreiber opened her eyes in fright, only to shut them again.

She could hardly stir. Her every limb seemed dislocated and throbbed with pain; her knuckles and toes felt as if they were coming apart. And hovering on the very verge of her mind was a question that had haunted her all night long: Was Ernestine really dead?

Only now, when Glikche reopened her eyes, did the conviction come that Ernestine had really died on Friday.

What was to be done? Postpone the funeral until Sunday, as was customary in America? In Preschburg, where Glikche's parents, grandparents, and great-grandparents had lived out their days, the custom was quite different. When someone in the family died he or she had to be buried the same day.

But it was already Friday afternoon, and Ernestine had failed to provide so much as a shroud for herself. True, she was a cousin of Glikche's; she was an Eiger, a great-granddaughter of Reb Akiba Eiger himself. But she had gone over to the reformed synagogue all

Female Corpse,
Hyman Bloom, 1945.
The Jewish Museum, NY/
Art Resource NY.

of fifty years ago, back in Preschburg. Ernestine's angel (since every human being has an angel up there, in heaven) had turned a deaf ear to her ever since. He never heard her pleas, since she had strayed so early from the path of true Jewishness. There was her very name: Ernestine! Both cousins had been named Glikche, after the same great-grandmother. Yet one of these Glikches had turned into an Ernestine. And why did she put on such airs, this Ernestine? Just because her husband happened to be an eye specialist? Or because she could speak Hungarian, German, French, and English? Well now, Glikche's husband, a heart specialist, had been a professor in Budapest and, right here in New York, had lectured at Columbia University. And what about

Wedding Dress,
Persia, late 19th century.
The Jewish Museum, NY/
Art Resource, NY.

Glikche herself? She had been more versatile than Ernestine from her very childhood, when it came to languages. Glikche could also interpret a portion of the Pentateuch or a passage from the Psalms. What, then, had made Ernestine so proud that she had to stray from the path of orthodoxy? And her dying, too, had been so very stupid: she hadn't even provided a shroud for herself.

So Glikche had gotten out her own shroud and yielded it to Ernestine. And when they had come back from the cemetery it had been just in time for the lighting of the Sabbath candles. Glikche perceived the graciousness of God in all this and, raising her eyes in gratitude, uttered the name of the Father in Heaven. Streaks of light came through the two windows that overlooked Central Park and fell tremulously on the southern wall of the room, resting uncertainly now on this photograph, now on that. Glikche gazed intently at these brightened faces, framed in old-fashioned beards and earlocks, their wise eyes looking down upon her pensively. Her great-grandfathers, two of them: Reb Moishe Schreiber, the Rabbi of Preschburg, and Rabbi Akiba Eiger, the Rabbi of Posen.

Glikche felt a glow at the sight of them. Nor was it Glikche alone who delighted in these forebears. Her two sons, doctors both, who refrained from writing on the Sabbath, as well as her son-in-law, a wealthy manufacturer who kept his shop closed on that day, also rejoiced in these ancestors. Every Sabbath eve one of her grandsons would drop in on Glikche to pronounce the benediction over the Sabbath wine. The grandson would sleep over and escort her next morning to the synagogue. For that matter, what about her sons and her son-in-law? Why, they would be welcomed in Paradise if only for the way they honored their mother (even the son-in-law called her that).

Glikche was saddened by the rate at which her contemporaries were vanishing. They had departed, one by one. For she had friends whom she had acquired both in Preschburg and in New York, where she had lived for almost threescore years. She ticked off on her fingers those of her friends who were still among the living: Radisch, and Freidche, and Shaindel, and Braindel, and Sorele—may they be spared long!

She had ticked off five names, and could see every one of these friends of hers standing before her, and could tell the age of each. The youngest was in her late sixties, the oldest in her nineties. Her friends were standing in a row, lined up before her, and she pondered: Whose turn would it be next?

Not Freidche's, she knew. The ninety-year-old Freidche was quite a doctor herself. Was there anything she couldn't cure? When someone fell ill she could tell days ahead whether the illness would pass or prove fatal. She had known as far back as last Wednesday that Ernestine was dying.

Glikche had asked her, "Freidche, darling, what do you say?"

And Freidche had replied, "Glikche, you want to know whether the illness is serious? Take a piece of soft bread, wipe the sweat off the patient's brow with it, and throw it to a dog. If the dog will eat it, it's a good sign; if it won't, things are all over for Ernestine."

Glikche had stared at Ernestine's black dog, which refused to budge from the side of its mistress's bed. The dog would not touch the sweat-soaked piece of bread which Freidche tossed to it. Glikche had sworn at the dog and had left Freidche in a huff. Of course the incident had rankled: Freidche could, indeed, foretell things. How did she do it?

The telephone on the night-table began to ring and Glikche picked up the receiver.

"Hello! Radisch? Good morning, Radisch; may we no longer know sorrow! Will you be welcome if you come? Of course! But why so early? I'm still in bed; I haven't said my prayers yet. Come after my morning prayers. All right then, Radisch darling."

What the old lady had forgotten was that in the mornings this friend of hers was a bundle of aches and pains, as if all her bones had been broken.

Glikche got off her bed and called to her maid, "Elizabeth, are you still asleep?"

"Who's sleeping, Missus Schreiber?" The maid, an elderly colored woman, entered the room. "Here I am, ma'am."

"Be a good girl, Elizabeth, and tidy up the room."

"What's the rush, ma'am?"

"We're going to have guests."

"This early?"

The older woman shrugged like a child and smiled. And, as soon as Elizabeth had tidied up the room, Glikche sat down with her prayer book near the southern wall, hung with the photographs of her ancestors. She prayed aloud, in the singsong peculiar to Preschburg, oblivious of the sound of her voice, of the noises which drifted in from the kitchen, where Elizabeth was preparing breakfast.

No sooner had Glikche concluded the Prayer of the Eighteen Benedictions than the doorbell rang. Crowded in the doorway stood Radisch, Freidche, Shaindel, Braindel, and Sorele, wealthy old ladies, all of them, their arms loaded with pastry, delicacies, and bottles of wine. And they had also brought their sewing.

Beaker of the Polin Burial Society, Bohemia, 1691. The Jewish Museum, NY/ Art Resource, NY.

"Good morning, Glikche," they hailed her in chorus.

Surprised, she exchanged kisses with her guests. As they sat down at the table, spreading out the good things they had brought and opening the bottles of wine, they got ready their sewing kits.

Radisch, the oldest among the callers, took a length of Irish linen from her kit and spread it out on the floor. "Glikche, do you know why we have come here today?" she asked. "Your friends have to sew your eternal wedding dress for you. You deserve it, Glikche. You gave your own to Ernestine and were left without one. So we got busy and here we are—"

Old Glikche had tears in her eyes as she embraced one friend after the other; then she sliced a cake and poured out glasses of wine. Her callers drank her health and nibbled at the cake. Radisch, the oldest among them, tried the shroud on Glikche, with all its points and knots.

The old women threaded their needles with long white threads. And as they bent over, sewing the eternal wedding gown, death began to spin its web.

A KINDNESS TO THE DEAD

—BY MICHA JOSEF BERDYCZEWSKI, translated by I. M. Lask

Here is a story of Jerusalem. In former years there was an exceedingly wealthy old man to whom an only son was born in his old age. When the boy was about six years old and could distinguish between good and evil, and his father saw that he was very wise, he decided to keep him away from the vanities of this world—which are but as a passing shadow that is gone—and to teach him only the commandments and Torah of the Lord—from which come the life of this world and the World to Come—in order that he might be an honor and a glory, for his son was more precious to him than all his wealth. So he gave him a special room and a fine tutor to instruct him in the Book of the Torah in its entirety, and the words of Torah did not depart from them by day or by night. He did not withhold any of the dainties of the world nor precious garments in order that the lad should not need to leave his room. Likewise he supplied his tutor with all he might desire. This he did for ten consecutive years. And the boy progressed exceedingly well and became a great and distinguished scholar, versed in the Talmud and the Rabbinical Authorities, which he knew almost by heart, as well as countless other works.

Now his father had become exceedingly ill, and he saw that his son was about seventeen years of age and a mature young man. He said to himself: "My days draw near and the time has come to restore the pawn to its owner. Now what shall I do with all the wealth that will remain in order that all my toil and labor should not prove to be in vain? My only son has never known what is in the house and is not familiar with trade and trafficking. How can I permit my wealth to be lost? Shall my dear son who is the delight of my heart have to hold out his hand for alms?" So he took his son to show him his glorious riches and ample wealth and taught him the nature of trade and trafficking and took him through the markets and the streets and showed him all kinds of wares. Then he said to him: "My son, be wise, and my heart will also rejoice, yet nevertheless let not the Lord's Torah depart from your lips! Torah is good with a knowledge of the world."

The son was exceedingly intelligent and understood one thing from another, and his father rejoiced greatly at his wisdom. And before very long the time to mourn for his sire drew near, for he went the way of all flesh, aged and replete with years.

Then the son took all the wealth he had inherited and set out to go from city to city in order to comprehend the nature and affairs of the world in which he lived. And he went with a considerable purse of money until he came to Constantinople, where he wandered through the markets and the streets. He came to a certain market where he saw a great iron case hanging on a chain with a soldier going before it bearing his weapons in his hand to guard it. The son stood and asked the guard: "What is this?" And he said to him sternly: "Get away with you, it is none of your affair." But he entreated him exceedingly, and after

Sabbath Afternoon (detail),
Moritz Oppenheim,
Germany, 1866.
From the HUC Skirball
Cultural Center and
Museum, Los Angeles, CA.
Gift of the Jewish Cultural
Reconstruction, Inc.

he gave him some money, the guard told him this tale:

"The sultan had a Jewish moneychanger whom he honored exceedingly. But after a great many years the Ishmaelites began to envy him and denounced him to the sultan, saying: 'All his wealth has been stolen from you, and whatever he has to show comes from what is yours.' Then the king sent for him and said: 'Come make an account since bygone years and ever since you have been a head man.' At this the moneychanger began to tremble and his knees knocked together, for who can give a correct account for twenty years and more? Yet his entreaties were of no avail in the day of wrath. When the king saw that by his own account there was a shortage of a very great sum, he grew exceedingly enraged and ordered that he should be put to death. So he was slain and embalmed and placed in this casket until such time as the Jews paid all the money that he had stolen to the very last farthing. Then his body would be released for burial."

When the young man heard this, he could not refrain from asking: "How much was lacking according to the tally?" And the guard said: "So much and so much, a very vast amount." And thereupon the young man went to the royal court and said to those in charge: "I have a secret matter of which I must inform the king." The sultan was told of this and gave him permission to enter. So he appeared before the sultan and uttered the proper blessing that is to be recited in the presence of a monarch, and then saluted him wisely and clearly so that he found exceeding favor in his eyes. And the sultan said to him: "Tell me what you desire and it may be given to you." And the young man answered: "My request is that your slain moneychanger be released for burial, and I shall pay your majesty whatever money may be owing."

The king approved of this and ordered that the poor and innocent moneychanger should be buried, while he took all his father's money and placed it before the sultan. But he requested the sultan to announce throughout the city of Constantinople that any man or woman who did not attend the burial of the moneychanger should be slain. And the king acceded to this request as well, for he approved of the young man, so not a single child was left in his cradle. They all went to the funeral and he was greatly honored and lamented for exceedingly.

A few days later the king sent for the young man and said to him: "One thing I ask of you and do not refuse it." "Indeed," said he, "I am your servant and shall do whatever you command." "My will and desire, then," said the king, "is that you should permit me to inherit the reward of this commandment which you have done." And the young man said to him: "Whatever you say to me I shall do with all my soul, but this is beyond my power, for what is man and what the purpose of his life except to fulfill the commandments of the Lord? All my life long I have regretted that the time has not come for me to perform some great commandment such as this, which will be invaluable even in that day which will last forever. So how can I give its recompense to my lord? For who knows whether an opportunity for fulfilling such a commandment will come again throughout the days of my life, no matter how wealthy I may become."

The king and the ministers approved of this, and they saw how wise he was. And the king went walking with him through the gardens and showed him all his fine estate and permitted him to depart in peace.

From there he departed and went from city to city, and a few years later boarded a ship in order to return home. Now it came about that there was an exceedingly great storm, and the sea rose and tossed until the ship was wrecked, and they all fell into the depths of the sea. And when the young man found himself in these perilous waters, it seemed to him that a great stone pillar emerged and led him to the seashore. He mounted to the dry land where he sat alone on the shore weeping bitterly. For he did not know what his end might be or where he was. Then he raised his eyes aloft and saw a great white eagle that came flying. It descended and stood beside him and began twittering and crying for maybe a full hour. Then he understood that this could not be a trifle but this must be some messenger of the All and Ever Present. Full of trust in His Blessed Name, he mounted the back of the eagle, which spread its wings at once and rose. Within a few moments it brought him to Jerusalem and set him in his own courtyard. Then it rose again and vanished. In the dark of the night he saw before him a man clad in white, and he trembled exceedingly. But the man touched him and said: "Have no fear. I am the moneychanger for whom you did that last true kindness and therefore I delivered you from death. I was the stone pillar and I was the eagle. Happy are you in this world, and it will be well with you in the World to Come. Your reward is very great indeed. Vast is the good that lies in wait for the righteous and the saints, and it is hid in store for you as well. No man has seen God except you."

Until the day of his death he was wealthy and honored and lived at ease. He saw the third generation of his offspring, and he engaged in the Torah of Moses by day and night and saw God in all truth, being most charitable and munificent in his distribution of charity to Israel.

BEFORE THE LAW

—*BY FRANZ KAFKA*, translated by Willa and Edwin Muir

Synagogue Lions, Marcus Charles Illions, New York, early 20th century. From the HUC Skirball Cultural Center and Museum, Los Angeles, CA. Museum purchase with Project Americana Acquisition Funds provided by Irvin and Lee Kalsman, Peachy and Mark Levy, and Gerald M. and Carolyn Z. Bronstein.

Before the Law stands a doorkeeper on guard. To this doorkeeper there comes a man from the country who begs for admittance to the Law. But the doorkeeper says that he cannot admit the man at the moment. The man, on reflection, asks if he will be allowed, then, to enter later. 'It is possible,' answers the doorkeeper, 'but not at this moment.' Since the door leading into the Law stands open as usual and the doorkeeper steps to one side, the man bends down to peer through the entrance. When the doorkeeper sees that, he laughs and says: 'If you are so strongly tempted, try to get in without my permission. But note that I am powerful. And I am only the lowest doorkeeper. From hall to hall keepers stand at every door, one more powerful than the other. Even the third of these has an aspect that even I cannot bear to look at.' These are difficulties which the man from the country has not expected to meet; the Law, he thinks, should be accessible to every man and at all times, but when he looks more closely at the doorkeeper in his furred robe, with his huge pointed nose and long, thin, Tartar beard, he decides that he had better wait until he gets permission to enter. The doorkeeper gives him a stool and lets him sit down at the side of the door. There he sits waiting for days and years. He makes many attempts to be allowed in and wearies the doorkeeper with his importunity. The doorkeeper often engages him in brief conversation, asking him about his home and about other matters, but the questions are put quite impersonally, as great men put questions, and always conclude with the statement that the man cannot be allowed to enter yet. The man, who has equipped

Torah Case (Tik),
India, early 20th century.
From the HUC Skirball
Cultural Center and
Museum, Los Angeles, CA.
Museum purchase with funds
by The Maurice Amado
Foundation at the behest of
the Tarica Family.

himself with many things for his journey, parts
with all he has, however valuable, in the hope of
bribing the doorkeeper. The doorkeeper accepts it all,
saying, however, as he takes each gift: 'I take this only
to keep you from feeling that you have left something
undone.' During all these long years the man watches
the doorkeeper almost incessantly. He forgets about
the other doorkeepers, and this one seems to him
the only barrier between himself and the Law.
In the first years he curses his evil fate aloud;
later, as he grows old, he only mutters to
himself. He grows childish, and since in his
prolonged watch he has learned to know
even the fleas in the doorkeeper's fur collar,
he begs the very fleas to help him and to per-
suade the doorkeeper to change his mind.
Finally his eyes grow dim and he does not
know whether the world is really darkening
around him or whether his eyes are only
deceiving him. But in the darkness he can
now perceive a radiance that streams immor-
tally from the door of the Law. Now his life
is drawing to a close. Before he dies, all that
he has experienced during the whole time of
his sojourn condenses in his mind into one
question, which he has never yet put to the
doorkeeper. He beckons the doorkeeper,
since he can no longer raise his stiffening
body. The doorkeeper has to bend far down
to hear him, for the difference in size
between them has increased very much to
the man's disadvantage. 'What do you want
to know now?' asks the doorkeeper. 'You are
insatiable.' 'Everyone strives to attain the
Law,' answers the man. 'How does it come
about, then, that in all these years no one has
come seeking admittance but me?' The doorkeeper perceives that the man is at the end
of his strength and that his hearing is failing,
so he bellows in his ear: 'No one but you
could gain admittance through this door,
since this door was intended only for you. I
am now going to shut it.'"

A HILL IN BERGEN BELSEN

—HASIDIC TALE, retold by Yaffa Eliach

Soul Series 1975-All that Remains (in Memory of the Six Million), Harold Paris, 1975. Courtesy of the Estate of Harold Paris.

Anna was among the tens of thousands who succumbed to the typhus epidemic in Bergen Belsen. Her friends gave her up for dead and told her that her struggle with death was useless. But Anna was determined to live. She knew that if she lay down, the end would come soon and she would die like so many others around her. So, in a delirious state, she wandered around camp, stumbling over the dead and the dying. But her strength gave way. She felt that her feet were refusing to carry her any farther. As she was struggling to get up from the cold, wet ground, she noticed in the distance a hill shrouded in gray mist. Anna felt a strange sensation. Instantly, the hill in the distance became a symbol of life. She knew that if she reached the hill, she would survive, but if she failed, the typhus would triumph.

Anna attempted to walk toward the hill which continually assumed the shape of a mound of earth, a huge grave. But the mound remained Anna's symbol of life, and she was determined to reach it. On her hands and knees, she crawled toward that strange mound of earth that now was the essence of her survival. After long hours passed, Anna reached her destination. With feverish hands she touched the cold mound of earth. With her last drop of strength, she crawled to the top of the mound and collapsed. Tears started to run down her cheeks, real human, warm tears, her first tears since her incarceration in concentration camps some four years ago. She began to call for her father. "Please, Papa, come and help me. I know that you, too, are in camp. Please, Papa, help me, for I cannot go on like this any longer."

Suddenly, she felt a warm hand on top of her head. It was her father stroking her just as he used to place his hand over her head every Friday night and bless her. Anna recognized her father's warm, comforting hands. She began to sob even more and told him that she had no strength to live any longer. Her father listened and caressed her head as he used to. He did not recite the customary blessing but,

instead, said, "Don't worry, my child. You will manage to survive for a few days, for liberation is very close."

This occurred on Wednesday night, April 11, 1945. On Sunday, April 15, the first British tank entered Bergen Belsen.

When Anna was well enough to leave the hospital in the British Zone where she was recovering from typhus, she returned to Bergen Belsen. Only then did she learn that the huge mound of earth in the big square where she spent the fateful night of April 11 in her combat with typhus was a huge mass grave. Among thousands of victims buried beneath the mound of earth was her father, who had perished months earlier in Bergen Belsen. On that night when she won her battle with death, Anna was weeping on her father's grave.

Based on an interview by Kalia Dingott with Anna, May 1976 (family name withheld by request).

THE DEATH TRAIN

—BY ELIE WIESEL

Indescribable confusion reigned.

Parents searched for their children, children for their parents, and lonely captives for their friends. The people were beset by loneliness. Everyone feared that the outcome of the journey would be tragic and would claim its toll of lives. And so one yearned to have the companionship of someone who would stand by with a word, with a loving glance.

Afterward, an ominous silence fell upon us. We squatted on the soft snow that covered the floor of the railroad car like a carpet, and tried to keep warm by drawing closer to our neighbors.

When the train started to move, no one paid any attention to it. Careworn and burdened with conflicting thoughts, each of us wondered if he was wise to continue on the journey. But in our weariness, whether one died today, tomorrow, a week or a generation later, hardly seemed to matter.

The night dragged on interminably, as though it were to go on to the end of time. When the gray dawn appeared in the east, I felt as though I had spent a night in a tomb haunted by evil spirits. Human beings, defeated and broken, sat like dusty tombstones in the dim light of early dawn. I looked about the subdued throng and tried to distinguish one from another. And, indeed, perhaps there was no distinction.

My gaze fell on one who stared blankly ahead. A wry smile seemed to play on his ice-encrusted face. Those glazed eyes, whether living or dead, seemed to ensnare my gaze. A hundred and twenty captives, shadows of human lives, extinguished flames of burned-out candles lit on the anniversaries of the deaths of their loved ones.

Wrapped in a drenched blanket, his black cap pulled down over his ears, a layer of snow on his shoulders, my father sat beside me. Could it be that he, too, was dead? The thought flashed across my mind. I tried to talk to him. I wanted to shout, but all I could do was mutter. He did not reply, he did not utter a sound. I was certain that from then on I was to be all alone, all alone. Then I was filled with a numbing sense of indifference to everyone and to myself. Well, the Lord giveth and the Lord taketh away. The struggle was over. There was nothing and no one for whom to fight now.

The train ground to an abrupt halt in a snow-covered field. Awakened by the jolt, a few curious captives struggled to their feet to look out. The scene was reminiscent of cattle staring stupidly from a livestock car.

German S.S. guards surrounded the human cargo, shouting, "All the dead are to be thrown out! All the dead are to be thrown out!"

The living were pleased; there would be more space. It would not be as crowded now.

Strong men appeared and examined each one who could not stand up, and rapped out, "Here's one! Get hold of him!"

Whereupon two men would pick the corpse by the shoulders and feet and fling it out of the car like a sack of flour.

Concentration Camp,
Ben Shahn, 1944.
© Estate of Ben Shahn/
Licensed by VAGA, NY.
Courtesy of Sotheby's, NY.

From various parts of the car came such cries as, "Here's another—my neighbor! He doesn't move. Help me get rid of him!"

Two deportees stepped forward and tried to lift a form beside me. It was only then that I was aroused from my stupor, and realized the seriousness of the situation. And to this day I cannot understand how I summoned the strength and courage to save my father from the lurking death. I knelt over him, tearing at his clothes, slapping his face, kissing him and screaming, "Daddy, Daddy—wake up! Get up, Daddy! Don't let them throw you out of the car. . . ."

As he failed to respond, the two men said to me, "There's no use your screaming, little fellow. He's dead! Your father is dead, do you understand?"

"No! He is not dead! He's not dead!" I wailed, repeating the words over and over indefinitely. For some reason, I seemed to fear the death of my father more than my own. I tried again and again to release him from the embrace of the angels of death, and I succeeded at last.

My father opened his glazed, ice-encrusted eyes, and regarded me in a dazed way, unable to understand what I was trying to convey to him or the commotion that was being made over him.

"See for yourselves, you murderers. He's alive, he's living!"

The two men eyed my father for a moment, then shrugged their shoulders and muttered, "Not for long," and turned to other silent forms.

There were twenty-odd dead in our one car, and after they were stripped of their clothes, which the living snatched up, they were flung out of the car.

This task took several hours. Then the train chugged along, and as icy gusts shrieked about it, it seemed that through the accursed world about us could be heard the far-away, muffled wail of the naked bodies that had been abandoned on Polish snow-covered fields.

The journey was insufferable; and everyone who lived through it later questioned the natural laws that their survival seemed to disprove.

We were deprived of even bread and water, and snow was our only source of water. Cramped for space and thoroughly chilled, we were very weak by the third day of the journey. Days were turned into nights, and the nights cast a shadow of doom over our very souls.

The train plodded along for what seemed countless days, and the snow fell, fell, fell incessantly. And the exhausted, travel-weary unfortunates lay huddled for days on end, without uttering a word, eyes closed, waiting for one thing only—the next station, where the new yield of corpses would be got rid of. That was what we looked forward to.

The journey lasted ten interminable days and nights. Each day claimed its toll of victims and each night paid its homage to the Angel of Death.

We passed through German settlements, generally in the early morning hours, only in a few instants. Sometimes men on their way to work would halt in their tracks to glare at us as though we were animals in a kind of demonic circus. Once a German hurled a chunk of bread into our car and caused pandemonium to break out as scores of famished men fought each other in an effort to pounce upon it. And the German workers eyed the spectacle with sneering amusement.

Years later, I chanced to land in the Oriental port of Aden. Some of the ship's passengers, looking for excitement and exotic thrills, tossed coins into the water to be retrieved by native boys who arrived on the scene to entertain the pleasure-seeking travelers by diving into the deep waters for the coins. At times the young divers would remain underwater for several minutes, and the passengers cheered the novel sport that could be enjoyed for a mere sixpence. . . .

I had once before witnessed such a scene. An elderly aristocratic woman from Paris, holding a handful of coins, stood on the deck amusing herself by throwing them one at a time to a dozen young dark-skinned swimmers. Each time she tossed a coin into the stream, a fierce fight ensued among the divers—a fact that seemed to delight her no end, judging by her peals of laughter. Revolted by the scene of children trying to choke each other under water for the possession of a coin, I pleaded with the woman not to throw any more coins.

"Why not?" she replied. "I love to give charity."

She loved almsgiving—and to see six- and seven-year-old children fighting each other for a worthless coin.

Then I looked back upon that morning when our train, carrying its human cargo, had halted near the German city and the worker had thrown a piece of bread into our car, perhaps in compassion, although that is hard to believe. At any rate, the morsel of food caused the death of a number of men. The scramble for bread! The fight for life! The chunk of bread brought about its own kind of war to the death. The wildest instincts of the primeval jungle had seized all of us, and we pounced upon the bread with all the savagery of enraged beasts. An atavistic throw-back?

Unfortunately, the Torah does not relate how the children of Israel received the first manna in the wilderness. Did they fight over it, and were there any casualties? And did scenes like the one in our car take place there? The German workers tarried a while, gazing at the amusing spectacle, and perhaps assuaging their conscience at the same time with the thought of their benevolence in giving bread to the hungry.

All the other German workers soon followed the example of their kindhearted townsmen. Pieces of bread were cast into all the cars. Bread and victims. And they—the good, gallant Germans—were pleased with themselves and smiled.

Strange, even while jotting down these words, the event seems incredible to me. I seem to be writing a horror novel—a novel that should not be read at night. It is hard to believe that what I set down in writing is really true, has actually happened to me.

And—only ten years ago!

I think to myself: if all that is alive in my memory, and that is seething in my heart, is really true, how am I able to sleep at night? How can I eat my food in peace?

I can still see the scenes I experienced that early morning when the bits of bread fell from heaven.

Unfortunately, the bread also fell into our car. Though I was very hungry, my exhaustion was stronger. So I didn't budge from my spot, refusing to take part in what was going on. Let bread drop down—even from heaven. I would not risk my life to get it. I lacked the strength not only to fight for the hard crusts, but even to eat them. So I squatted in my corner, watching how human beings turned into animals as they attempted to snatch the morsels of food from each others' mouths.

A piece of the heavenly bread fell in a corner of the car; the next moment another corner was emptied of its occupants. Not far from me a young lad bit the ear of someone standing in front of him, in order to get to the priceless bread first. The injured person, bent only upon reaching the bread, was oblivious to the pain. I suddenly beheld a frail, elderly Jew crawling along the floor, one hand clutching his chest. At first I thought that he had been hurt in the fight. But then I saw him take a handful of crumbs from his bosom and devour them almost with ecstasy.

A sly smile played upon his deathly pale face for a moment, and disappeared. Then someone pounced on the old man like a phantom, and the two engaged in a death struggle, clawing, biting, trampling, kicking one another. The old man managed to raise his head, a glint of joy in his bloodshot eyes.

"Little Meyer! Meyer, my son," the graybeard mumbled. "Didn't you recognize me? You have hurt me so much. . . ."

Meyer still struggled to retrieve a piece of bread from his father's bosom. Then the dying man groaned, "Meyer, you're beating your own father . . . I brought bread for you, too. I had risked my life . . . and you're hitting, beating me—your old father. . . ."

The old man seemed on the verge of death, he no longer made any sound. Meyer had triumphed: his right hand clutched the small piece of bread, and his left wiped the blood trickling from one of his eyes. The old man held a piece of bread in his clenched fist and tried to bring it up to his mouth—to die with the taste of food in his mouth. His eyes were alert now; he was clearly aware of the situation. He was at the portals of death—a condition in which one comprehends all that goes on about him. As he brought the hand with the bread closer to his half-opened mouth, his face glowed with lust for the bread. . . . It seemed as though the old man was holding back the bread intentionally, so that the pleasure of the anticipated feast should last longer. The eyes seemed about to burst from their sockets. And as the old man was about to bite into the bread with his darkened, broken teeth, Meyer once more pounced upon him and snatched the bread from him.

The old man muttered, "What? A last will and testament?" But, except for me, neither his son nor anyone else heard him. At last he breathed his last; and his orphaned son ate the bread. He was sprawled on the floor of the car, his right hand stretched out as though protesting to God, who had transformed Meyer into a murderer.

I could not bear to look at the old man for long. The son soon found himself engaged in a new struggle. Catching sight of the bread in his hand, others then pounced upon him. He tried to defend himself, but the furious throng, thirsting for blood in their frenzy, killed him. And so the two of them, father and son, victims of the struggle for bread, were trampled upon. Both perished, starved and alone.

Suddenly, I had the feeling that someone was laughing behind me, and I wondered who it was. But I was afraid to look around for fear of learning that the laughter was not coming from behind me, but from myself. I was fifteen years old then. Do you understand—fifteen? Is it any wonder that I, along with my generation, do not believe either in God or in man; in the feelings of a son, in the love of a father. Is it any wonder that I cannot realize that I myself experienced this thing, that my childish eyes had witnessed it?

Meir Katz, a robust, energetic Jew with a thundering voice, an old friend of my father, was with us in the car. He worked as a gardener in Buna. He conducted himself gallantly, both physically and morally. He was placed in command of the human cargo in our car because of his strength. It was thanks to him that I finally arrived alive in the Buchenwald concentration camp.

It was during the third night of our journey—or was it some other?—we lost track of time. We squatted, trying to doze off, when I was suddenly awakened by someone choking me. With superhuman effort, I managed to shout one word—"Father!" That was all I managed to get out, as the unknown attacker was choking off my breath. Fortunately, my father awakened and tried to free me from the stranglehold. Unable to do so, however, he appealed to Meir Katz for help, whereupon the latter came to my rescue.

I didn't know the strangler or the reason for his violent act. After all, I had carried no bread with me. It may have been a sudden fit of insanity, or—just a case of mistaken identity.

Meir Katz also died during that journey. A few days before we reached Buchenwald, he said to my father, "Shloime, I'm on my way out. I can't stand it any longer."

"Meir, don't give up!" my father tried to hearten him. "Bear up! You've got to! Try to have courage!"

"Shloime, it's no use—I'm washed-out," Meir muttered. "I can't go on."

Then the sturdy Meir Katz broke down and sobbed, mourning his son, who was killed in the early days of the Hitler terror.

On the last day of the journey, bitter cold, accompanied by a heavy snowfall, aggravated the situation even more. The end seemed to be near. Then someone warned, "Fellow Jews, in such weather, we've got to move about; we must not sit motionless—or we'll all freeze to death!"

So we all got up—even those who seemed to be dying—and wrapped our drenched blankets around our bodies. The scene was reminiscent of a congregation wrapped in prayer shawls, swaying to and fro in prayer. The snow, the car, even the sky (heaven?)—everything and everybody seemed to be swaying, worshipping, communing with God, uttering the prayer of life, the prayer of death. The sword of the Angel of Death was suspended above. A congregation of corpses at prayer.

A shout, an outcry like that of a wounded animal, suddenly rent the air in the car. The effect was terrifying and some of the people could not endure it silently, and themselves began to scream. Their outcries seemed to come from another world. Soon the rest of us joined in the uproar; screaming and shrieking filled the air. The defining roar rode the gusts of wind and amid the swirling snow soared to heaven, but, echoing from the closed gates there, reverberated back to earth.

Before long, twenty-five cars crowded with deportees joined us in the hysterical song of death. Everyone had reached the breaking point. The end was drawing near. The train was struggling up the hill of the Thyring forest. The divine tragi-comedy was approaching its finale. There were no longer any illusions about surviving; the thousands of deportees were aware of their doom.

"Why don't they mow us down on the spot?" Meir Katz asked through tears. "We could at least be spared further agony."

"Reb Meir, we'll soon arrive at our destination," I tried to comfort him. But the wind drowned out my words. We stood in the open car, under the falling snow, screaming hysterically.

Ovens,
Mindy Weisel, 1980.
Courtesy of the artist.

❖

We arrived at the Buchenwald concentration camp late at night. "Security police" of the camp came forward to unload the human cargo. The dead were left in the cars. Only those who were able to drag their feet got out. Meir Katz was left in the car; like so many others, he had frozen to death a short time before we reached our destination. The journey itself was the worst part of the ordeal. About forty of the deportees were claimed by death on that one day alone. Our car had originally started out with a hundred and twenty souls; twelve—among them my father and I—had survived the ordeal.

233

WHY THE NIGHT WATCHMAN WAS DENIED A RAISE

—*CHELM TALE*, retold by Irving Howe and Eliezer Greenberg

It was once rumored that the Messiah was about to appear. So the Chelmites, fearing that he might bypass their town, engaged a watchman, who was to be on the lookout for the divine guest and welcome him if he should happen along.

The watchman meanwhile bethought himself that his weekly salary of ten gulden was mighty little with which to support a wife and children, and so he applied to the town elders for an increase.

The rabbi turned down his request. "True enough," he argued, "that ten gulden a week is an inadequate salary. But one must take into account that this is a permanent job."

The Blessing of the Moon,
Harry Lieberman, c. 1977.
Private collection.

235

BEGIN WITH YOURSELF

—HASIDIC TALE, retold by Ellen Frankel

OPPOSITE: *Torah Curtain*,
Adoph Gottlieb, 1950–51.
The Jewish Museum, NY/
Art Resource, NY.
© 1997 Adolph and Esther
Gottlieb Foundation/
Licensed by VAGA, NY.

When Hayyim of Zanz was a young man, he set about trying to reform his country from its evil ways. But when he reached the age of thirty, he looked around and saw that evil remained in the world. So he said, "Perhaps I was too ambitious. I will begin with my province." But at the age of forty, his province too remained mired in evil. So he said, "I was still too ambitious. From now on I will only try to lift up my community." But at fifty he saw that his community had still not changed. So he decided only to reform his own family. But when he looked around, he saw that his family had grown and moved away, and now he remained alone.

"Now I understand that I needed to begin with myself."

So he spent the rest of his life perfecting his own soul.

LITERARY CREDITS

Produced by Fair Street Productions
and Welcome Enterprises, Inc.
Project Directors: Susan Wechsler, H. Clark Wakabayashi
Editor: Susan Wechsler
Designer: Jon Glick
Production Coordinator: Sara Baysinger
Art Coordinator/Photo Researcher: Stephanie Lieblich/
Photosearch, Inc.
Text Coordinator: Shaie Dively

Published and distributed by
Stewart, Tabori & Chang,
A Company of La Martinière Groupe
115 West 18th Street, New York, NY 10011

Export sales to all countries except Canada,
France, and French-speaking Switzerland:
Thames and Hudson Ltd.
181A High Holborn
London WC1V 7QX
England

Canadian Distribution:
Canadian Manda Group
One Atlantic Avenue, Suite 105
Toronto, Ontario M6K 3E7
Canada

Library of Congress Cataloging-in-Publication Data

The Jewish spirit: a celebration in stories & art / edited by
    Ellen Frankel.
        p. cm.
        "A Fair Street/Welcome Book."
        ISBN 1-55670-623-5 (hardcover)
        1. Legends, Jewish. 2. Short stories, Jewish.
    I. Frankel, Ellen.
        BM530.J49   1997
        296.1'9—dc21
                                97-2752
                                   r97

Printed in Japan by
Toppan Printing Company
10 9 8 7 6 5 4 3

PHOTOGRAPHY CREDITS

ACKNOWLEDGMENTS

*Levites Playing Music
in the Holy Temple,*
Shalom of Safed, 1972.
The Jewish Museum, NY/
Art Resource, NY.

For Rachel Falkove, whose friendship has sustained me.

The editor of an anthology plays the role of midwife, bringing to life the fruits of others' labors while coping with the mess and commotion that accompanies birth. In putting together this book, I have been spared much of the normal fuss and bother of this process, thanks to the professional support of the Fair Street/Photosearch staff. I am especially indebted to Susan Wechsler for her indomitable good humor, unflappability, competence, and good sense; I am also grateful to Stephanie Lieblich for her imagination and doggedness with the picture research, and to Shaie Dively for keeping track of all the text. A special thanks to the people at Welcome—Jon Glick and Sara Baysinger—for their good design taste and hard work. Ellen Scordato, Mairead Stack, and Kathy Aster, must also be commended for taking care of all the details.

Many people contributed to this volume, some directly, others by serving as mentors and trailblazers. I am especially grateful to Peninnah Schram for recommending me for this project; to Dov Noy, Howard Schwartz, and Barbara Rush, for pointing me toward so many sources of Jewish folklore; to the many Jewish storytellers who have collectively renewed the tradition of telling Jewish tales; and to W. S. Penn, for paving the way.

I also want to thank my colleagues and the Trustees at the Jewish Publication Society for their continuing support of my writing life. And as always, I owe a special debt to my secretary, Mrs. Eunice Dixon Smith, who has taught me so much about the human spirit through her own shining example.

Lastly, I want to thank my family—Herb, Sarah, and Les—for giving me a sufficiently wide berth when I was in "laser-beam mode," for being tolerant of my endless paper trails, and for cheering me on so enthusiastically. Herb, in particular, helped me think through and assemble much of this volume, lending me his expertise, insight, and helping hands.

I dedicate this anthology to my beloved friend Rachel Falkove, whose steadfast companionship and greathearted spirit have never failed me.

The editors acknowledge the many artists and institutions who provided us with illustrations and support, and especially thank the following individuals: Dalia Migdal; Claudia Goldstein/The Jewish Museum /Art Resource, NY; Jenny Page/The Bridgeman Art Library, London; Thomas Holman/Forum Gallery, NY; Susanne Kester/HUC Skirball Cultural Center and Museum, CA; Ann Prival/VAGA, NY.

E. F.